Edwin Cameron

JUSTICE

A Personal Account

TAFELBERG

Tafelberg
An imprint of NB Publishers, a division of Media24 Boeke (Pty) Ltd
40 Heerengracht, Cape Town, 8000
www.tafelberg.com
© 2014 Edwin Cameron

Set in Veljovic
Cover design by Michiel Botha
Cover photograph by Phyllis Green
Book design by Nazli Jacobs
Edited by Alison Lowry
Proofread by Linde Dietrich
Index by George Claassen

Printed and bound by Interpak Books
First edition, first printing 2014
Fourth printing 2014

ISBN: 978-0-624-06305-6
Epub: 978-0-624-06306-3
Mobi: 978-0-624-06307-0

Product group from well-managed forests
and other controlled sources.

Even the most benevolent of governments are made up of people with all the propensities for human failings. The rule of law as we understand it consists in the set of conventions and arrangements that ensure that it is not left to the whims of individual rulers to decide on what is good for the populace. The administrative conduct of government and authorities are subject to the scrutiny of independent organs. This is an essential element of good governance that we have sought to have built into our new constitutional order . . .

It was, to me, never reason for irritation but rather a source of comfort when these bodies were asked to adjudicate on actions of my Government and my Office and judged against.

FORMER PRESIDENT
NELSON ROLIHLAHLA MANDELA

Contents

Introduction
About this Book

This is a book about our country's most inspiring and hopeful feature – its big-spirited, visionary Constitution. And it tells the story of my journey from a poverty-stricken childhood to becoming a lawyer and eventually a justice in the country's highest court, which has the duty to interpret and guard that Constitution.

In telling that story, I blend my own life experiences, growing up as a white child from a poor home, who later worked against apartheid as a human rights lawyer, with what I hope are enthralling and inspiring stories of how citizens, lawyers and judges can make the law work to secure justice. I explain some features of the pre-democracy legal system, and how our country made the extraordinary transformation from apartheid to democracy, under the world's most generous-spirited Constitution.

Chapter one starts at my very first encounter with the law. I was seven years old. My sister Jeanie and I were in a children's home. It was a time of trauma, for we had just lost our elder sister Laura. It was then that a riveting confrontation with the law occurred. It left a profound impression on me, marking my consciousness for life.

Growing up under apartheid, I had the law all round me. For the distinctive feature of apartheid is that it was enforced by law – minute, exhaustive, detailed, and often cruelly enforced legal prescriptions. But what fascinated me was that the law, apartheid's oppressive instrument, could also be employed against apartheid. It could be used occasionally to mitigate its effects. Properly employed, it could be used to repair, not to break down or damage.

I saw this when, just out of school, I witnessed a famous trial, whose dramatic outcome I describe in chapter one. This chapter explains how, amidst oppression, resolute activists and human rights lawyers could also secure a limited measure of justice and fairness in the courts. It was their work that laid the foundation for our Constitution, in which our founders resolved that the law would embody our country's best and highest hopes for itself. The law would continue to be the centre point of the country's development. But henceforth it would be used as an instrument not of injustice, but of justice.

After recalling law under apartheid (chapter one), I describe my own encounter with one of our young democracy's most momentous challenges – AIDS. I explain how heavily this fearsome disease burdened our transition from apartheid to constitutional democracy (chapter two). I then recount the judiciary's transition from being an enforcer of apartheid law to becoming one of our new democracy's three arms of government (chapter three).

In chapter four I recount the drama of the biggest test the new Constitution has so far faced – President Mbeki's questioning of AIDS science, which tragically caused untold thousands of unnecessary deaths. But fortunately our Constitution is supreme. And the activists turned to the courts to enforce it. The courts responded justly. They ordered President Mbeki's government to start making anti-retroviral (ARV) treatment available, and to the President's credit, he eventually accepted the ruling. Today South Africa has the biggest publicly provided ARV treatment programme anywhere in the world. This massive achievement shows the immense power of law and of reasoned constitutionalism.

In chapter five, I explain the unspoken value that powerfully underlies all the ambitious promises of our Constitution – the value of diversity. I explain it from my perspective as a proudly gay man, one who grew up fearful and ashamed of my own sexuality, and who now serves my country without disqualification because of who I am. The Constitution affirms us in all our differentness. But we have a very long way to go before we can say we as a country have fully accepted its invitation to rejoice in our differences.

Chapter six celebrates the Constitution's promise of social justice. My whiteness bought me the privileges apartheid was designed to secure for whites. It secured for me access to a first-rate high school and an excellent university. These opened the way for me to get a Rhodes Scholarship to Oxford, and to start my legal career. I was a beneficiary of apartheid's affirmative action for whites but, growing up poor, my life also benefited lavishly from private gestures of generosity and support. Our Constitution seeks to offer this generosity and support justly to all. It gives us a framework for a society in which mutual support and generosity are the key. And it obliges government, on behalf of all of us, to create a society in which all of us can live in dignity.

In the concluding chapter, chapter seven, I reflect on where we are after nearly two decades of constitutionalism. There is much reason to feel disquiet and dismay. But there is also some basis for the sober belief that we, as an engaged, purposeful citizenry, can create a prosperous future. We need honest leadership and vigorous commitment from ourselves. What we already have are the constitutional fundamentals. The Constitution's values and structure are sound – twenty years of rowdy contestation have proved this.

The law offered me a chance to remedy and repair my life. The Constitution offers us a chance to repair and remedy our country. It is an opportunity we should seize with eager determination.

So I invite you to turn over the page, to start with me on the path that took me to the law, and that took our country to democratic constitutionalism. It is an engrossing and wonderful journey, full of ups and downs, but at its end there lie the practical possibilities of hope.

Chapter One

Law Under Apartheid

I A first encounter with the law

My first encounter with the law was at the funeral of my elder sister Laura, just before I turned eight. In the back row of the Avbob chapel in Rebecca Street, Pretoria, my father sat stiffly between two uniformed prison guards. They had slipped in discreetly late, after family and friends were already settled. My sister Jeanie and I, uncertain whether he would be allowed to come, squirmed round from our front-row seats alongside our mother to snatch a glimpse. He gave no signal in return. Despite the desperate reaches to which his alcoholism often took him, he carried himself with a natural dignity, and sat silently, motionless, between his captors.

Why he was in prison was not clear to us. There was so much else to deal with. Laura – the brilliant eldest child, about to enter high school, felled on a bicycle trip to the corner shop by a delivery van. It was Jeanie's eleventh birthday, the twelfth of January, and Laura had set out to buy golden syrup to bake cookies for a treat. A hot January afternoon in Pretoria cracked, life-swervingly, by the news, breathlessly brought by a neighbour's son, that she lay lifeless at the stop street below my aunt Lydia's house. There followed a harrowing succession of callers at the house, some kindly leaving envelopes with small sums of money. The next week, Jeanie and I were due to return to the

11

children's home in Queenstown, where she and Laura and I had spent the last bleak year.

The events were enough to split off an internal part of my engagement with the world. In the days after Laura's death, unlike my mother and Jeanie, who lay in the darkened back bedroom of my aunt's house, sick from shock and grief, I felt no pain. Only numb denial. Over the next years, instead of mourning, I withdrew into what seemed like the safety of a crabbed inner space. I reinvented myself in the guise of a clever schoolboy who, despite family tragedy, managed to excel at school. That my father was in Zonderwater, and had arrived late for Laura's funeral between two prisons guards, was a far distant detail.

I imagined that Zonderwater was a rehabilitation centre for alcoholics. That must be why he was there. My mother did not discourage this belief. Perhaps she encouraged it. Only much later did I realise that he was serving a jail term for car theft.

This first encounter with the law, as it held my father captive to exact accountability for a wrong he had committed against society, left in me a deep layering of thought and emotion. What was the law? In what lay its power? Was it only an instrument of rebuke and correction and subjection? Or could it be more? I did not know it then, but this vivid encounter imprinted and impelled my future life and career.

II A second encounter with the law – and a first lesson in lawyering

My next encounter with the law was a decade later. The meeting was also dramatic, though much less personal. Jeanie and I spent the desolate years that followed Laura's death in the children's home. My mother eventually managed to get us out. As a boy child, in contrast to Jeanie, for whom a commercial school was deemed enough, lofty things were planned for me. My mother set her sights on nothing less than excellent schooling and, in my second year in high school, she succeeded. She got me into Pretoria Boys' High. Then, as now, the school was a paragon of public-funded excellence. The teachers demanded concentration and hard work, and nurtured critical, open-minded thinking. They offered me a chance to change my life. With an eager hunger, I cast my entire self at it.

In January 1971, immediately after finishing high school, I was a 17-year-old conscript in apartheid's army when the security police made a sensational arrest. The Very Reverend Gonville Aubie ffrench-Beytagh, an English immigrant who was the Dean of the Anglican Cathedral in Johannesburg, was apprehended under the Terrorism Act and locked up in solitary confinement without being charged. As his detention without trial continued, an international campaign pressed the apartheid authorities to charge him or release him. Cathedral bells throughout South Africa pealed out daily in protest. My year-long compulsory army service ground slowly by, month by month. With excited apprehension, I alleviated its tedium by following the drama of the Dean's arrest and detention.

At last, in August, he was put on summary trial, accused of terrorist activities. The judge was an apartheid stalwart, Mr Justice Cillié, the Judge-President of the Transvaal. He presided over the tense contest in the Old Synagogue in Pretoria's city centre. Converted to a courtroom after the Jewish community moved to the suburbs, its dark wooden dock had confined many famous political prisoners, including Nelson Mandela and those arraigned with him eight years earlier in the Rivonia Trial, and six years before that in the Treason Trial. As a young white teenager, I knew nothing about the Rivonia and Treason trials, and barely anything at all about Nelson Mandela.

The Dean's trial during my army year was for me the start of a very slow, fitful and protracted coming to consciousness.

Defending the Dean was Sydney Kentridge, who later gained international fame for his withering cross-examination of the security policemen who bludgeoned Steven Bantu Biko to death in September 1977. In the hot afternoons of Pretoria's late winter, as temperatures rose before the spring rains started, I would slip away from my desk at the army's monthly journal, *Paratus*, and walk the few blocks to the Old Synagogue. Conspicuous in my army fatigues, I sat in the public gallery, listening to Kentridge grilling the police witnesses.

Some had befriended the Dean, or worked their way into his confidence as his congregants; others attended meetings he addressed. Now they testified that he furthered the aims of the banned African National Congress by inciting violence and by distributing money to its supporters.

The Dean denied the charges. He virulently opposed apartheid, but insisted that his warnings that violence would inevitably result from its injustices did not amount to advocating bloodshed. One charge was that he had incited the women attending a meeting of the Black Sash, an organisation opposing apartheid, to commit violence. The meeting was at the home of its founder, Mrs Jean Sinclair, in the middle-class, white suburb of Parktown North, Johannesburg.

The charge seemed plain silly, but it was earnestly levelled. It revealed the security police's apprehensions about the Dean's anti-apartheid work, and that of other outspoken white critics. And history showed this concern was not misplaced. Apartheid was defeated by internal uprising, township defiance, international isolation and sanctions, a banking boycott, armed insurgency and the country's increasing ungovernability. But its power was also sapped, crucially, by internal moral challenges to its legitimacy.

Internal opponents, and the legal challenges that were part of their armoury, proved vitally important to this strand of opposition.

The Dean's confrontation with the security police was a historic marker in that battle. And lawyers and the legal system played a central role in it.

A considerable part of the Dean's trial was devoted to a visit that a wealthy Englishwoman, Alison Norman, paid to the Dean in 1970. She was the channel through which much-needed funds flowed for the Dean to distribute to the families of activists who were facing trial or who were already in prison – and the charge sheet named her as a co-conspirator with the Dean. The question was whether the funds she sent to the Dean were ANC funds. On an overnight train trip to Pietermaritzburg, a security police-man, Major Zwart, posing as the liberal 'Mr Morley', contrived an introduction to Ms Norman. The day after the train trip, accord-ing to him, after several beers and brandies in a Pietermaritzburg hotel, she tried to recruit him for the banned London-based De-fence and Aid Fund, which gathered funds to help detained sup-porters of banned organisations and their families.

Kentridge's cross-examination was meticulously detailed, but mesmerising. Trudge, trudge, trudge. Question by question. Seated in the stuffy upper gallery, reserved for women during ortho-dox religious observances, I learned my first lessons about good lawyering.

There are few flourishes and grandiose gestures. Much more grinding slog. And intense concentration on detail, amidst the high technical demands of legal form and process.

But something else also became clear as I followed Kentridge's questions from upstairs, staring down at the inscrutable features of the Dean. If convicted, he faced a minimum of five years in jail. Kentridge's commitment to avoiding that result, and his mas-tery of the minutiae of whether Ms Norman had or had not drunk brandy with Major Zwart, was propelled by an underlying, smouldering, incensed rage at the injustice of the system that was trying to imprison the clergyman.

Kentridge achieved renown as a lawyer not only because of his intellect and his mastery of the technical rules of procedure and hearsay. He made an impact because of his fervour in employing those skills against a system he abhorred. My 18-year-old self, gazing down through the upstairs railings, began to understand that effective lawyering lies in a combination of heart and mind and very hard work.

Despite Kentridge's best efforts, Judge-President Cillié found the Dean guilty of terrorism. It was said of Judge Cillié that he had never been known to disbelieve a senior police officer. His judgment lived up to this expectation. When he sentenced the Dean to five years in prison, women in the courtroom gasped and sobbed. As he left the court, they began singing the stirring nineteenth-century English hymn 'Onward, Christian Soldiers'. But their defiance was edged with fear. The Dean's conviction sent a chilling warning to all outspoken internal anti-apartheid activists. Their work put them at risk of conviction for terrorism, plus a long time in jail.

III The Dean takes his case to the appeal court

Judge Cillié did not have the last word, however. Kentridge took the case to the appeal court in Bloemfontein, then the highest court in the land. Pending the appeal, the Dean was allowed to remain out on bail.

The appeal court moved swiftly to put the Dean's case on its roster. It came up for hearing a short while after sentence was imposed, in the very month when, freshly freed from my army service, I began my law studies in Stellenbosch, a famously beautiful university town in the winelands bordering Cape Town. I was able to attend university only because I had won an open scholarship sponsored by the mining corporation Anglo American. The scholarship covered my academic and residence fees, and gave me generous pocket money – and a first taste of material sufficiency. Between initiation procedures at my men's residence and trying to find my feet in the lecture halls, I kept watching the newspapers for news of the Dean's appeal.

On a hot morning in the last week of February 1972, the appeal of *ffrench-Beytagh v The State* was called. The hearing was in the main courtroom of the imposing 1920s appeal court building in President Brand Street, which stands opposite the Free State Republic's beautiful nineteenth-century Raadsaal.

Chief Justice Ogilvie Thompson presided. All appeals in Bloemfontein are called with utmost attention to propriety. I learned this in the eight years, rich and experience packed, that I spent as a judge in that court from 2001 to 2008. When I arrived to take my appellate seat in January 2001, Judge Ogilvie Thompson's reputation as a stickler for precise timekeeping and rigorous decorum still lingered in the corridors.

And, even now, the protocols instilled over decades are followed. First, the judges assigned to hear an appeal assemble in the gallery outside the courtroom. They do so five minutes before the case is to be heard, to make sure proceedings start precisely on time. At exactly 9:45, the court orderly enters the courtroom, and summons all to rise. Then with a swish he tugs the drawstring that opens a maroon velvet curtain screening the judges' gallery from the public. The judges file in, in strict order of seniority, and take their places on the Bench – the senior judge in the middle, the next most senior to the right, and third most senior on the left, and so on.

The judges bow gravely to the lawyers and members of the

17

public, and take their seats. The advocates, the attorneys and the public sit. The presiding judge's registrar gets up and calls the case for hearing. After a moment of shuffling papers and pens and checking books, the presiding judge signals that counsel for the appellant may rise to address the court.

Even in Bloemfontein's fiery Februaries, the high-vaulted main courtroom is comparatively cool. It has to be, for its severely elegant, stinkwood-panelled walls have witnessed many heated legal battles.

IV A brave history – the 1950s appeal court confronts the apartheid government

In 1952, twenty years before the Dean's appeal, the appeal court gave two of its most dramatic rulings. To the fury of the apartheid government, which came to power in 1948, the court under Chief Justice Centlivres declared invalid a law that stripped coloured voters in the Cape of their voting rights on the common voters' roll. The coloured vote was the sole racially liberal remnant of the settlement that consolidated white supremacy under British authority in South Africa in 1910. Parliament had removed African voters in the Cape from the roll in 1936. Now in its quest for all-white racial purity, the apartheid government was determined to expunge even this last trace of racial commonality.

But the coloured vote was 'entrenched'. A special parliamentary procedure had to be followed to abolish it. This demanded a two-thirds vote of both houses of Parliament, sitting together. The new government's lawyers advised that these restrictions, which the British Parliament enacted when it passed the South Africa Act in 1909, were no longer binding on Parliament, since it was now a fully autonomous legislative body, no longer subject to the mother legislature in Westminster, England.

The logic was bad, however. The Cape Town Parliament, no matter how autonomous, could act only within the limits of the powers conferred on it at its creation. It could not invent new powers for itself, or ignore the procedural limitations by which it was constituted. Nor could it make itself into a 'high court of Parliament' – as it proclaimed itself after the appeal court's first ruling against the coloured vote abolition – to reverse the judges' decisions. That, too, flouted the foundational principles of parliamentary power. Twice, Chief Justice Centlivres's court bravely called out the flawed logic, and threw out the bad statutes.

The rulings delayed the coloured vote debacle by four years, but the apartheid hardliners won in the end. They gerrymandered the Senate, or upper house of Parliament, by vastly expanding it, to secure the combined two-thirds majority they needed. The manoeuvre was rightly regarded as a fraud on coloured voters' rights. In addition, they stacked the appeal court with five extra judges to ensure the court toed the line. The extra appointees weren't necessary. In 1956 the court ruled that the Senate-packing legislation stood – and the vote was ten to one. Coloured voters disappeared from the common roll. It would be nearly forty years before a white and a coloured South African could once more stand in the same voting queue and vote alongside each other.

But the ruling in the Senate-packing case was not unanimous. One judge wrote a dissenting opinion, saying why he thought the majority was wrong. He was Oliver Schreiner, next most senior after Chief Justice Centlivres. He said that ordinarily Parliament could create any form or type of Senate it wanted using ordinary procedures. However, when it came to the protection guarding the coloured vote, which required the Senate to sit with the House of Assembly, the court had to look not at form, but at substance. In other words, the court's job was to assess not how well the conjuror concealed the trick, but whether there *was* a trick. The

Senate-packing legislation was a trick or fraud (Schreiner politely called it 'a legislative plan') designed to get round the protection afforded to coloured voters on the common roll. This was because government enlarged the Senate for the sole purpose of getting past the two-thirds majority requirement. The court should therefore strike the plan down as invalid.

Schreiner did not carry the day. His more conservative colleagues, even Chief Justice Centlivres and others sickened by the Senate shenanigan, concluded that the apartheid hardliners' manoeuvre now passed legal muster. But, as with other powerful dissenting judgments, Schreiner's reasoning ignited a flicker of light. His views in the Senate-packing case on substance versus form in legal devices eventually took flame, and have prevailed. To this day, they are cited in judgments. His views shape how South African lawyers approach contracts and tax havens and trusts and statutory bodies. Judges look first to see if there *is* a trick, not how well it is covered up.

More importantly, together with the bold earlier judgments, Schreiner's stand left a moral and political legacy. It laid a paving stone that would eventually open a path to a constitutional future. The appeal court's decisions striking down apartheid legislation, and the dissent in the Senate-packing case, showed what principled judges might achieve if they remain true to legal values. They can provide a bulwark for legal rights and civil liberties, even when powerful lawmakers try to undercut them.

V The appeal court wavers in defending liberties

That brave legacy did not stand unblemished. In the decades after the coloured vote cases, the appeal court stumbled away from principle shamefully often. In one notorious case in 1964, it ruled that security police detainees, even though not yet convicted of any crime, could not, in contrast to awaiting-trial prisoners, enjoy access to books, pens and paper. Parliament did not intend, the court ruled, that security police arrestees should be allowed 'to relieve the tedium of their detention with reading matter or writing materials'. To the contrary, the court said, the object of the legislation was to get the detainee to talk. Reading and writing went against this. So the ban was valid under the powers the statute conferred.

The detainee who went to court to claim his right to read and write was an advocate in Cape Town, Albie Sachs. A soft-spoken intellectual with a passionate commitment to a just legal system, Sachs nearly lost his life in 1988 while in exile in Mozambique, when the security police detonated a bomb under his car. But Sachs survived, and just six years after the car bomb, and thirty years after the appeal court ruled against his rights in detention, President Mandela appointed Sachs a judge in democratic South Africa's new Constitutional Court.

The judge who wrote the ruling denying him books, pens and paper was none other than Justice Ogilvie Thompson – who, after becoming Chief Justice, now, in 1972, presided over the Dean's appeal.

Opponents of apartheid, in South Africa and abroad, responded with furious dismay to the ruling in *Rossouw v Sachs*. Judge Ogilvie Thompson was condemned for bending over to please the executive at a time of 'white fright', when he should have stood firm in defence of vulnerable detainees. Critics pointed out that, until his ruling, South African law provided plainly that unsentenced detainees had the right to reading and writing materials. The only poser was one of legal classification: how to slot in the new category of security police detainee between the two existing categories – an awaiting-trial detainee, on the one hand, and a convicted criminal, on the other.

Apartheid critics thought the answer was obvious. Despite being a detainee in the hands of the security police, the prisoner had not yet been convicted of any crime so the awaiting-trial category should apply – therefore affording all pre-conviction rights. And indeed, when the case was first heard in Cape Town, two judges were faithful to this principled logic. They ruled that the security police had to allow Sachs to read and write while in detention.

But the police appealed against this finding. And, led by Ogilvie Thompson, five judges in Bloemfontein reversed the decision. The appeal court found in favour of the police. It said the purpose of security police detention – unlike pre-trial detention – was to extract information. This made security police detainees different from ordinary awaiting-trial prisoners. Hence ordinary rights did not apply.

Worse, Ogilvie Thompson's judgment made a general statement. He said that in deciding cases of this sort, judges shouldn't bend over backwards either to favour government or to protect liberties. They should take Parliament's will, as they find it in the words of the legislation, and enforce it.

This abdicated the courts' long-standing role as defenders of the weak and the vulnerable. And it rough-shouldered legal tradition out of the way to help the security police squeeze detainees to talk. The highest court in the land gave its blessing to the coercive power of solitary confinement and detention without trial. The judgment gave the security police wide leeway in dealing with anti-apartheid activists they arrested. It signalled to them that once they had a detainee in their grasp, the courts would be loath to supervise what they did.

In effect, the court washed its hands of those who were in security police hands. It is not far-fetched to see the results of the ruling in the dismal list of more than seventy brutal detainee deaths that took place from the mid-1960s to 1990, including many deaths the police claimed were suicides.

VI The appeal court decides the Dean's appeal

Now Ogilvie Thompson was Chief Justice. His imposingly tall frame rightfully occupied the high-backed, throne-like stinkwood centre seat in the main courtroom in Bloemfontein. The Dean's fate was in his and his fellow judges' hands. What would they decide?

The Terrorism Act was extremely wide. The statute was passed in 1967, just months after apartheid's chief conceptual planner, Hendrik Frensch Verwoerd, was assassinated on the government front bench in Parliament. The new statute gave the security police fearsome powers against opponents of apartheid. Under the law, you participated in terroristic activities if you did anything 'with intent to endanger the maintenance of law and order'. But, more widely even, you also committed the crime of terrorism if you took any action that 'aided' or 'encouraged' someone else to commit an act with that intent. These provisions were so wide that the threat of being prosecuted for 'terrorism' might shut down internal activist opposition to apartheid. A judge even vaguely inclined to help government in its war against apartheid opponents, as in Advocate Sachs's case, could give these terms their wide ordinary meaning – and the effect would be to smother internal anti-apartheid work.

The Dean's case was the first chance the appeal court had to pronounce on the statute's provisions. The appeal was a marathon. Chief Justice Ogilvie Thompson and his panel heard argument from Kentridge and the prosecution lawyers over ten full court days. The lawyers pressed their contesting positions on every fact, each legal angle, every statutory nuance. Then the judges reserved their judgment. When the appeal court adjourns after hearing argument, it almost never says when its ruling will be handed down. The parties leave Bloemfontein in suspense. When judgment is ready to be delivered, the court's registrar contacts the parties' local attorney. Everyone waits anxiously for the phone call from Bloemfontein.

In the Dean's case, it was five long weeks before word came. On 14 April 1972, ten days after Easter, the verdict was announced – as always, in the morning at 9:45 sharp. The judges must have laboured over the Easter weekend to finalise their judgment. The outcome was as dramatic as the Dean's arrest, detention, trial, verdict and sentence over the previous sixteen months. Kentridge had won. The Dean was acquitted. The appeal court set aside his criminal convictions and sentence. The appellate judges disbelieved the security police witnesses whom Judge Cillié had credited.

I heard the sensational news reports of the Dean's acquittal in Pretoria during the Easter break from my first-year law studies at Stellenbosch. I was spending the April vacation with my sister Jeanie, who was now a lodger in the home of my aunt Lydia. After a few years in the Pretoria flatland suburb of Sunnyside, we no longer had a home of our own. This was after my mother remarried, eighteen months before I finished high school, and moved to a faraway town. My bond with Jeanie, already intensely powerful after our years together in the children's home, became more intense even. This was because, as I sat hunched over my books for my crucial school-leaving examination, Jeanie had cooked my suppers and prepared my lunches, every single day, until I left school and entered the army.

But even after I left high school, she continued to provide a home for me. When she moved into my aunt Lydia's home, she paid board and lodging to make sure that I had somewhere to go during the university vacations. It was there that I heard the dramatic news that the Dean would no longer go to prison. He was a free man.

Later, in the law library back in Stellenbosch, I read the appeal court verdict. Chief Justice Ogilvie Thompson's judgment was meticulously detailed and carefully reasoned. It was written in the thick judicial style of the time, when judges didn't show much appreciation that their most important audience members are not the lawyers before them, nor even the litigants in the case – but the wider public beyond.

Wrestling with the judgment, and others even more opaque, I used to wonder why judges couldn't write clearly and understandably. The most important job of a judgment is to be clear. The public whom it affects must be able to understand it. This lesson has, I hope, stayed with me during my own twenty years as a judge – I have tried to remember that judges write for people, not for lawyers. Any literate person should be able to follow a judgment, even if it demands effort and concentration. A lawyer's skills should not be needed to be able to understand a judgment.

But the Chief Justice's ruling in the Dean's case was entirely unswayed by considerations of popular accessibility. Dense and long sentenced, it gave no glimmering of the human drama of the Dean's arrest, the Black Sash meeting in Parktown North, and Ms Alison Norman's eventful train trip to Pietermaritzburg. If within it were buried any delights, it did not easily yield them up.

Instead, what emerged very plainly was that, as with all judges, Chief Justice Ogilvie Thompson's personal history and social class played a part in how he assessed the witnesses who took the stand against the Dean. Ogilvie Thompson attended an elite private school in Grahamstown, and made his career as an advocate and a judge while living in the affluent English-speaking suburbs of Cape Town.

This personal history now hindered the prosecution and helped the Dean. On the credibility of Major Zwart versus Ms Norman, he made it plain that Ms Norman's upper-class social standing carried clout with him. 'She comes from a wealthy English family and is in her own right financially well off,' he noted, adding approvingly that she had taken 'a first-class degree in history at the University of Oxford'.

Would a woman of such quality have blown her cover drinking beers and brandies with an Afrikaner security policeman posing as a liberal? Chief Justice Ogilvie Thompson could not bring himself to think so. 'It is difficult to credit,' he said, 'that a woman such as the evidence indicates Miss Norman to be, would, in the middle of a hot day, consume not only three beers but two double brandies as well.' The latter, he said, noting a typically rigorous detail, 'being pre-metrication tots'.

Ms Norman later revealed that in fact she *had* drunk those brandies with Major Zwart. But her high-class credentials helped her earn credibility where it mattered – with the Chief Justice and his colleagues who decided the Dean's appeal.

But Ogilvie Thompson was an impressive lawyer, with a penetrating legal mind and some liberal sentiments. And, though he betrayed those in the Sachs appeal, he knew full well what he was doing in the Dean's case. Perhaps stung by the scathing criticism directed at *Rossouw v Sachs*, he now came out ringingly on the right side. Apart from freeing the Dean from the threat of long years in jail, his judgment significantly cut down the extraordinarily wide scope and application of the Terrorism Act.

It was plain, even to a fresher law student, that his judgment was a major setback for the apartheid Parliament's efforts to create a police state in South Africa.

VII Civil liberty, anti-apartheid activism and the Dean's judgment

Chief Justice Ogilvie Thompson's judgment drily pointed out that the prosecution had led 'no evidence to show that any member of the ANC, or any other political offender, terrorist or saboteur, entered upon, or continued to engage in, the activities of that body because of any assistance obtained, either by himself or by his family' from the funds the Dean administered. The Judge was saying that for the prosecution to succeed, it had to bring proof that the unlawful deeds of an anti-apartheid combatant resulted from the help the non-combatant gave.

For the prosecution to present evidence of this sort was almost impossible. Which anti-apartheid operative, even one who had turned to give evidence for the police, as some did, would say in court that money for studies, or food for the family, or legal fees, had boosted revolutionary anti-apartheid operational activities? The truth was that the Chief Justice was setting an extremely high bar – one the prosecution would rarely be able to surmount.

And that provided an answer to the crucial legal question in the case. Did doing what the Dean did – helping people who were on trial or in prison for opposing apartheid, and their families – 'aid' or 'encourage' terroristic activities within the words of the statute? The answer might well have been Yes. The statutory wording was wide enough to mean that anyone providing support to anti-apartheid causes was participating in terrorist activities. If that was what the appeal court had decided, the result would have been the police state that many feared Verwoerd's hardline successor as Prime Minister, Balthazar Johannes (John) Vorster, was seeking to establish.

But Ogilvie Thompson's deft ruling put an end to that. With an elegant sweep of his judicial pen, he brushed away the prosecution's insistence that supporting ANC trialists and prisoners amounted to supporting the ANC: 'Knowledge that his family is receiving some assistance while he is serving a prison sentence (or while he is outside the Republic's borders engaged in terroristic activities) is no doubt some solace to the individual concerned; but that can hardly be regarded as an intended boosting of morale in such a degree as to qualify as promotion of the activities of the ANC.' So providing 'some solace' to revolutionary operatives was not in itself unlawful. The Dean was in the clear.

The practical impact of these rulings was momentous. They sliced through the potentially unlimited scope of the Terrorism Act. And since it was almost impossible for prosecutors to provide evidence of the kind the Chief Justice required, his ruling blasted a torpedo through the hull of some of the statute's most menacing provisions. In doing so, it opened a life-sustaining space outside the whites-only Parliament inside which opponents of apartheid could continue to breathe and work inside the country.

Little did I appreciate, as I pored over Ogilvie Thompson's dense words in the whites-only students' law library at Stellenbosch, that his judgment would pave the way for my own legal practice and activism ten years later, when, after a byway into Latin and classical culture, and three privileged years at Oxford as a Rhodes Scholar, I eventually embarked on my career as a practising lawyer at the end of 1982.

Still less did I appreciate that, with the brave decisions on coloured voters, and Oliver Schreiner's dissent, the ruling in the Dean's case tremulously lit a pathway towards a future constitutional state for our country.

Ogilvie Thompson's judgment setting the Dean free meant that lawyers and philanthropists and activists could support ANC- or PAC-aligned causes as long as they steered clear of advocating violence and of direct links to the organisations themselves. Over the following two decades, the activities of countless internal activist organisations like the United Democratic Front, the Release Mandela Campaign, the Soweto Parents' Crisis Committee, the Detainees' Parents Support Committee, the black trade union movement from 1979, and independent white-led organisations like the End Conscription Campaign and the Black Sash itself, remained possible because of the lifeline Ogilvie Thompson's judgment threw them. My own work with many of these organisations in the 1980s was possible because of the Dean's judgment.

VIII White judges, the Defiance Campaign and attorney Mr Mandela

All that lay in the future. For now, spending long hours browsing through the books in the university library – often reading anything but the cases our lecturers said we must read – I came across a decision that immediately soared to the top of my list of all-time most favourite judicial decisions. It was the first judicial ruling involving Nelson Mandela – and it cast vivid light on President Mandela's subsequent personal stand on judges and the rule of law, and on what judges can mean to a democracy. Delivered in April 1954, just over a year after I was born, it was called *Law Society v Mandela*. It concerned the Defiance Campaign – and the role in it of a tall, ruggedly built, charismatic and impressively talented 35-year-old attorney, Nelson Rolihlahla Mandela.

The white supremacist National Party's hardline racial policies after 1948 caused the ANC to rethink its strategies. It decided on a radical shift. For forty fruitless years it had tried the gentle-handed route of petitions, deputations, meetings and polite persuasion. Now, roused by its imposing Youth League leader, Nelson Mandela, it embraced a new tough line: militant nationalism, mass action, boycotts, strikes and civil disobedience. The aim? To scrap all laws differentiating between white and black, to obtain full and equal voting rights for all, with direct representation in Parliament, and to abolish the pass laws and other unjust statutes.

The main tactical vehicle for the new strategy was the Defiance Campaign. It was the biggest organised programme of non-violent resistance South Africa had ever seen – and the first political operation pursued jointly by blacks, whites, coloureds and Indians.

The apartheid hardliners did not sit quietly by. In response to the ANC's change of tack, Parliament passed a tough new law in 1950. It became a crime for anyone to advocate or encourage, or even defend, any 'scheme' aiming to bring about change in South Africa 'by unlawful acts or omissions'. Breaching the law carried a possible ten-year jail sentence.

This only spurred the ANC and its allies on. In July 1951, at a joint conference they resolved 'to declare war on Pass Laws' and on segregation, and to embark on a mass campaign to repeal 'oppressive laws'. The strategy? 'Defiance based on non-cooperation'.

Civil disobedience involves breaking the law for moral reasons. The Defiance Campaign was in its very conception a scheme to bring about change in the country by unlawful acts. So by definition it flouted the new law.

At the forefront of the Campaign was the young attorney Mandela. He was a leading figure at the ANC's 35th annual conference in Bloemfontein in December 1951, which endorsed and adopted the Defiance Campaign, and he played a key role in taking the idea from conception to the streets.

In May 1952 Mandela addressed a crowd of 500 black people. As always, security police moles were present, taking notes. Mandela, they reported, called on black people to resist implementation of objectionable laws 'over our dead bodies'. He asked his audience to bear in mind that 'you must do this in a peaceful manner – the greatest discipline is required of you'. But there was steel inside his glove: 'We shall not rest,' he told his audience, 'until the gaols are filled.'

As the Defiance Campaign reached an uncertain peak, Mandela, the firebrand leader, doubled as Mandela, the practising attorney. Amidst his crowded political programme, he had to make arrangements for an effective professional life. In August 1952 he formed a law partnership with his fellow ANC leader, Oliver Reginald Tambo. They set up practice under the style and title of 'Mandela and Tambo' in Chancellor House, near the magistrates' courts in downtown Johannesburg.

But a question mark hung over the new law firm. The meeting Mandela addressed under the watchful eyes of police informers endangered the future of Mandela the lawyer.

The apartheid authorities quickly arrested Mandela and other Defiance Campaign leaders. They charged them with breaking the tough new 1950 law by advocating change through 'unlawful acts'. The Campaign leaders were brought to trial in Pretoria before Judge Frans Rumpff, whom the apartheid government had freshly appointed to the Bench in 1952. Defending the accused was a distinguished King's Counsel at the Johannesburg Bar, Bram Fischer. A courageous man of singular principles, Fischer came from an elite Afrikaner background. His father was Judge-President of the Free State, and before him his grandfather had been Prime Minister of the pre-Union Orange River Colony. Eschewing elite family connections, Fischer joined the SA Communist Party to dedicate himself to the cause of non-racial democracy and social justice.

In his autobiography Mandela describes Rumpff as 'an able man' who was 'better informed than the average white South African'. He also said he was 'fair-minded and reasonable'. But

Mandela's statements at the May 1952 meeting provided crucial evidence against him. He denied nothing he had said or done. Judge Rumpff convicted Mandela and the other Campaign leaders of breaching the statute. Mandela recounts that although Rumpff found that the accused had instigated acts that ranged from 'open noncompliance of laws to something that equals high treason', he accepted that they had consistently advised their members 'to follow a peaceful course of action and to avoid violence in any shape or form'.

Despite convicting the accused, Judge Rumpff showed unexpected leniency. From time to time in his later judicial life, he would surprise detractors by coming up with pro-liberty rulings. Instead of the ten-year maximum sentence, the accused were each sentenced to only nine months' imprisonment. And even more strikingly, the judge suspended the sentences entirely. No one would go to jail immediately. The condition was that the accused should not be found guilty of the same contravention within two years. Mandela's work as a politician and also as a lawyer could continue.

But the Law Society, a statutory body representing the country's attorneys, thought differently. Mandela's criminal conviction raised pressing questions about his status as a practising lawyer. How could an attorney, who is an officer of the court, urge organised resistance to the law? How can a guardian of the law advocate that it be undermined? Lawyers must uphold the law. They can surely not be allowed to subvert it.

On this line of argument, the Law Society moved to take action against Mandela. The criminal conviction – Mandela's first run-in with the law – gave them the trigger. They applied for the court to strike him off the roll of attorneys. The society argued that respect for the law was demanded of all advocates and attorneys. They were officers of the court. They had to encourage obedience to the laws that Parliament enacted, even laws they considered unjust. Mandela's deliberate defiance of the law made him unfit to continue to practise as an attorney. The court should disbar him from practising.

The Law Society's case was heard in Pretoria in March 1954. As always, because of the importance of a case concerning an officer of the court, two judges instead of only one were assigned. On the Bench were two English speakers, William Henry Ramsbottom and Edwin Ridgill Roper. Both were appointed before the National Party takeover in 1948, Ramsbottom in 1938, Roper in 1945. Judge Ramsbottom was a beloved and highly respected liberal judge, whom the apartheid government grudgingly appointed to the appeal court only very belatedly, when he was already ill: he died after serving less than two years on the appeal court.

Two experienced senior advocates appeared before the two judges to press the Law Society's argument that Mandela should be disbarred. But Mandela himself came to court with powerful legal backing. He put his faith in a team of distinguished liberal advocates from the Johannesburg Bar – Walter Pollak, who wrote a famous textbook on jurisdiction (the power of a court to hear a case and grant judgment), and Blen Franklin, who later became a judge in the Johannesburg High Court.

As the two opposing teams of lawyers filed into the spacious, light-filled courtroom of Pretoria's elegant nineteenth-century Palace of Justice on Church Square, what was at stake between them was much more than only Mandela's fitness to practise as a lawyer. What was on trial was the moral standing of the Defiance Campaign, with Mandela at its forefront, and, beyond that, the profound ethical questions its challenge to apartheid's oppressive laws posed.

How would the court respond? Would the judges react with crusty snootiness, like Winston Churchill, Britain's Prime Minister at the time? Churchill denounced the Campaign as counterproductive and 'very stupid'. Would their reaction be similar? Or would their judicial vision be sensitive to the longer, deeper moral issues of racial injustice and oppression?

After hearing argument, Judges Ramsbottom and Roper reserved their judgment for five weeks. At last, in April, they handed down their finding. It was a stunning reverse for the Law Society. The application to strike Mandela's name from the roll of attorneys was refused. Mandela had triumphed. He would remain a practising lawyer.

In a stirring judgment, Judge Ramsbottom reasoned that 'the mere fact that an attorney has deliberately disobeyed the law does not necessarily disqualify him from practising his profession or justify the court in removing his name from the roll'. He pointed out that though Mandela had engaged in misconduct – inciting disobedience to the law – the misconduct had not been committed in his professional capacity. On the contrary, the offence of which he had been convicted 'had nothing to do with his practice as an attorney'.

Hence, the question wasn't simply whether Mandela had been convicted of a crime. It was whether that crime showed that he was 'of such a character that he is not worthy to remain in the ranks of an honourable profession'. And on that question, Judge Ramsbottom was unequivocal. There can, he said, be 'only one answer'. 'Nothing has been put before us which suggests in the slightest degree that [Mandela] has been guilty of conduct of a dishonest, disgraceful, or dishonourable kind.' Nothing he had done, the judge said, driving the point home, 'reflects upon his character or shows him to be unworthy' to continue practising as an attorney.

On the contrary, Judge Ramsbottom said, using the racial terminology of nearly fifty years ago, Mandela's motives were pure:

in advocating defiance, he 'was obviously motivated by a desire to serve his fellow non-Europeans'. The intention was 'to bring about the repeal of certain laws which [he] regarded as unjust'. The method of producing that result was unlawful, 'but his offence was not of a personally disgraceful character'. Hence there was nothing that rendered him unfit to practise as an attorney.

What about the fact that Mandela was unrepentant? He denied nothing. On the contrary, he remained defiant. He embraced his leadership of the Campaign, and refused to disavow anything he had said or done. The Law Society urged the court to take disciplinary action because despite being convicted of a crime he had 'not expressed regret'.

This point was a potential winner for the Law Society. Most practitioners carpeted for wrongdoing ooze humility and repentance. Not Mandela. He remained unbowed in the face of possible professional ruin. But Judge Ramsbottom also dismissed this attack. He did so in a rousing codicil to his judgment. He said that if Mandela's actions did not justify the court disciplining him, he could not be required to express regret: 'If what he did was not dishonourable, his failure to express regret cannot make it so.'

It was an extraordinary judgment. In effect, it was a ringing endorsement of Mandela's character and the motives behind his political work. Urging disobedience of apartheid laws was 'not dishonourable'. On the contrary: it was 'obviously motivated' by a desire to serve. This came as close as two white judges of the courts of apartheid South Africa could come to saying that Mandela's motives were noble, and that his support for the Defiance Campaign was righteous.

Mandela was deeply affected by the judges' decision. He cited it later, when, after being released from prison, he addressed the very Law Society that forty years earlier had moved to disbar him. 'Here I am,' he proudly exclaimed, 'with my name still on the roll.'

IX Justice and the courts under apartheid – the Treason Trial

The apartheid authorities, though dismayed by the judgment, did not sit still. They acted forcefully to hobble Mandela's mobility and to mute his public voice. The police tried to punch him down with successive banning orders. These restricted his movements, forbade him from holding office in any organisation, and muzzled his public speaking. But government had to do this through ministerial diktat and security police action. Until his conviction of conspiracy, in effect treason, ten years later, the courts and the law did not disown Nelson Mandela. And he remained a lawyer and an officer of the court.

Most importantly, the decision showed that, even in a wicked legal system, judges committed to justice and fairness may do more good than harm.

The judges in the Law Society case were appointed before the apartheid hardliners came to power. After 1948, government vigorously set about appointing Afrikaners, many of them apartheid supporters, to the Bench but, to the surprise of many, quite a number of the new judges also showed an aptitude for independence, a commitment to the rule of law, and a readiness to respect fundamental legal principles.

The Afrikaner nationalists were proud of the Roman and Roman-Dutch legal heritage the white colonists brought to South Africa in 1652. They saw themselves on a mission of civilisation in Africa, and they considered their legal heritage an important part of their calling. The effect of this was that, even though the legal system was grotesquely disfigured because it enforced apartheid, occasionally some justice could prevail. I was an Afrikaans speaker myself – my mother was an Afrikaner Schoeman, whose forefather came to the Cape in 1724. Though my primary language has long been English, before Pretoria Boys' High I went to Afrikaans schools. In literal terms both my first language and my mother tongue were Afrikaans. Hence my upbringing gave me a first-hand sense of the Afrikaners' sense of mission: both its racial condescension, and its claim to elevation.

Afrikaner pride in 'their' legal system helps to explain why Judge Rumpff, against expectation, let the Defiance Campaign leaders escape jail. And it explains the reaction of Judge Quartus de Wet, who later determined Mandela's fate in the Rivonia Trial, when a troublesome magistrate questioned Mandela's status as a lawyer, demanding to see his certificate to practise, and addressed him disrespectfully ('Hey, you'). Mandela brought a petition to remove the magistrate from the case. His motion succeeded. De Wet was outraged: 'This is the sort of thing that brings the administration of justice into disrepute in our country,' he said. He removed the magistrate, and ordered the case to start afresh before a new, presumably more respectful, presiding officer.

But Mandela's confrontation with the apartheid legal order was only beginning. On 25 and 26 June 1955, barely a year after Judges Ramsbottom and Roper affirmed his status as a practising lawyer, a 3000-strong 'Congress of the People' at Kliptown in Soweto adopted the Freedom Charter. In defiance of his ban, Mandela covertly attended.

The Charter proclaimed that South Africa belongs to all who live in it, black and white, and that no government can justly claim authority unless it is based on the will of the people. It demanded democratic government by the people, equality and human rights for all, and a share for all in the country's wealth. It proclaimed that the land shall be shared amongst those who work it.

It concluded in rousing terms. 'Let all who love their people and their country now say, as we say here: "These freedoms we will fight for, side by side, throughout our lives, until we have won our liberty."'

To the apartheid authorities, determined to perpetuate white dominance, this was intolerable provocation. Heavily armed policemen disrupted the second day of the Kliptown meeting. They said they were investigating high treason, and were searching for subversive documents. Their quest culminated within a few short months. Before the end of the following year, at dawn on 5 December 1956, only a few months after the rigged Parliament voted to cut coloured voters from the common franchise, the police swept through the country, arresting 140 people. Sixteen more followed shortly after. Among the very first seized was Nelson Mandela.

All those arrested were brought to the Old Fort prison in Johannesburg, which stands on the high knoll between Braamfontein and Hillbrow, commanding both the northern and the southern approaches to the city. Its northern ramparts now shelter the Constitutional Court from the icy southerly winds that sweep through downtown Johannesburg in wintertime. The Fort was built on the instruction of President Paul Kruger at the end of the nineteenth-century to defend the Transvaal Republic against British gold-seeking imperialists.

Now, a half-century later, it held captive the most prominent extra-parliamentary opponents of apartheid. They were a distinguished array of churchmen, lawyers, writers, trade unionists, teachers, manual workers, businessmen, academics and community activists. They included blacks, coloureds and Indians, and also 23 whites.

The arrests signalled the start of the biggest trial in South African history. Two weeks later, those arrested were brought to face the charges. They appeared before a magistrate in a makeshift courtroom set up in downtown Johannesburg's Drill Hall –

because no court was big enough to accommodate them. All were charged with the offence of high treason under the Roman-Dutch common law. The charge, if proven, carried the death penalty.

The trial was in two stages. First there was a preparatory examination to see if there was enough evidence to formally try the accused in a superior court. For those against whom enough preliminary evidence was presented, a full trial then followed. (This two-stage process, though not abolished, fell into disuse when the current criminal procedure statute came into force in 1977.)

But if the apartheid authorities thought that arrest, arraignment and treason charges would silence the accused, they were badly mistaken. The accused and their legal team sprang a surprise. Far from adopting a defensive posture, they came out fighting from the very start. Instead of allowing the proceedings to focus on the technical question of whether the accused had engaged in acts that made them guilty of subverting the state, their defence turned the spotlight on the high ethical issue of how apartheid laws oppressed South Africans.

Under scrutiny were not so much the actions of those struggling for freedom and equality, but government's intransigent and oppressive racial policies. The accused and their lawyers used the court proceedings to put apartheid on trial. This was to be a pattern over the next forty years. Apartheid hardliners sought to enforce their policies of racial domination by using the law against their opponents, and by using criminal trials, and the prospect of jail, to smother their work. In response, anti-apartheid activists and their lawyers used every public appearance, every procedural loophole, every legal opening and every conceptual ambiguity the law and its processes offered to thwart apartheid.

As the preparatory examination started in the Drill Hall, the silver-tongued advocate leading the defence, Vernon Berrangé, audaciously took the battle onto apartheid's territory. He announced that 'what is on trial here are not just one hundred and fifty six individuals, but the ideas which they and thousands of others in our land have openly espoused and expressed'. He went on: 'A battle of ideas has indeed been started in our country, a battle in which on one side are poised those ideas which seek equal opportunities for all, and freedom of thought and expression by all persons of all races and creeds; and, on the other side, those which deny to all but a few the riches of life, both material and spiritual, which the accused aver should be common to all.'

His words rang out in media reports in South Africa and across the world. Those accused of treason were putting apartheid in the dock, and shaming it. I read Berrangé's words years after I became a lawyer. They stirred my pride in what my profession could achieve. Far from being just grey-suited factotums, lawyers could help shape history – on the side of justice and fairness.

Twenty years after the start of the Treason Trial, public interest lawyers continued to embrace these very strategies to counter apartheid. At Wits University, John Dugard in 1978 established the pioneering Centre for Applied Legal Studies (CALS), which created an academic base for practitioners to attack apartheid while seeking to pave the way for a more just legal system. And Felicia Kentridge and Arthur Chaskalson were amongst those who soon after, in 1979, founded the Legal Resources Centre (LRC), a pioneering firm of public interest lawyers, which gained and has sustained enduring international admiration for its work. After three years in commercial and general practice at the Johannesburg Bar, Professor Dugard invited me in 1986 to move my practice to a base at CALS. I was excited to accept. My idea that the law could be more than only a rebuke, a restraint – as it had been to my father – and more than an instrument of oppression and injustice – as it was to millions of black South Africans – was confronted with an exciting challenge. CALS invited me to come and help put my lofty aspirations of legal challenge and reform into practice.

When as lawyers from the LRC and CALS we engaged in court-room confrontations, we aimed to set the same battle lines as the lawyers in the Treason Trial had set. Time and again, we adopted tactics and brought forward witnesses and testimony that shifted the courtroom contest from focusing on the strict legal issues to the moral repugnance of the apartheid laws the authorities were seeking to enforce.

From the Treason Trial on, public court hearings under apartheid became a contest of right and wrong – but not right and wrong according to apartheid law. One set of norms, those of the apartheid legal system, determined that breaking the law was illegal, and that those guilty of it were criminals. Another set – the moral values that showed that racial subordination was abhorrent, and that any system premised on it was indefensible – determined that apartheid's opponents were fighting a just cause, in a necessary struggle, and were guilty of no moral wrong in breaking its laws.

The legal system under apartheid, employed to perpetuate racial supremacy, became one of the instruments for its subversion.

However, as I was to discover in my own years in legal practice, using the law against apartheid was often a tedious and long-winded business. It demanded much patience.

The preparatory examination in the Treason Trial dragged on for over a year, but in January 1958, 61 of the accused, including Chief Albert Luthuli and Mandela's law partner, Oliver Tambo, were discharged for lack of evidence. They walked free. For the 95 accused who remained, Mandela amongst them, the daily burden of trial attendance and preparation continued.

The trial proper started on 3 August 1958. A special court of three judges was put together to try the accused. Presiding was the same Judge Rumpff who had previously convicted Mandela and the other leaders guilty of breaking the law, but had given them wholly suspended sentences. Together with him sat Judge Kennedy, and Judge Ludorf – all had been appointed to the Bench by the apartheid government. In his autobiography Mandela bleakly describes the panel, with its links to government and apartheid-supporting organisations, as 'not promising'. (Ludorf later, after the accused successfully challenged his impartiality, was replaced by Judge Bekker.)

To many it must have seemed inevitable that this panel would render guilty verdicts and long sentences.

The daily slog that a long-running trial demands continued for the accused even, as outside the courtroom, tense events were shaping our country's momentous and sometimes horrifying history. Robert Mangaliso Sobukwe and others, objecting to the Freedom Charter as too conciliatory, broke away from the ANC in April 1959 to form the Pan Africanist Congress (PAC). Mrs Helen Suzman and eleven other parliamentarians split from the main white opposition to form the Progressive Party. In Cape Town and Johannesburg, the newly formed PAC pre-empted the ANC by leading mass protests against the pass laws. On 21 March 1960, to the aghast horror of South Africa and the world, police shot dead 69 unarmed protestors at the Sharpeville police station. Eighteen days later Parliament passed a special law banning both the ANC and the PAC. South African whites voted just months later, in October 1960, to become a Republic, which Prime Minister Hendrik Verwoerd soon took outside the Commonwealth.

The grim thirty-year end-phase to apartheid, which was to see decades of isolation and oppression, had begun.

Amidst these momentous events, the leaders who remained on trial had to travel to Pretoria every day, where the trial proceeded in the Old Synagogue, and sit through the long, dense hours of court process. The trial absorbed the energies and time of all, taking them away from their work, their families and their political activity. But the proceedings – and especially the belligerent defence – also soaked up the resources of the apartheid state, its prosecutors and police and officials. At least some of that energy would have been spent enforcing the increasingly rigorous racial separation the hardliners demanded, uprooting families and communities from 'black spots', and victimising black people without passes in urban areas. Because of the combative tactics of anti-apartheid lawyers, time, money and resources had to be diverted from enforcing apartheid into the courtroom battle.

The legal fight was surely worth it.

And most importantly and practically, the protracted Treason Trial ended in a sensational acquittal of all the accused. After Mandela and other accused had testified in their own defence, and the state and defence had closed their cases, Judge Rumpff told the defence the court did not need to hear further argument. He said that the panel of judges had reached a unanimous verdict. This cut the proceedings dramatically short. It was an outcome that freed all the accused. For the prosecution, this meant the trial had proved a catastrophe.

In his judgment on 29 March 1961, Rumpff explained that although the ANC was intent on replacing the government, and had used illegal means of protest during the Defiance Campaign, the prosecution had failed to show the organisation was using violence to overthrow the state. Hence the prosecution had failed to show that the accused acted with revolutionary intent.

The last 30 accused were all pronounced not guilty and discharged.

Mandela recounts that when Judge Rumpff finished delivering the court's verdict, 'The spectators' gallery erupted in cheers.

We stood and hugged each other, and waved to the happy court-room. All of us then paraded into the courtyard, smiling, laughing, crying. The crowd yelled and chanted as we emerged.'

The most massive legal contest in South African history had ended in disaster for the prosecution. The accused and their law-yers had torn the state's accusations to shreds. The attempt to use treason charges to stifle extra-parliamentary anti-apartheid opposition had been calamitously thrown out of court. As Man-dela recounted, 'After more than four years in court and dozens of prosecutors, thousands of documents and tens of thousands of pages of testimony, the state had failed in its mission. The verdict was an embarrassment to the government, both at home and abroad.' Yet, he reflected, 'the result only embittered the state against us even further. The lesson they took away was not that we had legitimate grievances but that they needed to be far more ruthless.'

And Mandela did not regard the verdict as a vindication of the legal system – or as evidence that a black man could get a fair trial in a white man's court. His own assessment was much more constrained. 'It was,' he said, 'the right verdict and a just one, but it was largely as a result of a superior defence team and the fair-mindedness of the panel of these particular judges.'

X Law and armed resistance to apartheid – the Rivonia Trial

Mandela was correct when he had predicted that enforcement of apartheid would take a ruthless turn after the Treason Trial acquittals. Government pushed even tougher statutes through Parliament to make it easier for prosecutors to secure convictions against extra-parliamentary apartheid opponents.

Without a bill of rights, the courts had no power to question what the legislature enacted. Parliament was supreme, and courts had to enforce its will – or that, at least, was the doctrine most white judges accepted under apartheid.

A brave minority on the Bench thought differently. They fought to find ways to uphold long-standing Roman and Roman-Dutch legal precepts. These included equal treatment, unless a statute expressly commanded otherwise, and elementary procedural fairness. They fought for these to prevail, even in the face of rancid apartheid legislation. And, indeed, occasionally the laws Parliament enacted did leave enough room for determined lawyers, and fair-minded judges, to try to secure just outcomes. In addition, fair procedures could generally still be demanded in the courtrooms of apartheid.

Only months after the treason acquittals, events occurred that would put those courtroom processes to further test. On 16 December 1961 Mandela and other leaders founded the ANC's armed wing. They called it uMkhonto weSizwe (MK), the 'Spear of the Nation'.

The armed struggle had begun.

But on a wintry day just a year and half later, on 11 July 1963, most of the high command of the ANC leadership was arrested in a dramatic police raid on a secret hideout at Rivonia, north of Johannesburg. During the raid, the police arrested seven people. They also seized a crucial six-page document headed Operation Mayibuye ('Let Africa come back'). The document had been drafted by the ANC high command, excluding Mandela, who had previously been arrested. He was already in the Old Fort prison in Johannesburg, serving a sentence of five years' imprisonment. This was for incitement and for leaving the country illegally, when he received military training in March 1962 from the Algerian National Liberation Front.

When those arrested at Rivonia fifteen months later were put on trial, Mandela joined them in the dock. Others on trial included Govan Mbeki, Raymond Mhlaba, Walter Sisulu, Ahmed Kathrada, Elias Motsoaledi, Denis Goldberg, Lionel Rusty Bernstein and Andrew Mlangeni.

But the prosecutors had learnt from the Treason Trial fiasco. This time, they were careful to avoid the pitfalls of bringing charges under the common law. Instead, they adopted a much safer ploy. They used the newly enacted 1962 Sabotage Act against the accused. The charge sheet confronted the accused with charges of statutory sabotage and conspiracy. The statutory charges were no less grave than those under the common law. They too carried the death penalty. The crucial difference was that the statute made the prosecution's task easier, by providing important procedural help in proving vital elements of the charges against the accused.

As in the Defiance Campaign prosecution twelve years before, the lead counsel for the accused was Bram Fischer. By now, alongside a busy commercial practice, representing corporate giants like the Anglo American gold-mining corporation, Fischer was also an underground leader of the Communist Party. And he was still deeply involved in anti-apartheid work. It was by simple happenstance that he had not been at the Rivonia hide-out when the security police arrested the ANC leadership there.

For Bram Fischer, defending the Rivonia accused entailed taking extraordinary risks. While defending them as an advocate, he was also engaged in a high-stakes double game. He was an officer of the court, with a duty to it and to his clients, but he was also an underground leader in the anti-apartheid opposition, with a commitment to securing a just society. During the trial, Fischer the advocate obtained crucial documents from the state. Fischer the underground activist then made these documents available to fellow underground activists to use in their struggle.

Presiding over the Rivonia accused was Quartus de Wet, now Judge-President of the Transvaal. He was the judge who ten years earlier had rebuked a magistrate for disrespecting Mandela. Of him, Joel Joffe, the attorney for Mandela and the other accused in the Rivonia Trial, said he 'did not have the reputation of being a puppet of the Nationalist Government who would take orders directly from politicians'. While the accused and their lawyers felt that they could have done much better, 'we could also have done much worse'.

Before the trial started, the defence lawyers went on the attack. They applied for the dismissal of the indictment on the grounds that it did not set out clearly enough the precise charges the state was levelling against the accused. Their strategy succeeded. Judge-President De Wet handed the defence a symbolic victory – he quashed the indictment. This was a slap in the face for the prosecution. It meant it had to go back to the drawing board to reformulate the charges. It had to set them out with more precision and clarity. The victory was short-lived. The prosecution fixed its sloppy work, and was allowed to proceed. But the judge's ruling was important. It showed that he was not prepared to give the prosecutors a free ride. Procedural justice, by his lights, would prevail in his court.

Operation Mayibuye detailed ambitious plans for military insurrection. In his autobiography, Nelson Mandela describes the document as 'the keystone of the state's case' against the Rivonia accused. It sketched out in general form, he explained, 'the plan for a possible commencement of guerrilla operations, and how it might spark a mass armed uprising' against the apartheid government.

The state argued that the ANC executive, including Mandela, had endorsed and approved Operation Mayibuye, and that MK had adopted it as the operating model for armed revolution. As

Joel Joffe, the Rivonia accused's attorney, explained, this meant that 'the lives of the accused were at stake. The state's case alleged that they had already embarked on the organisation of armed insurrection and guerrilla warfare', involving foreign military intervention and general mayhem. If the court accepted this, 'the peril to the lives of the accused was real and grave'.

The accused denied that Operation Mayibuye was already operational. They contended the high command had never formally adopted it. It was, they said, still being considered as a possible plan of action.

The accused made it plain to their legal team, which included Arthur Chaskalson, that they would never deny membership of the ANC or the SA Communist Party. Nor would they disavow the ideals and aims of the organisations. Through skilful cross-examination of the police witnesses, and adroit testimony by the accused who took the witness stand, the accused's version prevailed. The trial judge accepted that Operation Mayibuye had never become operational.

The trial offered the accused an important opportunity. Most of them had, like Mandela, long been banned from public speaking and from being quoted in the media. Now the courtroom confrontation gave them a platform from which to voice their principled opposition to apartheid. And the newspapers were entitled to report on courtroom proceedings.

In particular, Nelson Mandela's statement from the dock rang across the world. It became a classic enunciation of a people's claim to dignity and freedom. He explained his commitment to non-racial principles. He emphasised his support for independent institutions and the rule of law. And he detailed the ravages apartheid's unjust racial laws inflicted on black South Africans.

He ended by explaining that the struggle of the African people was a national struggle, 'inspired by their own suffering and their own experience'. It was, he said, 'a struggle for the right to live'.

'During my lifetime I have dedicated myself to this struggle of the African people. I have fought against white domination, and I have fought against black domination. I have cherished the ideal of a democratic and free society in which all persons live together in harmony and with equal opportunities. It is an ideal which I hope to live for and to achieve. But if needs be, it is an ideal for which I am prepared to die.'

Judge-President De Wet eventually convicted eight accused in the Rivonia Trial of statutory sabotage – the equivalent of treason. They were, in the order in which the judge announced his verdict, Mandela, Sisulu, Goldberg, Mbeki, Kathrada, Mhlaba, Mlangeni and Motsoaledi. Only Bernstein was acquitted.

Mandela was prepared to face death for opposing apartheid, but that price was not exacted of him. Instead of the death sentences many expected, the trial judge on 12 June 1964 imposed imprisonment: life sentences. This was imprisonment for life – but, it was for life. The accused all left prison, years later, living. All eight lived to see democracy established in South Africa. One of them became democratic South Africa's first President.

XI Law and the struggle for justice under apartheid – the legacy for democracy

Soon after the Rivonia Trial ended, Bram Fischer, who had led the defence, was himself arrested. Released on bail, he obtained the court's permission to go abroad to argue an appeal for a mining corporation before the Privy Council in London. He returned. But then, on 25 January 1965, defying his bail conditions, he went underground, eluding the courtroom, to continue his anti-apartheid work.

Fischer was eventually re-arrested and he was put on trial. He was convicted of conspiring to commit sabotage. He, too, received a sentence of life imprisonment but, unlike the Rivonia trialists, he did not outlive the system that imprisoned him. He died in 1974. When he was already severely stricken by cancer, and close to death, the prison authorities released him. He died a few weeks later in the home of his brother in Bloemfontein.

Bram Fischer's life as a practising lawyer illuminates the complexity of the apartheid legal system. He thought it worth sustaining the struggle for justice through the law, and treasured his position as legal counsel. When he estreated his bail, the Bar Council, which he himself had previously chaired, hastily brought proceedings to strike his name from the roll of advocates. Fischer knew that more was required to attain a just system than only legal work. Unlike many other lawyers, including me, he sacrificed his legal practice, his home and his comforts to devote his life unconditionally to the struggle for justice.

But Fischer felt acute anguish at his colleagues' actions. He felt they were precipitate. It pained him that they did not accept that his motives were always in pursuit of justice.

Throughout his struggle against apartheid, Mandela, too, thought it worth fighting to keep his status as a lawyer inside the South African legal system. This was even though the law was the chief instrument through which racial privilege, the pass laws and segregation were enforced. Why did he fight to remain a lawyer in such a pernicious system? Mandela explained that, as a young law student, it was one of his ambitions 'to try to use my professional training to help tilt the balance just a wee bit in favour of the citizen'. Later, as President, he explained that under apartheid, 'The law was used not as an instrument to afford the citizen protection, but rather as the chief means of his subjection.'

But even in the harshest period of apartheid law enforcement,

Mandela recognised that there was a balance that lawyers and judges could try to tilt in favour of justice – even if only 'a wee bit'. In its very nature, the legal process afforded lawyers that chance.

Mandela's biographer Anthony Sampson records that Mandela was occasionally surprised by the fairness of judges, but at the same time he knew apartheid laws severely limited the courts as the guardians of civil liberties. As Mandela wrote in jail, 'In our country where there are racial laws, and where all the judges and magistrates are white and reeking the stale odour of racial prejudice, the operation of such principles is very limited.'

The apartheid legal system was evil. It enforced a system that sought to degrade, subordinate and dehumanise the majority of South Africa's people because of their race. But, though limited in their operation, the principles Mandela spoke of were never obliterated. For most of apartheid, the candle of hope for justice under law flickered low and the space within which its light shone was often stiflingly small. Apartheid law was the instrument through which 'a stubborn, race-blinded white oligarchy', as Mandela called it, enforced its will.

Even so, the law continued to provide a means through which creative lawyers and principled judges could oppose apartheid, or at least try to ameliorate its harsh effects. This was what propelled my own choice of law as a career. I became a human rights lawyer in the early 1980s. Human rights practice in these years was sometimes dark and difficult, but it could also be hopeful and exciting.

By the end of the 1970s government realised it could no longer suppress black worker organisations. In 1979 it changed the law to allow black people to join and form trade unions. As a result, unions flourished. When I started practising from CALS in 1986, I formed part of a group of activist lawyers who were committed

51

to thwarting apartheid's effects through legal strategies. Led by labour organiser Halton Cheadle, we fought cases on unfair dismissal, trade union rights and worker security and safety. Unions used the new fair labour practice protections aggressively to give workers job security and to secure better pay and benefits for them.

The apartheid government thought that by drawing workers into the labour relations structures it created, it could contain them. It was wrong. It had let the genie of mass activism out of the bottle. By working within the new system of labour protections, the unions did far more than only secure legal rights. Strengthened by repeated court victories under the new law, they became joint leaders of the mass internal activist alliance that swept the country from the mid-1980s. They and other activist organisations were at the forefront of insisting on equal rights for all in a democratic South Africa.

We also fought cases in which we resisted forced removals from land, and defended ANC fighters charged with treason, and white conscripts refusing to serve in apartheid's army. And legal victories in many cases meant that, in effect, lawyers were working in tandem with internal activists opposing apartheid. Arthur Chaskalson, who later became Chief Justice of democratic South Africa, with his team of LRC lawyers, a team that included Geoff Budlender, successfully fought pivotal cases against the pass laws and forced removals and suppression of anti-apartheid organisations. Their litigation helped thwart apartheid's grand design.

Two cases put a virtual end to enforcement of the notorious pass laws – the very laws that, thirty years before, formed the centrepiece of the Defiance Campaign.

The first case involved Mrs Nonceba Komani. She moved from the Eastern Cape in May 1974 to Gugulethu, to join her husband, Mr Willie Komani. He had been working in Cape Town since

July 1960. The pass law authorities initially allowed her to stay but then, as part of the crackdown on 'urban blacks', in January 1975 they instructed her to go back to the Eastern Cape.

She refused to leave. The pass regulations required that, as the wife or customary union partner of a long-term resident, she had to have what was quaintly called a 'lodger's permit'. The Cape Town court enforced this requirement. Chaskalson appealed the verdict to Bloemfontein. He argued that the lodger's permit requirement was inconsistent with the statute under which the regulations were promulgated. He said the lodger's permit regulation was invalid.

The appeal court upheld his argument. The judgment was written by Judge Rumpff – the judge who in 1952 sentenced Mandela to a suspended jail term for his part in the Defiance Campaign, and who in 1961 acquitted him in the Treason Trial.

Now it was August 1980, and Rumpff was Chief Justice. He found for Mr and Mrs Komani. He wrote a judgment scrapping the iniquitous system of 'lodger's permits'. Mrs Komani's case established that, as Mr Komani's spouse, she did not need a separate permit to live with her husband.

Less than three years later, Mr Tom Rikhoto, again with Chaskalson's advocacy, struck what was to prove a probably fatal blow at the pass laws. To become entitled to live permanently in the urban areas, a black person who was born in the 'homelands', and not in a city, had to have 'worked continuously' in an urban area for ten years.

Since August 1970, Mr Rikhoto had been working for the same employer, and living in Germiston, an industrial and gold-mining city close to Johannesburg. The regulations enforcing the pass laws required him to leave every year, and to return to his 'homeland'. So he did. For a few weeks each year, he returned to his rural home in Gazankulu, in the remote northeast of the country.

Every year, early in the new year, he returned to Germiston, knowing that his employer needed him, and that his employer would give him back his job for another year. And when he returned in January each year, this is indeed what happened. For over ten years, year by year, like clockwork, his employer re-employed him.

Did this mean that Mr Rikhoto had 'worked continuously' in Germiston for more than ten years? If the answer was Yes, he was entitled to stay permanently in the urban areas. He would have security of tenure as a city dweller. But the pass law authorities said No, and they refused Mr Rikhoto and others in his position the right to live permanently in the cities.

The LRC took Mr Rikhoto's case to court. Government argued strenuously in support of the pass law officials. It pointed out that Mr Rikhoto took leave every year. And his contract was renewed from year to year. It was not 'continuous'. Hence, government argued, Mr Rikhoto had not worked continuously. For all those years, he had been employed only for separate one-year fragments. This meant that he had no right to live permanently in the urban areas.

The LRC lawyers contested this. The courts' answer was crucial to enforcement of the pass laws, since there were millions in Mr Rikhoto's position.

The tight legal question was what constituted 'continuous' residence and employment. But behind the legal issue was the human question of residential security for a significant segment of urbanised South Africa. And behind that social question lay a blunt political question. This was whether it was still practical for apartheid ideologues to dream of enforcing 'grand apartheid'. To be practicable, grand apartheid wanted to make black South Africans identify with their 'homelands'. It wanted them to plan their lives and future in their own areas and to accept that their time in the 'white' cities was just a temporary sojourn.

The Rikhoto case put this cruel and absurd logic to a legal test. The courts failed this logic. Both the Pretoria court and the appeal court in Bloemfontein, following on its humane ruling in Mrs Komani's case, ruled in Mr Rikhoto's favour. Even though Mr Rikhoto went back home every year, and even though his job contract was renewed year by year, he had in fact lived and worked 'continuously' in the urban areas. He was entitled to stay permanently.

This decision meant not only that a huge group of black people gained legally secure status in the urban areas, but that it became practically impossible to enforce the pass laws. Further legal activism nailed the lid on the pass law coffin. In addition to the Komani and Rikhoto victories, in the early 1980s Lawyers for Human Rights and CALS provided mass defences for city dwellers prosecuted for contravening the residential segregation laws. Then they launched a campaign to provide free legal representation in pass courts. Once pass law accused had lawyers to represent them, the pass courts simply could not work. What had previously been a quick two-minute hearing now took a day.

The lawyers' interventions eventually forced the apartheid government to see the folly of its ways. On 23 July 1986 the apartheid government gave up on the pass laws. The pass law statute was repealed. The lawyers' work and the courts' decisions had rendered a pivotal piece of the grand apartheid design unenforceable.

Amidst the brutality and turmoil of the 1980s, my CALS colleagues and I sometimes even managed to turn apartheid's logic against itself. In two cases, we managed to thwart government's plans to split off pockets of the rural areas, under oppressive pro-apartheid traditional leaders, to set up further 'independent'

Bantustans. We did so with legal arguments that gleefully turned the grand theory of apartheid against the evil system itself.

Government tried to incorporate the relatively prosperous Moutse area, northeast of Pretoria, into the impoverished Ndebele-speaking homeland KwaNdebele, to make it viable for 'independence'. John Dugard, head of CALS, devised a clever argument. Surely this offended apartheid's own legislative principles of ethnic purity, he argued. After all, the population of Moutse was not Ndebele. It was predominantly Pedi speaking. By apartheid's own logic, Moutse's Pedi speakers could not be dragooned into an alien-cultured homeland.

I helped Dugard formulate the court papers and the evidence, and acted as his junior counsel in the high court and the appeal court. We lost in the Pretoria High Court, but the appeal court reversed the high court judgment. It upheld Dugard's argument. It found that government could not use a statute based on distinct ethnicities to create a single homeland by forcing other ethnicities into it. The court set aside Moutse's incorporation into KwaNdebele. As a result, 'independence' was put on hold.

But the apartheid planners persisted. Even though Moutse could not be tagged onto KwaNdebele, they proceeded with 'independence' plans. So, in another case, Geoff Budlender from the LRC briefed me to challenge the State President's official proclamation announcing pre-independence elections. The proclamation allowed only Ndebele-speaking men to vote. Women were barred. This, surely, was not acceptable! Or so we protested in court papers on behalf of Ndebele-speaking women objecting to their exclusion.

Of course the women we represented did not want to vote in an 'independent' homeland. They wanted freedom in their own country. But our argument used principles of Roman and Roman-Dutch law to thwart the grand design of apartheid. The common law, much prized by Afrikaner judges, forbade unequal treatment and discrimination, unless legislation in express terms authorised it.

And the legislation said nothing that empowered the State President to bar women from the vote. So we urged that the elections were illegal. Without express legislative sanction, women had to be allowed to vote. The court agreed. It upheld our argument. The effect was that the KwaNdebele elections were trash-canned – and, as a result, KwaNdebele independence never happened.

These legal ploys were possible because, in its essence, apartheid was a project that used the law as its instrument. For most of its history, most of those enforcing it saw themselves as subject to the law and its constraints. This changed radically in the 1980s, when 'dirty tricks' campaigns were sprung, and murderous 'third forces' were unleashed.

Until then, security policemen, bureaucrats, politicians and lawyers, including apartheid-minded judges, thought of themselves as operating within the values of an ethically sound and respected legal system. They knew apartheid was criticised around the world, and that most black South Africans rejected it vehemently, but they told themselves that there was a logic and justice to it.

Because of this, the legal system offered space to thwart apartheid's plans and grand designs. And hence the legal system often did operate as a brake. On occasion, the courts were a real constraint on what the apartheid apparatus was able to achieve. Apartheid bureaucrats found that implementation of their orders was sometimes slowed down. They found the courts served as a check on government and police action.

And it was the very legal trappings of apartheid, despite the evil they engendered, that laid the foundations for the constitutional system that followed.

To say this is not uncontroversial. The role of judges and the courts under apartheid inspired impassioned debate. Some argued that the legal system provided a cloak that legitimated apartheid – enabling it to be enforced for longer under a guise of respectability. Others urged that the legal system offered important opportunities to ameliorate and sometimes halt, or even reverse, abusive injustice.

Both sides were right, for without the law, apartheid may not have been as efficient as it was for so long. But without the law, it would undoubtedly have been an even harsher, more vicious, destructive and degrading system. Anti-apartheid legal activism played an important role both in slowing its implementation and in alleviating its injustices. More importantly, together with the honest and principled judges who refused pro-apartheid rulings whenever they could, legal activism opened a way to a better legal system – one where the law seeks to secure justice and equality, and not their opposite.

XII The apartheid judiciary and the Truth and Reconciliation Commission

In 1997 the Truth and Reconciliation Commission (TRC), chaired by Archbishop Desmond Tutu, called for submissions and evidence from judges and the legal profession on their role under apartheid. The country's five top judges put in a joint submission. They were Justice Chaskalson, the new President of the Constitutional Court, his deputy, Justice Pius Langa, and the two senior judges in the appeal court in Bloemfontein, Judge Ismail Mahomed and his deputy, Judge Hennie van Heerden. Recently retired Chief Justice Corbett, whom the new democratic government had asked to stay on in 1994, joined them.

The five judges pointed out that law was the primary tool used to give effect to apartheid. From 1948, when apartheid became the chief focus of government policy, there were in effect two legal systems – one for whites and the other for blacks. Throughout the apartheid era, laws violated a host of human rights. These were introduced with muted protest from only a few judges and lawyers.

The five noted that the legal system generally treated whites benevolently but that the system for black South Africans did not meet the standards of the rule of law and respect for individual rights. In the magistrates' courts, and in pass law courts, they came into daily contact with the brutal side of apartheid law.

The judges pointed out that few of these cases came before the higher courts. But they noted a shameful thing about apartheid law. When confronted with these cases that came up from the lower courts, judges treated apartheid provisions as 'normal law'. It was very rare, they said, to find a judicial officer remarking on the racist and unacceptable character of apartheid law. The judges pointed out how the courts also failed to protect detainees held without trial. Courts should have been vigilant to provide protection against abuse, but they were not.

The submission noted that lawyers' challenges did reduce apartheid human rights violations and provide some protections. People charged with political offences pleaded not guilty and mounted careful defences. Sometimes they succeeded, and avoided conviction. 'For all the deep injustices perpetuated by law,' the five judges argued, 'there remained a real sense in which the techniques and procedures of law remained independent from the gross manipulation of the executive and in which justice was sometimes seen to be done. No account of these years would be accurate if it were not accepted that justice was done and seen to be done in some cases.'

To this, Justice Langa added a deeply personal submission. His words were humble, direct and powerful. He described how he had risen from being a court interpreter to qualifying as a public prosecutor and then becoming a magistrate, and later an advocate, a senior counsel and eventually a judge of the Constitutional Court.

He had seen the system at its worst. He described his 'frustration, indignity and humiliation' of being subjected to the pass laws, which included degrading medical examinations. To watch how pass law officials, both black and white, enforced the law was 'soul-destroying'. 'No one,' he said, 'can ever forget the experience.' And the role of the judicial system in this, Justice Langa pointed out, 'was to put the stamp of legality' on a framework designed to perpetuate disadvantage and inequality.

I also made a personal submission to the TRC. In it, I pointed out how all of us who participated in the apartheid system were responsible for its injustices. In a passage the TRC included in its final report, I said that all lawyers and judges, whatever their personal beliefs and whatever the extent of their participation, were in some way complicit in apartheid. But this did not mean, I said, that there were no degrees of complicity or moral blame.

The TRC found that the legal system and all its members – judges, magistrates, prosecutors, advocates, attorneys and law teachers – were deeply complicit in apartheid. This was because, as it rightly noted, the apartheid leaders 'craved the aura of legitimacy that "the law" bestowed on their harsh injustice' – therefore, superficially, they adhered to the rule of law. The consequence was longer and harsher apartheid law.

Yet, for all this, the TRC noted that there were always a few lawyers who were prepared to break with the norm. These lawyers used every opportunity to speak out publicly against laws sanctioning arbitrary conduct and injustice. They explored the limits in defending those on trial for anti-apartheid offences. They worked ceaselessly to defend those whom apartheid targeted, often under difficult circumstances and for little reward.

The TRC also recognised those judges who found in favour of justice and liberty wherever proper and possible.

Importantly, the TRC remembered not only lawyers operating in the courts, but also those operating outside the courts. It mentioned lay activists and community advisors, serving the rural poor and workers through advice offices and religious bodies. It also mentioned legal academics, who challenged their students to understand how law was related to justice, and to work to attain their ideals.

On this evidence, the TRC was able to reach an overall conclusion. It said that to practise as an anti-apartheid lawyer under apartheid was justified. It found that what anti-apartheid lawyers had done to diminish suffering 'substantially outweighed the admitted harm done by their participation in the system'.

XIII Apartheid law and the constitutional transition

It was the legal clothing apartheid wore that made it possible for some judges of honour to remain on the Bench, and for lawyers opposing apartheid – including Nelson Mandela and Sydney Kentridge and Arthur Chaskalson and George Bizos and Pius Langa – to challenge it through the very legal processes that were designed to enforce it. This is because law can provide a cloak of legitimacy to the exercise of power only for so long as it really does curb power. If it does not, there is no longer law. There is only brute force.

So it was under apartheid. Though apartheid's brutality was enforced through the law, the law also inhibited some of its excesses. And it was the work of anti-apartheid lawyers, and some honourable judges, that made it possible for those who negotiated the end of apartheid after 1990 to enshrine our country's future aspirations in the form of legal principles and values.

Many of those leading the negotiations to end apartheid and create a constitutional democracy were lawyers. Mandela and De Klerk both were. Mandela's long memory of fragments of honourable justice meted out in the apartheid courts played a part. Joe Slovo, Cyril Ramaphosa and Roelf Meyer were also lawyers. The negotiators found a tattered, partly discredited, but still-functioning and partially credible legal system.

They took it and salvaged it for better service under democracy. The constitution they crafted took the best from what preceded, and placed it at the service of a new, larger and more hopeful legal order.

This act of salvage was for a public who understood that the law in South Africa was, at least occasionally, a potential mechanism of right rather than exclusively an instrument of oppression. Under apartheid, the law was a 'site of struggle'. As a result, a wide array of trade unions, community organisations, guerrilla fighters, detainees, politicians and ordinary people believed, from their own experience, that the law could be used to protect and to afford dignity.

The new Constitution was designed to foster the best in that tradition.

XIV Law as a reparative project

Our new legal order offered our country an opportunity to engage in the greatest reparative project of all – to repair the injury of apartheid.

When I started as a human rights lawyer in the early 1980s, it was twenty long years after my father had appeared between two prison guards at the funeral of my sister Laura. My personal quest was to make the law more than only an instrument of confinement, more than only an implement of reproof, rebuke and correction. The law's role, as I saw it, was also to repair.

The law could be confining, and oppressive and unjust. But it could also afford a means of healing, and restoration. In the law, while working with the often grimy realities of injustice, I found also a means of channelling my life's aspirations, for social justice and for healing, into my daily work.

It was a long way from Laura's funeral.

Chapter Two

AIDS and the Constitutional Transition

I Illness and shame

Late on Friday afternoon on 19 December 1986, at about four o'clock, I received a telephone call from my doctor. He told me that I had HIV, the virus that causes AIDS. It is never good to be diagnosed with a fatal disease, but that seemed a particularly bad time. I was 33 years old and working as a human rights lawyer at Wits's Centre for Applied Legal Studies (CALS). The work was hard, but at times it felt hopeful and inspiring. My diagnosis with HIV seemed a certain death sentence, one that would bring my life and my work to an imminent and traumatic end. There was no cure for AIDS. And no effective treatment to ease it.

My doctors were kind, but I could sense their horror at the condition they were trying to manage. This reinforced the isolation I felt. They explained that there was nothing they could do to slow the virus. The HIV organism back-doors its way into the genetic material of your immune system (hence 'retrovirus') by attacking its most active cells. Once lodged there, deep inside, it multiplies, systematically taking over and destroying the very defender cells that are meant to help your body fight off alien organisms.

The virus, they explained to me, would continue to gather force in my bloodstream, where it would eventually seethe out of control. When it had fatally weakened my immune system, I would have AIDS – a syndrome of various rare illnesses that manifest because the body becomes so vulnerable. They are called 'opportunistic', because they take advantage of the obliteration of the body's defences.

How long I would live before this happened my doctors could not tell me. It could be anything from a few years to a decade or more. We agreed that, of course, I should not lose hope. My life had to carry on. But, eventually, the disease would prevail, even over hope.

I would not die from HIV itself. No one does. I would die from the multitude of infections, some common and some extremely rare, that beset the body once its weakness lets them in.

By late 1986 I had seen enough friends experience agonising deaths from AIDS to know what I could expect. I had watched them lose weight and weaken and die, big-eyed and emaciated, at home and in hospices and in hospitals. I had watched their families and doctors stand helplessly by. Young men, mostly. In the prime of their lives. Just like me. They died not from sudden trauma or from debility of a vital organ or from cancer or heart disease. Those deaths often come with merciful speed.

Not AIDS. AIDS is slow. Excruciatingly slow. What brings death is a lingering overall decline of the physique, as the body's capacity to defend itself against repeated attacks from hostile organisms is gradually worn away.

Now I faced this in my own life. My own body. I would become ill and die. I would probably not reach forty. Even less probably would I see our country attain democracy or a just legal system. In the mid-1980s those seemed unattainably far off. The end point of our work, for which my colleagues and I hoped, was one I would never see.

At that time AIDS was relatively unknown in South Africa. This, too, increased my sense of fright. Only a few cases had been noted – many in people I knew. The horrendous impact the epidemic was beginning to inflict elsewhere in Africa was only starting to emerge. There was controversy about whether our country, at the southern tip of Africa, would suffer the same fate as Uganda, 5 000 kilometres to the north, where reports told of a growing, mass, heterosexual epidemic, a nation at risk of its very survival. Surely that could not happen here?

Over the weekend that followed, all this hit me with a fell shock of horror. HIV was no longer outside, a scary sensation in the news reports, a dread condition that afflicted some of my friends. It was within myself. Within the building blocks of my own body's DNA.

But there was something worse, worse than the spectre of an impending mass epidemic, worse than the thought of my undone work, worse than my truncated lifespan: worst of all was the sense of shame I felt. I was ashamed that I had HIV.

More than ashamed. Aghast. Appalled at the organism that had infected my bloodstream and my body. HIV made me feel tainted. Contaminated. Dirty. Unclean, polluted, impure.

Why would someone feel ashamed to have an illness? Cancer, diabetes, heart disease – all these are life-imperilling conditions. To have them is distressful and often horrific, but do people feel ashamed of them? The answer seems No. The support and love of friends and family are lavishly available to help those receiving these diagnoses. And their help is usually accepted gratefully.

HIV is different. Why? After all, HIV is just a viral particle, trying its genetic best to survive in the human bloodstream. In this it is no different from other viruses. Because it is ingenious and, once inside, it replicates virulently, it has fatal effects. But the organism itself has no intrinsic genetic or virological attributes that make it shameful.

Like other diseases, HIV is a bodily manifestation of our human vulnerability and mortality. In these, we are all the same. And in preying on our bodily weakness, HIV is no different from any other infectious organism.

Yet shameful it is. On a flight abroad while writing this book, soon after take-off one of the cabin personnel came to crouch quietly next to my aisle seat. She was vivacious and extremely pretty. She rested her hand gently on my forearm and turned her face to me. When I leaned over to try to hear her, our temples briefly touched. She knew that I had HIV and that I was taking anti-retroviral medication. She murmured that she needed time to talk with me. Later, when all was quiet in the galley, we found solitary moments together.

Just two weeks before, she had been diagnosed with HIV. Behind her professional polish and impeccable deportment, her emotions were heaving. She had told no one in her family and none of her colleagues. She turned her troubled gaze to me as we spoke, searching my face for help. She was dealing with her diagnosis alone, terrified of others' responses.

But, more importantly even, she was ashamed that she had HIV.

I spoke words of comfort. I stated reassuring medical and scientific facts. But I sensed that the biggest struggle for my new confidante lay ahead. It was a struggle that had to be fought largely within herself. It was the struggle against shame.

Why the shame? The root cause is simple to state, but not easy to understand. It is sex. I felt ashamed because of how I had acquired HIV – through sexual contact.

Sex: an intimate act of intense bodily connection with another human being. When it is with another adult, consensual, and in a suitable place, it can be joyful, impassioned, liberating and beautiful. Between two persons of opposite sex, it may hold the immediate promise of new life. But in all who want it, it is an act that deeply affirms our human need, our shared human vulnerability, and our profound hunger for human connection.

The act of sexual connection affirms our bondedness as human beings. In this, it affirms life.

Shakespeare writes that the urgent need for sex is 'Before, a joy proposed; behind, a dream'. When one is diagnosed with an infection that has been transmitted during sex, the dream sours. When the infection is death-bearing, as HIV is, it turns to nightmare.

The embarrassment and shame seem to stem from the fact that an intimate bodily connection that should have exchanged life-affirming joy, instead becomes a source of possible illness and death. More, it becomes the basis for others' rebuke and reproach: You should have known better. What did you expect? Knowing that others may judge us stupid, irresponsible, immoral and unclean, shames us deeply.

In addition, the very fact of infection cruelly ruptures the seclusion and intimacy of the original act of connection. It broadcasts to the world – to the doctor's room, to one's circle of friends, family, colleagues, neighbours – the shared moment of bodily connection that would otherwise have remained deeply personal.

All this is hard to explain and understand. This is partly because almost everywhere the nature and practice of sex remain contentious. We still debate who should have it, when, how, and on what terms. Delicacy and embarrassment still surround it, and not wrongly so. Sex is the most intimate bodily act two humans can perform together. It is unavoidably fraught with complexity.

And it is never, ever expected to be the vehicle for a dangerous infectious agent to pass from one human body to another. When that happens, the delicacy, the intimacy, the vulnerability, the tenderness and the beauty of the shared act of intimacy turn to mortification and shame: additionally so when the act is shared between people of the same sex because of the irrational stigma heaped on same-sex relations.

In the case of HIV, which threatens death, the shame is over-poweringly profound.

II The mass epidemic of AIDS reaches South Africa

After my diagnosis with HIV, with despair sometimes welling up inside, I little foresaw the powerful part the disease would play in my country's future. Little did I realise it would become one of South Africa's most furiously debated post-democracy issues. And little could I predict it would confront our democratic Constitution and courts with their first truly momentous challenge, still less that the epidemic would be the occasion for the Constitutional Court's bravest judgment, with perhaps the most far-reaching practical impact of all its decisions so far.

In grappling with the HIV in my own body, I had no idea that within a few short years the virus would sweep through our country's people in catastrophic proportions. I did not foresee that the worst predictions of the demographers, who foretold nightmare rates of infection, would be fully realised, that many millions of my fellow countrymen and -women would join me in my HIV status. Like me, they would carry HIV in their bloodstream. Like me, they would fear discovery of their HIV and rejection by their family, friends and colleagues.

Just a few years after being diagnosed, in the late 1980s, I started meeting other South Africans with HIV. They came to me through my work with the National Union of Mineworkers, NUM, and with the labour federation to which it belonged, COSATU. I met miners with HIV. And I met miners' wives with HIV.

We sat on opposite sides of the desk in my office at CALS. They did not know that the burden they brought to me was one we shared. With rigid professionalism, though also in self-protection, I muted my fears to be respectful of theirs. But across the gulfs of language and race and job title and culture, an element of commonality pulsed in our beings. It was a tinge, and sometimes more than a tinge, of human desperation.

I knew that, like me, these men and women were battling isolation and despair that sometimes threatened to overwhelm them. I knew that, like me, their greatest fear was to be branded with stigma and to be condemned, and then to fall ill and die from AIDS.

Indeed, what I could least foresee, in those years of certain anticipation of decline and death, was that it would be the arrival of near-miraculously effective treatment – treatment that would save my life, and promise life to millions more – that would be the anvil on which the colossal issue of AIDS would be hammered out in our future democracy.

All this lay far in the future. The dramatic unfolding of events, and their agonising cost in human lives and suffering, was quite impossible to imagine – not only for a young human rights lawyer freshly diagnosed with HIV, but for anyone trying to peer ahead into our country's perilous future.

III Friday, 2 February 1990

Three years after my diagnosis, on Friday, 2 February 1990, President FW de Klerk made a dramatic statement in Parliament. The apartheid government astonished the world by announcing that it was abandoning its violent attempts to suppress the movement for democracy in our country. Instead, it said it was now willing to negotiate a transition to democracy. The ANC, PAC, South African Communist Party and other liberation organisations were immediately unbanned. Racist laws would be suspended or abolished. The execution of death sentences was suspended. And Nelson Mandela and other leaders who remained in prison would be released.

What, four decades before, Mandela and his fellow leaders had fought for in the Defiance Campaign, what he had gone to prison for nearly three decades earlier, at last lay within prospect – though only after blood and agony, and decades of internal dissent and struggle.

On the morning of President De Klerk's surprise announcement I was inside the imposing high court building in Johannesburg's Pritchard Street. The court was erected in 1911, the year after the Union of South Africa came into being, with a splendid bronze dome, a recessed, arched entrance and a cool, voluminous foyer where lawyers could meet with their clients. Outside the court building stands a statue of Carl von Brandis, the mining commissioner in 1886, after gold was discovered on the Witwatersrand. He became Johannesburg's very first magistrate. His statue looks westwards, towards the mine dumps that evidence the riches the gold-diggers feverishly extracted from the ridge's earth, and which made Johannesburg the most prosperous and developed city in Africa.

And indeed my business in court that morning concerned gold mining. I heard the news of President De Klerk's announcement as I stepped out of court with NUM's safety officer, Sazi Jonas, and the union's attorney for health and safety, Paul Benjamin. As we walked into the court's foyer, we spotted groups of lawyers and their clients, and even some of the registrar's staff, talking animatedly.

In court, we had heard Judge Goldstein deliver an important judgment. At stake was the conduct of a mining company that owned the Kinross gold mine, whose tunnels reach deep under the Highveld plateau 110 kilometres east of Johannesburg.

The case went back to a horrific event more than three years before. On 16 September 1986, during the day shift, a dreadful accident occurred in an underground tunnel of the mine. A gas tank welders were using to repair an underground railway line suddenly started sparking flames. These ignited a catastrophic fire. Within seconds, flames engulfed the tunnel. Most disastrously, the plastic piping and polyurethane cladding on the walls took flame. The fumes the burning material spewed out smothered hundreds of workers in toxic smoke. For those worst affected, asphyxiation was almost immediate.

One hundred and seventy-seven miners died almost instantly. Hundreds more survived, but suffered injuries from the toxic fumes.

Almost all of those dead and injured were migrant workers, from both inside and outside South Africa, workers who left their families for eleven months each year, year after year, to work deep underground, extracting the country's riches. They came from Mozambique, Malawi, the Transkei and Lesotho, often to work in extremely dangerous conditions. They were mostly young men in the prime of their lives. These were the very people most at risk of the emerging epidemic of HIV – it was men like these, and their wives, who were coming to confide in me at CALS. The Kinross fire left 177 of them dead, choked to death deep inside the earth by poisonous fumes from a fire that should never have happened.

It was one of South Africa's worst mine disasters. NUM, supported by CALS, said that the mining company and its responsible managers should be held liable. By 1986, it was well known that certain types of plastic used in underground tunnels and stopes, as well as polyurethane cladding, were highly toxic. Once they caught fire, they belched out deadly fumes. The materials were thus known to be a deadly hazard. Replacements for them had long been available. NUM claimed that they should long have been stripped out of all underground shafts and stopes. Not to do so was criminally negligent.

We said the mine's managers and executives were to blame. They should be sent to jail for their part in causing the disaster.

But the criminal prosecution that followed was a farce. The magistrate disregarded expert evidence NUM brought in from the United Kingdom. He acquitted all the company's managers, bar one, who pleaded guilty to two minor breaches of the statutory regulations on mines. He received a fine of R50.

Even in those days, R50 was a derisory amount. Less than thirty cents – bronze cents, not even pieces of silver – for every miner who died.

We had no control over these criminal proceedings. Even so, the outcome dismayed us. But the mining statute stipulated that an inquiry, presided over by a mining inspector, then had to be held into all accidents. We decided to pour all our energies into the inquiry. We amassed what we thought was overwhelming evidence of neglect and disregard by mine management. We were ready to grill the managers, and to call the witnesses we had on standby, including those the magistrate had disregarded during the criminal trial.

On a cold and fog-bound morning at the end of June 1988, nearly two years after the disaster, and more than eighteen months before Judge Goldstein gave judgment, the NUM safety team, together with its lawyers from CALS, including me, travelled to Secunda, the town closest to the mine. The mining inspector appointed by the government was ready to hold the inquiry.

But, again, there was no proper hearing. The presiding inspector cut our case short. On the first day, at the start of proceedings, he announced that he had already taken written statements from all the managers concerned. That was all the evidence he needed. In addition, there was the criminal trial. No more was required. So, he ruled, there would be no cross-examination of the managers. They had got away scot-free during the criminal proceedings.

Now they would do the same here. They would never be challenged in front of the widows and families and injured colleagues of the men who had died.

This seemed an outrageous affront to justice. We told the inspector and the mine's lawyers that we did not accept the ruling. It was, we said, clearly wrong. We would challenge it in the high court, so that a proper inquiry could be held. Pending our legal challenge, we said we would seek a temporary interdict from the high court to suspend the inquiry while it corrected the ruling. At this, all parties, including the presiding inspector, agreed to hold over the proceedings so that the high court could hear our challenge first.

Those proceedings, too, turned into a gruelling battle. Over the next year, we exchanged contesting sets of affidavits. Both government, defending the inspector's ruling, and the mining company, reaping the benefit of it, brought in senior counsel. Our opponents challenged us at the very doorstep of the court. They said that NUM had no legal standing to contest the inspector's ruling. Their argument was that the inquiry was not likely to hold any union members liable for the disaster. In any event, the inspector's ruling was right.

At stake were both factual and legal questions. The factual issue was what precisely the inspector had said when he started the inquiry. The legal questions were what his ruling meant, how much power he had to allow cross-examination, and whether, if the judge could not decide the facts on the affidavits before him, he should nevertheless give a decision on the key question of the inspector's power to allow cross-examination.

Behind all these complex technical legal points there was a vital issue. Did the criminal trial, where the mine's managers got off scot-free, make the inquiry pointless? The mine, supported by the government mining bureaucracy, said it did. We argued that it did not. The widows and families wanted their day in court with the managers. They should not be denied.

Over four heated days in November 1989, we argued the issues before Judge Goldstein, an intense, scrupulous and fair-minded judge. We wanted him to find the facts in our favour. But in any event, win or lose on the facts, we wanted him to decide the law points. We said NUM was entitled to have its say in the proceedings. Its interest lay not only in the risk that its own members might be found responsible for the disaster. This, we agreed, was obviously unlikely. NUM's interest was broader. It was to find ways to prevent more mine disasters and so its voice should be heard. And, we argued, the inspector got the law wrong when he barred all possibility of cross-examining the management witnesses.

After argument, Judge Goldstein reserved his judgment. Ever conscientious, he worked on his outstanding decisions over the Christmas recess. Then, at the start of the new court term, towards the end of January, his registrar let us know that he would give his decision on Friday, 2 February.

That morning in court we heard that we had partly won, and partly lost. The part we lost was the least important. Judge Goldstein said he could not decide on the conflicting affidavits before him what precisely the inspector ruled. He said this could be decided only on the basis of witnesses' in-person testimony (not written statements under oath) about what had happened that morning in Secunda.

But on all the other issues he found in favour of NUM. The statute gave the inspector power to allow cross-examination of witnesses who had given written statements. The post-criminal trial proceedings were not pointless. And, most importantly, NUM had a sound claim to have a voice in the proceedings. NUM should be heard. And the widows and families and injured mineworkers it represented should be heard.

Sazi Jonas and Paul Benjamin and I looked buoyantly at each other. We were overjoyed. The ruling would make NUM's job at other mining inquiries much easier. It might even make it easier to prevent more disasters. Later, legal action by the union forced the mine to agree to help the dead miners' families. It undertook to establish a fund to pay them compensation over and above the meagre sums the government-run compensation fund provided. When the mine later agreed to this, the union agreed to drop its demand for a full inquiry.

Judge Goldstein closed his books and adjourned the court. Though that morning we did not yet know the favourable details of the later settlement, our spirits were high as we rose to our feet. Then, when we heard the news that was awaiting us outside the courtroom, they soared: for now at least, it seemed, the apartheid regime had renounced its intransigence. Our country might at last be able to hope to achieve democracy, in a just system that included all its people.

IV AIDS and the path to democracy

The same virus that was coursing through my bloodstream that morning as we emerged from court was already spreading through the country with unnerving rapidity. As Nelson Mandela walked free from prison on Sunday, 11 February 1990, after twenty-seven years, and started negotiations with the apartheid government, the AIDS epidemic, already beginning to devastate populations and economies to our north, was reaching out to clasp South Africa in a deadly grip.

From early 1990, two powerful streams of history ran alongside each other through our country's affairs. One was of hope, the other of menace. The first was public, proclaimed and celebrated. It was the transition to democracy, a process of sometimes giddying expectation and promise. The other was silent and unstated. In truth, it was almost entirely unknown. It was the increasingly rapid dissemination of a fatal, unseen virus threatening the very life of the new democracy. For those who appreciated what was happening, this stream of history held only foreboding and fear.

Within a few years after democracy was attained, these currents would intermingle. The result would be powerful turbulence, unstable enough to capsize the new state.

The first talks between government and the ANC took place three months after President De Klerk's announcement, in early May 1990. They were held in Cape Town at Groote Schuur, the lovely Cape Dutch estate Cecil John Rhodes had bought with his diamond and gold-mining fortune and then bequeathed, in a forward-looking gesture when he died in 1902, to the leaders of a future united South Africa. In time, Nelson Mandela would rightfully occupy Rhodes's home at Groote Schuur but, for now, a perilous transition was only beginning – one whose progress was pock-marked with too many hazards to be predictable.

The talks started at a fraught time. Widespread violence plagued the townships. Its intensity was increasing. After three days of tough talking, the parties agreed on preconditions for ending political strife. These included releasing political prisoners, the return of political exiles, with indemnity from prosecution, and the lifting of the nationwide state of emergency that President De Klerk's predecessor, President PW Botha, had imposed four years before, on 16 June 1986. The agreement became known as the Groote Schuur Minute.

Violence continued, however, and even intensified. In July 1990, with the Minute barely sealed, brutal gunmen, both black and white, started perpetrating inexplicable attacks on the packed commuter trains that ferried black workers to their jobs in and around Johannesburg. What seemed at the outset merely random, unplanned acts of brutality began to take an increasingly sinister form. As the attacks became more frequent, they seemed to involve orchestrated incidents executed by large groups of hitmen. Men with firearms would start shooting from station platforms, or would direct murderous fusillades at commuters trapped helplessly inside coaches.

The perpetrators' prime objective seemed to be to cause general terror amongst the populace. At no point did they articulate any political objective or affiliation. Our receptionist at CALS, Ms Soneni Ncube, lived 60 kilometres south of Johannesburg in the Vaal dormitory township of Sebokeng. Her whole family found themselves enmeshed in horrific violence. In January 1991 her nephew Chris was killed by attackers the family believed were connected with Chief Buthelezi's Inkatha Freedom Party (IFP). During the night vigil for the deceased at her home, an attack they also attributed to the IFP left 33 mourners dead. These included her brother and his son. She herself was shot in the foot.

As if this was not enough, Soneni, who came to work by train, was caught up in the train violence too. One morning a gang of men entered her carriage, shooting wildly. Some in her carriage were killed. Many others died from attackers' bullets. Other commuters were flung randomly from moving trains, meeting pitiless deaths on the stony verges of the railway lines.

The attacks were baffling and their scale was horrendous. Between 1990 and 1993, about 572 people died in more than 600 incidents on commuter trains. Pro-democracy groups said the violence was started by those who were opposing a democratic transition and the possibility of an ANC-led government. Some evidence implicated members of the IFP, and members of the security forces, in the attacks. But a full understanding of how they were organised and their planners' objectives has remained opaque.

Despite the fact that bizarrely terrifying attacks were continuing, negotiations to found a democratic state in South Africa began at last. They were called the Convention for a Democratic South Africa, or CODESA, and the first plenary session took place at Kempton Park, just outside Johannesburg, in December 1991.

Two judges from the Johannesburg High Court shared the intricate task of chairing the proceedings. One was an intense and earnest Afrikaner, Judge Pieter Schabort, who had once belonged to the Broederbond, the secret organisation committed to maintaining Afrikaner rule in South Africa. He was one of the most senior judges in Johannesburg. The other was associated with liberation causes. He was Judge Ismail Mahomed, an irascible but brilliant man, whom President Mandela later appointed to the Constitutional Court, where he became its first deputy president. At that time, Judge Mahomed had just been appointed to the Bench in Johannesburg. Though he and Judge Schabort had fought many cases on opposing sides when they were advocates at the Johannesburg Bar, they liked each other and got on well. This helped.

The CODESA parties expressed a solemn commitment to bringing about a country that was undivided. There would be one nation sharing a common citizenship, patriotism and loyalty, 'pursuing amidst our diversity, freedom, equality and security for all irrespective of race, colour, sex or creed'. They pledged a country free from apartheid or any other form of discrimination or domination. Most importantly, there was agreement that there had to be a written constitution in which 'all shall enjoy universally accepted human rights, freedoms and civil liberties'.

The first plenary session of the talks, in March 1992, laid an important grounding for future talks involving all the major negotiating parties. The second session started in hopeful spirits on 15 May 1992, but it ended in disagreement when the parties could not agree on the form an interim government should take, and on the fundamental content of the future constitution.

And then, barely a month after the talks resumed, on 17 June 1992, killers perpetrated a horrific massacre in Boipatong township, south of Johannesburg. Boipatong borders its more famous neighbour, Sharpeville. Like Sharpeville, Boipatong had always been a hotbed of political activism. The attackers seemed to have come from the nearby KwaMadala hostel (its name means 'place of old men'). The hostel was known to house supporters of Chief Buthelezi's IFP, a party that operated under apartheid, and was hostile to the ANC.

The attackers moved randomly through the township, shooting some and hacking others. Precise numbers vary in different accounts, but about 46 people died and many more were injured, including women and children. Many believed that a secretive force associated with the apartheid government had organised the massacre. Dubbed 'the third force', it was believed to comprise right-wing elements in the apartheid police and security forces, colluding with IFP members. Their objective was to create terror and instability, and to disrupt CODESA. Both government and the IFP denied involvement. Indeed, the IFP asserted that its members were frequent victims of ANC-inspired attacks.

The ANC insisted that government forces were in cahoots with those who carried out the Boipatong horror and it condemned President De Klerk for not doing enough to halt violence against its supporters. As a result, on 21 June 1992, Mr Mandela, who was leading the ANC negotiations while the ANC president, Oliver Tambo, was severely indisposed, wrote a scathing letter to President De Klerk, accusing him and his government of turning a blind eye to the increasing violence. As a result, he announced that the ANC was suspending its participation in the CODESA negotiations.

The country entered a period of anxious uncertainty. No one knew when, or even if, negotiations would resume.

Through these tense times, many in the AIDS field had been working steadily to prepare a comprehensive response proposing policies for the new democratic government, which we hoped would take office sooner rather than later.

Participating in the work were officials from government's department of health, as well as doctors and health specialists from the ANC and other organisations, and activists from a wide range of non-governmental organisations. My involvement was not because I was living with HIV. That I still kept a dread secret. It stemmed from my work as a human rights lawyer. This enabled me to present a face of professionalism and competence and expertise without betraying the vulnerability that underlay them.

In the course of that work, in late 1991, I helped set up the AIDS Consortium, a national alliance of non-governmental organisations working in the AIDS field. The Consortium operated from CALS. And in the following year I started the AIDS Law Project (ALP), also at CALS.

V The trial of Barry McGeary

My own human rights practice increasingly included litigation for people experiencing discrimination from their doctors or employers or spouses or neighbours because of HIV or AIDS.

In the middle of 1990, a young man, Barry McGeary, came to see me at my office at CALS. He told me an unsettling story. A few months before, in April, he had applied for life insurance. As was usual, the insurer required an HIV test, so he visited his regular doctor in Brakpan to be tested. The doctor and his wife were friends of Barry's. After a few days, his doctor called him in. It was a Monday. He told Barry he had tested positive for HIV. Barry was devastated.

His distress was soon greatly compounded, however. On the Wednesday, the doctor played his regular mid-week game of golf. Two golfing buddies joined him. Both were colleagues with medical practices in Brakpan. In the small-town setting, both of them knew Barry. They and their wives moved in the same social circles as Barry, and dined in an elegant restaurant Barry and his partner Johan ran together.

As their game progressed from green to green, Barry's doctor told the other two that Barry had tested positive for HIV. By the end of the week, the news was no longer secret. It was obvious that almost everyone who knew Barry knew that he had tested positive. The news had spread with lightning speed. An icy chill fell over many of his relationships. The restaurant's business fell away.

Feeling betrayed by a medical confidant who should have protected him, Barry sought me out for advice. I thought about what he had told me. Then I spelled out the possibilities. A thoughtful and careful man, he listened intently. Under our pre-constitutional common law, breach of confidentiality in a professional relationship, like that between a doctor and patient, was an actionable wrong. The Roman-Dutch law, which applied in South Africa, regarded it as an affront to a person's inherent dignity. To prove our case, we would have to show that the doctor had wrongfully broken confidentiality. If he had, that violated Barry's rights of personality.

But suing the doctor was full of risks. To bring a lawsuit is always risky. Evidence that seems clear turns out to be muddy. New witnesses appear. Twists and turns eventuate. The law itself is never clear. Here, we knew that we would be making law. No one had ever brought a claim against a doctor for violating AIDS confidentiality. In addition, we knew that the case would be a newspaper sensation. Barry's face, and his HIV status, would be on every front page.

Barry thought hard about what I told him but he remained adamant. He felt strongly that his doctor had betrayed his friendship, and his trust. He also thought that other people with HIV or AIDS would suffer if he did not take a stand on their behalf. He insisted he wanted to sue.

I asked a young attorney colleague, Mervyn Joseph, with whom I had worked closely on other difficult cases, to help CALS with Barry's claim. Despite the fact that taking the case would cost Mervyn fees, he agreed. We issued summons. In it, we set out Barry's claim, and demanded that the doctor pay compensation.

His defence made matters difficult. On advice from his medical insurance, far from admitting the golf course conversation, the doctor denied everything. Only shortly before the date on which the trial was scheduled to begin did the doctor at last admit that it was he who had told the other two doctors. Then, after making the admission, he changed his pleadings. He claimed that because HIV was so dangerous, medical ethics required him to tell his two colleagues. After all, they might conceivably come into contact with Barry. This would mean that they would be at risk of getting infected from him.

We thought this far-fetched. By the late 1980s, less than ten years after the epidemic became known, the scientific evidence was already very clear. HIV is very difficult to transmit. It can pass from one person to another when a mother is giving birth to or breastfeeding her baby, and when two people have unprotected sexual intercourse. Casual transmission is impossible. And in a doctor-patient clinical setting, transmission is extremely rare. A direct injection, through the skin, of a significant quantity of body fluid with HIV must happen before a health worker is at risk. Studies had repeatedly shown this.

So it was far-fetched to claim that the doctor's colleagues needed the HIV status of every potential patient broadcast to them – particularly not on the golf course. To protect themselves all health care personnel needed to observe simple universal precautionary measures. These effectively precluded HIV transmission. Good medical practice required all doctors and health workers to observe them.

What we did not yet know was a lesson about law and legal personalities. This is that scientific evidence that is manifestly clear outside a courtroom may not carry enough weight inside to persuade a hostile judge.

Undaunted, we prepared painstakingly for trial. One weekend before the case began, we retreated with our law books and pleadings and court rules to a quiet country lodge in the bushveld north of Pretoria, which Barry and Johan had elegantly refurbished. We appreciated that bringing a claim for breach of confidentiality against a medical professional in HIV was pushing into unknown reaches of the law, but the best expert HIV physicians, social scientists and psychologists made themselves available to us to help explain Barry's case to the court. We went through their evidence carefully with them.

Despite our careful preparations, the strangeness of the issue, and deep stigma against AIDS, did indeed count against Barry. When the trial date the registrar had assigned to Barry's case dawned, we arrived at the Johannesburg High Court expectantly, only to find that all the available judges were already hearing cases. We had to wait. Eventually a judge became free. Our case was placed before an acting judge, Denis Levy. Nervously, together with my opponent who, instructed by the medical insurer, was appearing for the doctor, I observed the customary pre-courtroom courtesy and went to meet the judge.

Levy was a retired advocate of advanced years. He was well into his seventies, and of a testy disposition. He had never received a full appointment as a judge. But, on the basis of his seniority and experience, the Judge-President offered him repeated appointments as an acting judge in his retirement.

Acting Judge Levy's manner during the pre-trial courtesies was brusque but civil. But almost immediately the proceedings began in court, his brusqueness turned to hostility. He interrupted my opening address. He snorted sceptically when I mentioned that the disclosure of the plaintiff's HIV status had taken place on a golf course. What did that have to do with anything, he impatiently asked. Everything, I wanted to say. But, courteously, I replied, 'We will show you, My Lord.' All the same my heart sank. I knew we had drawn a tough nut.

And from early in the evidence, the judge made very plain his distaste for Barry and his lifestyle. Through frequent interventions, he made it clear that he regarded AIDS itself as repugnant.

Barry gave his evidence with difficulty. His main account of his dealings with his doctor was clear. When his doctor called him in to tell him he had HIV, Barry told him he was worried that others may get to know. The doctor had assured him the news would remain confidential. As Barry proceeded with his story, it was plain to us, who by then knew him well, that the burden of his illness was drawing his energies and his attention far away from the witness stand. The advanced stages of AIDS had already beset him. With no medications to slow the virus, or to ease its debilitating effects, he was mortally sick.

At the end of the first day of the trial, I had finished leading him through his evidence in chief but that was as far as his strength could take him. He was clearly suffering the effects of the onset of AIDS. He looked distracted, exhausted and weak. After we parted, he went home to rest where, suffering from the extreme stress of the day, he collapsed. We brought him back to the court the next day in a wheelchair. He entered the witness stand and sat composed and ready for the opposing advocate's questions. Clearly, though, he was in no state to give any evidence at all. His answers were slurred. Increasingly they became incoherent. He seemed to have suffered a stroke. The neurological effects of the virus were taking a heavy toll.

We asked the judge for an adjournment, although we could see that Barry would not return to resume his evidence. Having told his story of his doctor's betrayal in open court, to a packed public gallery, Barry seemed content, however. He had fulfilled his mission. The armed combat of the trial could proceed without him. Day by gruelling day we continued in the courtroom while Barry was cared for in a lovely hospice newly opened in nearby Houghton. A few weeks later, on 18 September 1991, surrounded by loving family and tended by devoted friends, he died. He succumbed to his illness the night before closing argument.

From a legal point of view, Barry's death weakened our case. The doctor's counsel never had the opportunity to cross-examine him. This meant that his evidence, being untested, counted for very little. We had to make the case for Barry on science and reason alone.

Hanging heavily over my role as advocate in the trial was my own HIV status. I shared it with no one. Not with Barry and his partner and family. Not with our expert witnesses. And not with my attorney Mervyn Joseph, who had become a valued friend. In all my dealings with Barry and his partner and family, and with all my other clients, all along, I kept my own HIV-positive status a fierce and at times desperate secret.

What was more, when talking at public forums on AIDS, I spoke as a lawyer and a human rights expert – not as someone who was living with HIV. I never revealed that I myself understood all too personally the complexities and anguishes of the issue.

86

There was one exception. As a patient, I had been to see a specialist HIV physician, Professor Stephen Miller. When Barry approached me for help, I referred him to Dr Miller. He became our expert witness both on the science of HIV and on Barry's treatment. My dual roles – as HIV patient myself, but also as counsel and advocate, battling for Barry's cause before a hostile judge – put me under pressure. But I determined to battle on. There was no choice.

Five weeks after Barry's death, on 16 October 1991, Judge Levy handed down his judgment. He ruled in favour of the doctor. We had expected an adverse outcome but, even so, the negative language of the judgment was a disappointment. The judge upheld the defence we considered fanciful – that of medical necessity. The doctor, he found, had been justified in telling his two medical colleagues, because they might conceivably come into contact with Barry as a patient. In effect, he found that doctors were free to tell each other whenever one of their patients tested positive for HIV. Even on a golf course.

We were dismayed, but also convinced the judgment was wrong. We were determined to appeal against it. We hoped that, away from the rough emotions of a trial court, which had worked against us because of the judge's hostility, we would get a better hearing. Five judges in the serene atmosphere of the appeal court in Bloemfontein would hear us calmly, and decide the case on the science and the facts.

But the trial judge was not yet done with us. He continued to make things difficult. After a first-instance hearing in the high court, a losing litigant cannot automatically appeal. He or she must ask the trial judge for leave to appeal. This seems anomalous, since the application is brought before the very judge who has just found against the litigant, but it serves as a useful filtering mechanism. If leave to appeal is wrongly refused, the loser can petition the appeal court in Bloemfontein – and now of course also the Constitutional Court.

Usually, if the issue is novel or involves difficult questions of law, a first-instance judge grants leave without a murmur. But not Judge Levy. Even though the issue was brand new, and the chances of differing judgments on it were great, he signalled in his chambers that he might not grant us leave to appeal. He said I must submit written argument to persuade him that there was a reasonable prospect that another court might differ from his conclusions. I gritted my teeth and did so.

He did eventually grant us leave to appeal, but while it stood, his judgment represented a painful reverse. It cast a pall over the hope many in the HIV community had felt. Instead of entering a new era of reason and respect, the judgment seemed to signal that people with HIV would continue to face stigma and discrimination. Most importantly, it signalled that judges would condone breaches of their expectation of confidentiality.

VI The media and AIDS

Barry's trial, as we had feared, had indeed elicited widespread media attention. Before proceedings got under way, we considered applying for an order to bar the media from publishing Barry's name. But we decided against it. Barry, after all, was fighting for a principle. His own right to confidentiality had already been torn to shreds. He would not now fight for justice for others from under a blanket of anonymity. He would stand up under his own name and speak in his own voice.

The result was that both Barry and his former doctor were on the television news almost every night, and on the front pages of most newspapers across the country. When on the second day of the trial, after Barry's collapse, my attorney Mervyn Joseph wheeled Barry into court, the photographers and headline-writers were waiting. The telling picture of Barry being wheelchaired up the ramp at the main entrance of the Johannesburg High Court, neatly dressed in a suit but desperately drawn and distracted, etched an indelible impression.

Some reporters did push the line. They badgered us for information and interviews that, with the trial under way, we simply couldn't give. For the most part, however, we knew all too well that the media were our friends. Barry's story had deep human interest. And the doctor-patient conflict was riveting in its implications. Above all, there was the powerful human interest in Barry's vulnerability to disease – a young businessman, in his thirties, cut down by a dread virus, which was transmitted through sex.

What was more, most reporters well appreciated the underlying issues – that the virus was seeping with increasing rapidity through our population, and that it was becoming a problem so big it could threaten to sap the country's well-being. They published helpful articles informing readers about the stages of HIV infection, how the virus was transmitted, and about seeming breakthroughs in treatment. And they responded positively to our requests to stop using sensational language and demeaning terms – like 'victim' or 'sufferer' – to refer to Barry and other persons living with HIV and AIDS.

It was hard to blame even the most intrusive of journalists. And the experience of dealing with the media during Barry's trial later proved invaluable to me. It helped prepare me for my own very personal encounter with the media's interest in AIDS, years later, when I made my own public stand. Then I would also appreciate fully that the immense power the media wield can be put to very good effect.

VII Preparing a future democracy for AIDS

Throughout Barry's trial my other legal and human rights work continued. This included a smattering of commercial work, and civil liberties work, as well as cases for young white conscripts who refused, for conscientious or religious reasons, to serve in the apartheid army. On 28 June 1991, in pursuance of the Groote Schuur Minute, the apartheid Parliament repealed the Population Registration Act, which classified all South Africans into rigid racial categories. That should mean, we thought, the end of whites-only conscription. In September 1992 I tried to persuade a full bench of three judges in the high court in Pretoria that conscription could no longer be enforced. Our ambitious argument lost.

In the meanwhile, I was also involved in efforts to try to help sketch a sound national policy on AIDS for the incoming democratic government. By the end of 1991, we realised that to make progress, there had to be an inclusive national meeting, attended by government officials, ANC leaders and others concerned with the epidemic. The meeting took months to prepare. It was scheduled to take place at the Nasrec facilities outside Soweto, south of Johannesburg, in October 1992.

Then, in June, the Boipatong massacre occurred and the negotiations between the ANC and government were abruptly halted. The rupture put the Nasrec meeting in peril. Would the cancellation of negotiations apply also to AIDS? Fortunately not. We received assurances from the ANC and from government that our meeting should go ahead as planned. The AIDS issue was big enough to trump the cessation of multi-party negotiations. All parties had expressly decided that the issue was so important that the Nasrec meeting should proceed.

As it happened, Mr Mandela and President De Klerk agreed late in September 1992, three months after the massacre, and a month before the meeting, that the parties should start talking again. Nevertheless, the fact that the AIDS meeting would have proceeded anyhow made it clear that all parties saw the importance of the issue.

On 23 October 1992 the conference started. AIDS activists, health officials and medical specialists from all over the country crowded into the hall. We waited expectantly for Nelson Mandela to arrive to give the opening address. As always, he arrived precisely on time. This was my first opportunity to meet him. The encounter was quick and formal but, like many before and after me, I felt honoured to have shaken the hand of the legendary leader.

Mr Mandela's speech was short, clear and well structured. He pointed to the growing menace the disease presented. He sketched the epidemic's socio-economic roots, and its disproportionate impact on women. These, he noted, were accentuated by apartheid policies of separation and racial injustice.

He underlined the importance of information and education and of efforts to prevent transmission of HIV. In carefully measured language – he clearly did not want to imperil the unitary commitment to co-operation in AIDS – he noted that the apartheid government lacked credibility to initiate effective information and prevention programmes. This was, he explained, because its efforts were 'viewed with suspicion and as a ploy to control the population'. The existing government, he stated, 'does not have the credibility to convince the majority of black South Africans to change their sexual behaviour'. He therefore called for unity and a 'broad front' to deal with AIDS.

One line in his speech hit me with especial force. Mr Mandela noted that 'AIDS exposes an aspect of our lives that we are most loath to discuss openly'. The wording was delicate. But this was an important acknowledgement from the ANC leader, who was 74 years old, and who had spent more than a third of his life confined within prison walls, while the sexual revolution of the 1960s and 1970s was occurring outside, that sexual transmission and the silence surrounding it were deeply complicating factors.

After the meeting we formed a widely embracing national organisation to co-ordinate AIDS policy, and to finalise a draft policy that would be ready for the new government to endorse. This we called the National AIDS Convention of South Africa, or NACOSA. I co-chaired the new organisation with Dr Clarence Mini, a returned exile and ANC health committee member. With him, too, I never discussed my HIV status.

Other returned exiles working with us included two ANC health leaders, Dr Nkosazana Dlamini-Zuma, and Dr Manto Tshabalala-Msimang.

Especially after Mr Mandela's speech at Nasrec, leaders on all sides spoke of their understanding of the problem, and of its urgency. By every means, we had to ensure that South Africa did not fall subject to a mass epidemic of the magnitude of those ravaging our neighbours to the north. But though we didn't yet realise this with any clarity, by 1992 the spread of HIV was already spiralling beyond any practicable measures that could be taken to try to control it.

The return of exiles from abroad, many of whom had taken shelter during apartheid in countries like Zambia, Tanzania, Zimbabwe and Mozambique, where the prevalence of HIV was high, contributed to an increase in the rate at which HIV was spreading. And the end of apartheid isolation meant that we opened our borders to the rest of Africa. That, too, meant that the rate at which HIV spread increased.

How could we know? The virus is mysterious, and moves from person to person mostly unseen. But science has reliable ways of keeping track of it. There are two ways to find out how widely HIV is distributed in a population. The most reliable is through a household survey, taken from door to door. This method tries to cover the country on the basis of a scientifically composed nationwide sample. The results are then multiplied to reach a reliable figure for how many people in the population as a whole are affected.

Two surveys of this kind have been done in South Africa. They were undertaken in 2002 and 2005 with the backing of the Nelson Mandela Foundation. Over time, their findings were shown to be remarkably accurate.

The other way is very different. It is to test 'sentinel groups'. This is less reliable, but can also be very informative. Sentinel groups are not chosen because they are representative of the population. In fact, they are unrepresentative – for instance, pregnant women, or people seeking treatment for sexually transmitted infections, or people in prison. They are not a sample. But they give valuable clues as to how people outside the sample are affected. Again, the information the group yields is projected, with necessary adjustments, onto the population as a whole, to reach a population-wide estimate of HIV prevalence.

Since the start of the epidemic, in most countries the most reliable sentinel group has been pregnant women. Most women, at some stage in their lives, become pregnant. This is true across all sectors and segments of the population. And at some point in their pregnancy, they must seek health care. In South Africa, most of them do so at public hospitals and clinics. This means that they can be reached by public health experts seeking to establish indicative figures for country-wide HIV prevalence. So it is to this group that epidemiologists – public health experts in mass disease – turn.

From 1990, the authorities started estimating the prevalence of HIV in South Africa by taking blood samples from pregnant women who attended public antenatal clinics. The samples were anonymous – they were not linked by name or number or code to any individual. So no woman's confidentiality was threatened. Their findings proved very helpful. For the last two decades, throughout Africa, findings from surveys like these guided governments, economists, health care planners and businesses in dealing with AIDS.

From the very start, the antenatal surveys in South Africa were deeply unsettling. The first national survey of women visiting public antenatal clinics found that just under 0.8% of pregnant women had HIV. In itself, this was not so bad. One per cent is high but it is still below the crucial level that signals that the disease might spiral dangerously out of control, and become a mass epidemic. We were not there. Yet.

What was more disquieting was the inference that most of these infections were relatively recent. The findings suggested that the incidence of HIV – which is the rate at which the virus is spreading within the population – was extremely high. In other words, HIV levels had by no means stabilised at under 1%. On the contrary, those who already had HIV in 1990 had all been relatively recently infected. The 0.8% prevalence showed that the incidence of the disease was beginning to skyrocket.

In blunt numbers, epidemiologists estimated that by the end of 1990, between 74 000 and 120 000 people in South Africa were living with HIV. Most were black. And a majority of them were women. That was a very large number of people with the virus in one country. They were people who would suffer the symptoms of acute HIV infection. Inevitably, with no cure or treatment for AIDS, they would die. They were like me.

Worse even, almost none of them knew that they had HIV. HIV testing was still in its infancy. Many health activists, even some doctors, counselled against it. The reason was the high level of discrimination against people with HIV – something we experienced from the hostile judge who conducted the trial of Barry McGeary.

Friends of mine, and clients who sought my help as a lawyer, found themselves ostracised, without a job, without a home, without friends and colleagues, when they were discovered to have HIV. For them, there was no insurance cover. Often you could not apply for a job because many employers had now started screening new job applicants for HIV. Those found to have HIV were 'weeded out' in the vain belief that this would secure an 'HIV-free workforce'.

Some pregnant mothers, diagnosed with HIV after consenting to be individually tested, returned home to share the news with their spouses – men who may well have infected them in the first place – only to be beaten up and thrown out of the home.

The fact that doctors could do very little to help someone diagnosed with HIV also discouraged many from being tested. Why have yourself tested when, if the result is positive, your doctors can do nothing to help you – and when the sole reward will be discrimination and stigma? Many preferred to live in ignorance rather than to learn of a terrifying fate, with the risk of harsh discrimination.

It was only fifteen years later, after anti-retroviral drugs started becoming publicly available, that mass programmes encouraging testing for HIV began to make a significant impact. For now, in the early 1990s, HIV testing was rare. So most people bearing the virus did not know they had it. Worse, they were passing it on to others in unwitting acts of sexual transmission.

From the approximately 100 000 people estimated in 1990 to have HIV in South Africa, the epidemic was already spreading, unsettlingly fast, to many hundreds of thousands, and eventually to millions, of others.

Between 1990 and 1993, the HIV prevalence among pregnant women increased more than fivefold. By 1993, as negotiations for an interim constitution and a governmental transition began to promise democracy for the country, the proportion of pregnant women who tested positive for HIV was not far below one in twenty (4.3%). By 1993 the department of health reported that in the preceding two years the number of recorded HIV infections had increased by 60%. The number was expected to double that year.

By 1994, as we entered our democracy, the estimated median prevalence of HIV amongst women attending public prenatal clinics was nearly 6%.

Just as we attained democracy, the epidemic hit us with full force.

VIII The appeal court decides
Barry McGeary's appeal

In September 1993, as the constitutional negotiators outside Johannesburg were putting the final touches to the agreement for national elections and a new democratic government, we argued Barry McGeary's case before five appeal judges in Bloemfontein. The atmosphere was very different from that in the trial court two years before. When we arrived at the President Brand Street building on the morning of the appeal, there was a buzz amongst the security personnel and the registrar's staff. International visitors were present at court. They were meeting the judges. There was to be an international seminar of judges that weekend.

With democracy within sight for South Africa, judges from throughout the Commonwealth had agreed to meet in South Africa. Part of their visit took them to the country's then judicial capital, Bloemfontein. The time and the setting offered us some promise of a more open-minded, less constricted approach to the issues.

There was a further surprise. As we unpacked our books and trial records onto the heavy 1920s stinkwood advocates' tables in the main courtroom in Bloemfontein – the same courtroom where Chief Justice Centlivres had sat alongside Judge Oliver Schreiner, and where, nineteen years before, Chief Justice Ogilvie Thompson had decided the appeal of the Dean of Johannesburg – we learnt that the Commonwealth judges would be present in court that morning to observe Barry's appeal.

And, indeed, as we returned from paying our respects to the presiding judge, just after 9:30, in time for the punctual start at 9:45, we found judges from the highest courts in Australia, India, England, Kenya and other countries from the Commonwealth of Nations seated in the front row of the public gallery. Their distinguished presence – unthinkable under apartheid – tellingly portrayed the profound transition in our country and its legal system.

The presiding judge was not a modernist, or a reformer. In fact, he was a cantankerous hardliner, Mr Justice CP Joubert. In all his judgments he showed determination to preserve as much as he could of South Africa's Roman and Roman-Dutch legal heritage. A former academic, he peppered his judgments with quotations from original Latin law texts. Often he didn't bother to translate them. His court manner was grumpy and pedantic. During my argument, he tried to show that the Roman-Dutch law had full answers to all aspects of modern medical confidentiality claims. But all the judges listened courteously to my submissions. My time at the podium was smooth. And it was soon over – almost always a good sign for an appellant seeking to overturn a first-instance judgment.

There is a morning tea break in Bloemfontein. It always lasts exactly fifteen minutes, from 11:00 to 11:15. After tea my opponent rose to defend the trial court's judgment. He was a highly respected and experienced senior counsel, Peter Solomon, whom the medical defence union had brought in to argue the appeal. From the start, the judges asked him many questions – also an indication that the appeal may turn out badly. One judge in particular, Mr Justice Kumleben, asked questions that seemed deeply sceptical about the doctor's defence.

But it was a question from a different judge that seemed to us to seal the day. It came from the second most senior judge in the case, Mr Justice Nestadt, sitting on the presiding judge's right. He came from a wealthy family that owned many properties in and around Benoni, close to where Barry and his doctors lived at the time of the incident. 'Mr Solomon,' he said, 'am I right that your defence is in essence one of medical necessity?' 'Yes, My Lord,' my opponent replied. Judge Nestadt persisted. 'I happen to know the golf course on which the defendant disclosed the plaintiff's HIV status. Can you confirm my understanding of the doctor's evidence? Would I be right that his disclosure took place at about the fifth or the sixth hole?'

Peter Solomon was himself a golfer, as Judge Nestadt well knew, as they had been colleagues at the Johannesburg Bar. Good-naturedly, he agreed to the judge's estimate. But behind the banter lay a sting, one the advocate knew was perilous to the doctor's defence. And Judge Nestadt struck home. 'But if the disclosure was performed under medical necessity, why didn't the defendant tell his colleagues right away, at the very first hole?'

To this, my opponent could offer no ready response. We kept our faces expressionless, but our pulses quickened hopefully. We concluded that, unlike Judge Levy, the judges thought the golf-course setting cast doubt on the doctor's defence. We also realised we had a chance of winning.

And indeed the appeal court judgment proved to be an important victory. The judgment was written by Mr Justice Louis Harms, the most junior member of the panel who heard the case, who was then an acting judge in the appeal court. His judgment engaged rigorously with the facts and the law and the science of AIDS. He reversed all Judge Levy's central findings adverse to the plaintiff.

Judge Harms's judgment was an eloquent rights-based illumination of the facts and the legal values of confidentiality and human dignity – an approach that prefigured the constitution the negotiating parties at Kempton Park were at that very time in the last stages of finalizing.

Judge Harms, with all his colleagues concurring, held that doctor-patient confidentiality should be maintained except where convincing grounds justified its breach. More importantly, even, his judgment accepted our experts' unanimous evidence that the stigma surrounding AIDS was very severe. This was a special reason, Judge Harms found, why the law should protect people with HIV and AIDS. And it was a special reason for valuing their right, except in cases of genuine necessity, to decide themselves who should know their status.

Judge Harms concluded that the doctor had no right to tell his colleagues about Barry's HIV. He had violated Barry's right to dignity and privacy. He was liable to pay damages to Barry's deceased estate. And he had to cover our legal costs.

We felt elated. The judgment was a profoundly hopeful portent. Although it dealt with the past, it seemed a pointer to the future. It offered hope that more reasoned, scientifically based approaches to the AIDS epidemic would prevail. But it did more. It suggested that our country's judicial system might be receptive to the power of the constitutional rights that were being negotiated for the new democracy at Kempton Park.

Chapter Three

The Judiciary in Transition

I Judicial office and mortal frailty

Towards the end of September 1997, nearly eleven years after my doctor had called to tell me I had HIV, and three years after our country became a democracy, I fell ill with AIDS. The illness hit me hard. Both my lungs were debilitated by pneumocystis pneumonia, or PCP. It is a rare form of pneumonia. Its cause is a fungus that is in the lungs of many people with normal immune responses. It does no harm there. But in people with a weakened immune system, the fungus opportunistically seizes control. It inflicts severe respiratory problems, and unless treated with strong antibiotics can be fatal.

This fungus was stifling my breath. I lay awake at night, trying to inhale. My lungs felt inefficient, distended, like balloons full of water. But what felt worse was another opportunistic ailment, gastro-intestinal thrush. This thickly coated my mouth, tongue, throat and stomach. The fungus is often found in healthy people too, where it causes no ill effects, but in my body's weakened state it bullied itself into control, forming a furry white layer that made it difficult to chew or to swallow. I lost my energy and my appetite. And, when I did manage to take in food, my stomach couldn't digest it. I was losing my weight as fast as my strength, and beginning to get the gaunt 'AIDS look'. I could not help thinking that fungus grows on decaying bodies. My body was dying.

I had hoped never to reach this pitch of decline and fear. A tiny fraction of people with HIV – less than one-fifth of one per cent – manage to elude AIDS. Medical scientists don't fully understand why. But if you have HIV it is on this group you pin your hopes. You yearn to be among the lucky who will never fall ill. My closest family and friends ardently shared these hopes. After three years of utter solitude, remaining silent while feelings of shame and fear churned inside, in 1990 I had managed to start speaking with my closest relatives about my HIV.

Like most families, my sister Jeanie, and brother-in-law Wim, and their children, Marlise and Graham, responded with unconditional love and support. Why would they not? So did the small group of friends and the tiny handful of colleagues I gradually began to tell. And they, too – how could they not react with acceptance and encouragement? Yet, knowing how often people with AIDS faced hatred and ostracism, I felt grateful for their support. I needed it.

By now I was a judge. Three years before, in the middle of 1994, the advocates' organisation, the Bar Society, nominated me for this position. In the old system, judges were appointed secretly. The Minister of Justice made recommendations, and after a Cabinet meeting, the President announced the appointment. No interview, no debate, no public participation, no fanfare. The new Constitution swept this closed system away. In its place, it created the Judicial Service Commission (JSC). This body interviews candidates for judicial office in full view of the public, and makes recommendations to the President.

My nomination meant I had to appear before the JSC. For me, becoming a judge had been a lifelong ideal. I never could have achieved this in apartheid South Africa. Now we had started on the road to democracy, with a constitution that included all South Africans equally in the rights it promised. To become a judge would be a fulfilment indeed. But something troubled me deeply. Should I publicly state my HIV status?

The question caused me much anguish. I was a vigorous campaigner for rationality and justice in the epidemic, but only a handful of family and close friends knew that I was campaigning for more than just the public issue. I was campaigning also for myself. Were the public, the JSC and President Mandela not entitled to know that I was living with HIV?

But, if they were, was I ready to deal with the intense media and public scrutiny that seemed inevitable? The Barry McGeary trial had shown me how powerfully intrusive media interest and coverage can be. The dilemma seemed impossible.

In this perplexity, I turned to an important mentor, Arthur Chaskalson. He was the country's most distinguished public interest lawyer. For many years he had been one of the Johannesburg Bar's most respected advocates in both commercial and public interest law. He had been among the defence lawyers in the Rivonia Trial. Then, in 1979, he agreed to head the Legal Resources Centre (LRC). It was the country's first public interest law firm. It offered free (*pro bono*) legal services to people oppressed by unjust laws. The impact of its work was deep. His and the LRC's creative legal arguments garnered many judgments that blunted the impact of apartheid laws, and sometimes thwarted their grand design. The pass law judgments the LRC secured made it impossible to enforce apartheid.

But Arthur's innovative public interest lawyering, which was his proudest creation, did more. He revolutionised legal practice itself. He made it possible, and even fashionable, to practise beyond the traditional enclaves of commercial law, family law and criminal defence work. He created a new terrain where it was possible, through the law, to dig at the very foundations of social injustice in our country.

At CALS, operating from the Wits campus in Braamfontein, just across the Queen Elizabeth Bridge from our colleagues at the LRC offices in downtown Johannesburg, we had our own rough-and-tumble style of lawyering. We had successes and we experienced reverses. But there was no question who the giant in the field was, and whose work we all sought to emulate. It was Arthur Chaskalson.

Arthur's focus on work was intense, and his commitment to principle profound. These qualities made him a formidably impressive, even severe, man. But he also had a tender side. Those who worked closest with him sometimes saw it. The first time I came close to engaging with that side was when I considered confiding in him that I had HIV.

It was when I had to argue Barry McGeary's appeal. It was hard to fight a trial for a dying client on an unpopular issue before a hostile judge. But this was all the more complicated because, as an advocate, I was fighting a cause whose agent was coursing through my own bloodstream.

Often, during the tense courtroom confrontations, I wondered how my own HIV was affecting my tactical decisions. Was it influencing my responses to Judge Levy's angry interventions during evidence and argument? Was I unduly sensitive, over-fraught? Or would any advocate in my position have felt the vexation? It was impossible to know.

These reflections took on new intensity after the judge granted us leave to appeal. The stress of the trial, and Barry's death just before final argument, combined with my anguish about my own condition, forced me to think carefully about how to proceed. Would I mishandle the case before the appeal court in Bloemfontein? Did I not need a powerful, experienced senior lawyer to lead me in arguing the case – one whose engagement in the issues of the case was not clouded by personal involvement in the issues?

I turned to Arthur. I called him at his offices in the LRC, and asked him whether he would be willing to lead me in arguing Barry McGeary's appeal. In his typically considered and thorough way, he did not say Yes or No immediately. He first asked for the transcript of the trial. In addition, several months before an appeal, all parties must lodge written argument with the registrar in Bloemfontein. I had prepared the argument. He asked to see this too.

Then Arthur called me in. It was early 1993. We were waiting for the court registrar to assign a date for the appeal. I hoped that when that happened I would have a distinguished senior counsel to manage the planning and the argument. When I arrived at the LRC, Arthur welcomed me into his sparsely yet elegantly furnished office. He invited me to sit at the plain wood table. Then he gave me his answer. He was quite matter of fact, even dismissive. He told me he would not do the appeal. 'Your written argument is fine, Edwin,' he said. 'You have this in hand. You don't need to call me in. Go to Bloemfontein and do it yourself.'

I felt severely disappointed, but Arthur was right. My fears did not stem from the legal principles, or the facts. Despite Judge Levy's hostile findings, we knew the law was on our side. My fears stemmed from the virus I was carrying in my blood, and from the dread secret I was carrying in my head. I feared it would spill out in the courtroom in Bloemfontein, as I often feared it might spill out in the wrenching battles of the trial court.

Looking back, I have often wondered why I did not tell Arthur, then, my real reason for wanting to bring him in. Why did I not confide in him? Tell him that I needed his strength and succour and stature not only because he was a brilliant and respected senior lawyer, but because I was scared that, like the plaintiff, I was going to die myself? I could have told him. For my own ease of mind, I should have told him, and in fact I came close to doing so. I sat at the pale-wooded conference table in his office, with him sitting next to me, earnest and business-like, and swallowed back the impulse to do so. The internalised stigma that is often the greatest burden that many of us with HIV carry stopped my words.

Arthur was right that we would manage in Bloemfontein. I asked my attorney, Mervyn Joseph, to brief a bright young junior advocate to help me instead. He was Danny Berger. He and I systematically worked through the facts and the issues. His fresh perspectives and energies were helpful. We travelled down to Bloemfontein the afternoon before the appeal. That night, we sat up late with Mervyn Joseph in my hotel room, preparing our strategy for the next day.

After all our concerted preparations and anxious anticipation, the hearing was an agreeable surprise. And the outcome – Judge Harms's forward-looking judgment – confirmed Arthur's assessment. He had not needed to divert his sought-after energies to this appeal.

But eighteen months later, when the Bar Society nominated me to become a judge, I knew the time had come. I had to turn to Arthur, not only to confide in him, but to seek his advice.

II The judiciary in transition from apartheid to democracy

When the Constitution took effect in 1994, it introduced a bold innovation to South Africa's court system – the Constitutional Court. From 1990, the negotiators debated intensely what to do with the existing judiciary. Some judges had bravely spoken out against apartheid. Others ruled in favour of just and equal treatment whenever they thought the law gave them an opening to do so. But these judges were a minority. Most judges thought they had no duty other than to apply the letter of the law as they saw it, and they did so in a mechanical and literal way. They saw no obligation to question the iniquitous statutes the apartheid Parliament had enacted, nor did they think they were called to apply legal principles and values so as to find ways to try to secure just outcomes in the cases before them.

Indeed, like most white South Africans, the majority of judges supported apartheid. From time to time, you could see this in their rulings. Some judges gave harsh treatment to those from the liberation movements who stood trial for waging war on apartheid. Some sentenced ANC and PAC soldiers, without misgiving, to long terms in prison. Others passed death sentences.

Would this Bench of judges be a fitting heritage for a new democratic and constitutional order? Some negotiators thought not. Some were in favour of appointing a new judiciary from scratch. Others thought all existing judges should be subjected to a process of scrutiny. Before they could take office under the new Constitution, they should be publicly quizzed about their role in enforcing unjust laws during apartheid.

There were also weighty considerations that pointed to a more cautious approach. South Africa faced an uncertain period of transition. The country would need continuity and stability. Keeping the judges could provide it. What was more, South African judges were experienced and well trained and internationally, the South African judiciary was relatively well regarded. The standards of procedural fairness the higher courts applied were, on the whole, considered impressive. The Bloemfontein appeal court, in particular, despite dismal rulings in the area of apartheid policies and legislation, had managed otherwise to retain its reputation as a scholarly court with serious standards of jurisprudence.

Mr Mandela and other figures in the liberation movements had intimate personal experience of the apartheid judges. They had suffered under the system. They knew the extent of its evil. But on occasion they had also felt the benefit of the space the system left for judges committed to justice and equality to try to make an impact.

The Kempton Park negotiators settled on a pragmatic compromise. The more cautious arguments prevailed. There would be no mass removal of judges, but the existing judiciary would not be untouched.

The compromise had three parts. First, the judges appointed to office under apartheid would stay in their jobs. The interim Constitution expressly stipulated that all judges holding office immediately before its commencement would be 'deemed to have been duly appointed' under the Constitution. They would 'continue to hold office in accordance with the applicable laws'.

Second, in future all new judges would be appointed through the new JSC. It would interview those who applied to be judges, and make independent recommendations to the President. Its objectives included renewal of the judiciary in accordance with the aims and principles of the Constitution.

Third, and most importantly, the interim Constitution created a brand-new court. This court was specifically entrusted with the task of interpreting and applying the Constitution. It would be the guardian of the new Constitution. The court had jurisdiction over all questions regarding the interpretation, protection and enforcement of the Constitution. This included fundamental rights violations, disputes over the constitutionality of state conduct, the validity of statutes passed by Parliament, and disputes between organs of state.

When he became President in May 1994, one of President Mandela's very first tasks was to appoint someone to head the new court. This had to be a person of powerful stature and integrity, a lawyer who could help transform the South African legal system from its role as an instrument of oppression to being a vehicle for justice. Despite intense personal lobbying from Judge Ismail Mahomed, President Mandela did not appoint him. Instead, he appointed Arthur Chaskalson. Leaders in both the legal and political spheres acclaimed his decision.

But first, careful thought had to be given to how the new court was composed. The negotiators decided on a large court – bigger than the highest court in Australia (which has seven members) and the Supreme Courts of Canada and the United States (which each has nine members). To ensure maximum diversity and inclusivity, the Constitutional Court would have eleven members. At least four had to be existing judges. President Mandela picked Judge Laurie Ackermann, Judge Richard Goldstone, Judge Ismail Mahomed, and Judge Tholie Madala.

Judges Mahomed and Madala had accepted appointment after the constitutional negotiations to end apartheid began in 1990. Some months later, after a public interview process, President Mandela added two further judges to the four already appointed to the court. They were Judge John Didcott and Judge Johann Kriegler. Both had held office under apartheid, but had earned reputations as unflinching critics of injustice. In addition to the six judges and Arthur Chaskalson, the new court's head, President Mandela appointed four non-judges: Pius Langa, Yvonne Mokgoro, Kate O'Regan and Albie Sachs. They served on the court for fifteen years, until their term limits forced them to retire, on 11 October 2009. All four made distinguished contributions to the court's jurisprudence, and Justice O'Regan, in particular, achieved worldwide repute as a jurist of profound thought and integrity.

Initially, the Constitutional Court's position in the judicial hierarchy was ambiguous. It was the highest court on constitutional matters, but the Constitution recognised other laws, too, like the pre-existing common law, though it stipulated that these were subject to the Constitution. The ambiguity meant that, for now, the appeal court in Bloemfontein remained the highest court in non-constitutional matters, including the common law. It would take some careful reasoning in contested cases, and even some judicial jostling, before the Constitutional Court established the place of the Constitution as supreme over all law, and its own pre-eminence as the champion of the Constitution.

As head of the Constitutional Court, Arthur's position had a similar shade of ambiguity. The Constitution was supreme – and the Constitutional Court, which the new Constitution specified would be based in Johannesburg, was its guardian and interpreter. But the Constitution also provided that the Chief Justice at the end of the apartheid era would continue in office. This meant that the head of the appeal court – whose seat would remain in Bloemfontein – would continue to be Chief Justice. The Constitution further specified that the Chief Justice would perform important functions of state. These included swearing in the new President and the provincial premiers.

The Chief Justice in 1994 was Michael McGregor Corbett. It was he who on 10 May 1994 at the Union Buildings in Pretoria swore in Nelson Rolihlahla Mandela before the eyes of the world as the first President of the democratic, constitutional state of South Africa.

Chief Justice Corbett, a deeply thoughtful, liberal-minded man, born and bred in Cape Town, was a protégé of Chief Justice Ogilvie Thompson. While he was an advocate at the Cape Bar in the 1950s, he had actively opposed the abolition of the coloured vote. After being appointed a judge in Cape Town, he gained a reputation as a meticulous lawyer with a penetrating legal mind, who did not flinch from giving liberal rulings. Despite his clear anti-apartheid track record, Chief Justice Ogilvie Thompson insisted that he be appointed to the appeal court in Bloemfontein. The apartheid government agreed.

In Bloemfontein, Judge Corbett's efforts to ease conditions under apartheid continued. During the 1960s and 1970s, government's prison policy was especially harsh towards political prisoners. They were segregated from all other prisoners – the black 'politicals' on Robben Island, and the whites in Pretoria Central Prison – and deprived of all access to current news. This was a vindictive gesture. It meant that political prisoners could not read any news magazines and that their newspapers were cut to shreds. Nor could they listen to news bulletins, not even on the government's own sycophantic radio services. One of those sentenced to life imprisonment at the same time as Nelson Mandela, Denis Goldberg, led a group of white political prisoners who challenged this policy in court. They failed. Both the high court and the appeal court upheld the power of the prison authorities to deprive political prisoners of all news of current events.

The majority of the appeal court applied an undemanding test. It held the prisons commissioner merely had to apply his mind to the matter and to exercise his own discretion in determining the conditions under which prisoners were held. Since the prisoners had not proved that he had erred in doing this, there was no basis to find that he had disregarded the prisons statute or the regulations under it.

Judge Corbett dissented. He alone held that the policy was unlawful. He wrote a stirring judgment. He found that, fundamentally, a convicted and sentenced prisoner retains all the basic rights and liberties of an ordinary citizen, except those the law expressly takes away or which are necessarily inconsistent with being in prison. Of course, the prisoner no longer has freedom of movement and only limited contact with the outside world, and the discipline of prison life and the rules and regulations must prevail. 'Nevertheless,' said Judge Corbett, 'there is a substantial residuum of basic rights which he cannot be denied; and, if he is denied them, then he is entitled to legal redress.' Because of this remaining reservoir of rights, he reasoned, the prison authorities could not ban political prisoners from receiving all current news.

Judge Corbett's dissent, like other great dissents before, prevailed in the long run. The appeal court in 1993 unanimously endorsed his approach to prisoners' rights as good law. More importantly, his dissent had immediate practical consequences. Despite winning the court battle, the prison authorities relented. They eased the rule barring political prisoners from current or political news. Goldberg's challenge, and Judge Corbett's dissent, must have shamed them. Again, legal process in the apartheid courts proved effective.

At the very end of the apartheid era, in 1989, the government appointed Corbett as Chief Justice. Judge Corbett, born in September 1923, was due to retire at the end of 1993, when he reached 70. The Kempton Park negotiations were at their crux. The new Constitution was about to be finalised. Everyone wanted a respected figure to head the judiciary as the country moved to democracy. Corbett was so highly respected that all parties asked him to stay on for a transitional period of three years. When he finally retired in 1996, President Mandela paid tribute to him at a formal state banquet. He spoke of his 'passion for justice', his 'sensitivity to racial discrimination', 'intellectual rigour' and 'clarity of thought'.

Apart from other important duties of state, like swearing in the new President, the Constitution also specified that the existing Chief Justice would chair the new JSC. Its first regular meeting was held in Bloemfontein, at the appeal court, in early December 1994. It was Corbett who would preside at the meeting where I would be interviewed and considered for appointment.

Before my own appointment, I had a warm relationship with

Chief Justice Corbett. He chaired the national committee select-
ing Rhodes Scholars when I was its secretary. And I knew that he
followed with sometimes amused interest and discreet approval
the scathing scholarly critiques I penned of the way some of his
colleagues supinely connived in apartheid. But, despite his wisdom and seniority, I did not feel able to turn to him for guidance
on my HIV. The issue was too difficult, too deep, and too fraught.
I needed a confidant whose political and personal reactions I
could trust utterly. The Constitution provided that the President
of the Constitutional Court was also a member of the JSC. That
was Arthur Chaskalson. I knew that he was the person to whom
I could and must turn.

III Joining the judiciary

Once again I called Arthur's offices to make an appointment. He
had moved from his modest accommodation at the LRC to equally
modest space at the new court. It did not yet have the spacious,
light open building it now occupies. Nor did it yet have the wonderful art collection for which it is internationally known.

Instead, the judges' chambers and registrar's offices, and the
courtroom itself, were temporarily housed in an office park in
Braamfontein, a busy area adjoining the city centre. In contrast to
other new constitutional entities, like the South African Human
Rights Commission (SAHRC), and the Land Claims Court, which
chose office space in the more affluent northern suburbs, the
judges deliberately located the court in the central heart of
Johannesburg. The site they chose placed the court on the high
ridge running east-west that serves as a watershed for the Highveld plain, with the city's residential districts in view to both north
and south.

Although the court is now accommodated in an imaginatively

designed and internationally acclaimed building, its location is still unapologetically inner-city. It is wedged into an urban space right alongside the crowded cosmopolitan flatland of Hillbrow, where surely nearly every language of Southern Africa, and most of those of the continent itself, is spoken.

When I made my appointment, I merely told Arthur's new secretary, Miss Fouché, a stern, hard-working Afrikaner, that it was a personal matter. He came to fetch me at front-desk security when I arrived. As he escorted me to his new judicial chambers, he pointed out some of the artworks that his colleague Albie Sachs had started collecting for the court. When we reached his chambers, he first offered me a cup of tea, which I was glad to accept. Then he gravely bade me sit down. As I did, I found myself battling an impulse to say nothing at all about HIV to him. Instead, I forced myself to blurt it out without ado. I said, 'Arthur, you know I've been nominated to become a judge. But I need to tell you something. I have HIV.'

A look of shock appeared on his face. It was clear that the news was unexpected. His first response was to express distress and concern. I murmured my thanks. He paused. Then, intently, he asked questions. How was my health? How was I feeling? What was the prognosis? Was there any hope of medical treatment? What did my doctor say?

I told him there was no cure, and that as yet there was no prospect of effective treatment. I also told him that it seemed certain that at some point I would fall ill and die of AIDS. Despite this, I was in fact still well. I was playing squash regularly with friends like Gilbert Marcus (whom I eventually told, together with his wife Jenny, of my HIV), and in generally robust health. But my declining CD4 count (which gauges the most important blood cells that fight off alien organisms, and serves as a marker of the body's resistance to disease) was showing my body's

113

vulnerability to the ravages of the virus. I told Arthur it was slowly but steadily tracking down.

Then our conversation shifted to my dilemma. Could I take appointment as a judge? And could I do so without a public statement about my condition?

Arthur did not rush in with an immediate disclaimer or assurance. He thought the matter through. He asked me more about living with HIV. And he asked about the laws in other countries. What did foreign legal systems say about stating one's HIV status before taking a job? And what did the International Labour Organisation (ILO) in Geneva say? I explained that many leading legal systems discountenanced an obligation to disclose HIV status when seeking a job. The ILO, too, recommended against any requirement of disclosure.

After considering carefully, Arthur came to a clear view. I should go ahead with the JSC process. And, if it recommended my appointment, as he thought was sure, I should accept. There was no reason to think that I did not have years of productive service ahead of me. Arthur mentioned Joe Slovo, the head of the South African Communist Party. He had recently accepted a job in President Mandela's first Cabinet, as housing minister, even though it was known that he was very seriously ill. No one suggested that he should not serve in the Cabinet because he was ill. The judiciary needed lawyers, Arthur said, who had been involved in human rights law. It was important for me to become a judge.

Finally, Arthur concluded, I need make no public statement. Since my health was still good, my HIV status was not of concern to the JSC or to the President. I left relieved. I was not ready to speak publicly. The dreadful burden of fear and inhibition that those of us with HIV internalise still weighed too painfully on me. But I knew this was only another step in time. In December 1994, I travelled to Bloemfontein to be interviewed for an appointment in the Johannesburg High Court. The JSC recommended me, along with three other judges. We were the first four judges President Nelson Mandela appointed to the high court. I felt overjoyed. All the same my HIV infection, and a feeling of frailty, shadowed my joy. Eventually, I would have to engage with the public, whom I proposed now to serve not as an activist lawyer, but as a judge under a highly aspirational Constitution.

IV ARV treatment and openness with the public

The next step came three years later. As the years passed, the disease at last caught up with my bodily frailty. I had lived to see democracy and a rights-based Constitution. I had lived to serve as a judge under it. Now, as my body weakened, I faced death from AIDS.

But there was help in store. Near-miraculous treatments had become available. My doctor explained that our immediate priority was to overcome the opportunistic diseases that were besetting my body. With some difficulty he managed to do so. The pneumonia proved hardy against my first two-week bout of antibiotics. I needed a second, stronger, course. And the thrush, which we had repelled with an expensive but wonderfully effective new antifungal medication, Diflucan (Fluconazole), returned.

In the meantime, I was intent on keeping up my judicial work. This was not just blind duty. It was also self-help. Continuing to work helped me to cling to balance in circumstances that imperilled it. Even so, it was not easy. Some months before, the Judge-President had assigned me to a duty that took me outside the high court's headquarters in Johannesburg. This meant that I had to preside in the circuit court sitting in Vereeniging, a riverside town near the famous Vaal townships of Sharpeville and Sebokeng. The journey added hours to the day. Each morning, I made the hour-long trip to Vereeniging. During the lunch break, I lay on the floor of the judge's room, trying to garner strength for the afternoon session.

Lying there, hearing my own torturous breathing, it was impossible to imagine how completely I would recover. For, after a grim fifteen-year period of relentless death and disease, with millions of lost lives, the landscape of AIDS had changed dramatically the previous year. Drug combinations had become available to manage AIDS. In 1996 doctors in North America announced that they were treating patients, including some who were extremely sick, and helping them to full recovery. Miraculous stories did the rounds of people on their deathbeds rising up to resume a vigorous life.

This fell also to me. It was an extraordinary joy. Experiencing it changed my life. And it happened with breath-catching rapidity. I started taking anti-retroviral (ARV) medication in November 1997. From crippling incapacitation with the disease's worst opportunistic afflictions, only a few weeks later, I was restored to health. The medications' effect on me seemed and felt little short of miraculous.

The first sign that I was getting better was that I became hungry. Not just hungry. Ravenously hungry. All the time. From being unable to eat at all, I now craved not three, but sometimes four meals a day. The weight I had lost quickly returned. From being exhausted and tired, and seeing the ravages of opportunistic illnesses in my body, vigorous energy returned to me. My skin tone – often a key sign of immune response – recovered. I looked as well as I felt.

But recovery was bought at a high price. Literally. The medications were extremely expensive. At that time, judges earned just less than R360 000 per year. To most South Africans, this was a fabulous figure. At that time, the household income of more than

116

three-quarters of my fellow South Africans was less than R4 000 per month. By contrast, every month, after taxes and other deductions, the Treasury paid about R16 000 into my bank account. My medications initially included a particularly rare and expensive drug, the protease inhibitor Norvir, or Ritonavir. The monthly cost of my medications was more than one-quarter of my income. For me, with my housekeeper's daughters whom I wished to send to a good school, with my home mortgage to pay off, and with ordinary household and living expenses, it was unaffordable.

But for many of the millions of people in Africa the cost was beyond imagination. Like me, they faced death from AIDS, yet they could not possibly afford the medications. I was buying my life with my position and my salary.

The statutory medical insurance that covered judges and parliamentarians barred support for AIDS. Illogically, and unjustly, it listed AIDS as an excluded condition. My colleagues battling high blood pressure, cancer or diabetes, could turn to the scheme to cover their doctors' visits, hospital stays and medication. During his last months in President Mandela's Cabinet, before he died on 5 January 1995, Joe Slovo needed expensive hospital treatments. The same medical insurance surely paid for these. Yet now it would give me no help in fighting AIDS.

My battle with it lay ahead. For now, to stay alive I had to find the money every month.

I was to be able to do so. I was acutely conscious of how lucky I was. One friend's gesture moved me deeply. It showed what all the friends and colleagues to whom I had spoken felt, even though they could not match it. One afternoon after court, with the bills for my anti-retroviral treatment streaming in, my former colleague at CALS, Gilbert Marcus, walked into my judge's chambers. Without comment, he dropped an envelope into my in-tray. Inside was a cheque for R4 000 – a month of life.

Zackie Achmat, a close friend and comrade who had worked with me at CALS for the AIDS Law Project, was deeply concerned for those who did not have judges' salaries, or generous friends. In 1998, a year after my own brush with death, Zackie founded the Treatment Action Campaign (TAC). Zackie had been schooled from childhood in the guileful art of politics. He joined the anti-apartheid struggle as a child. Now, shortly after going public with the news that he was himself living with the virus, he took on the life-and-death issue of drug pricing.

The TAC's target was the international drug companies who held patents on life-saving anti-retroviral drugs. Most of these drugs were quite cheap to manufacture, but the drug companies' patent rights meant they could, while producing the drugs cheaply, demand high prices for them. And they did. Their chief argument was that they needed to accumulate war chests for future life-saving research. Many regarded this argument with scepticism – particularly since the companies paid their shareholders fat dividends, and their executives received annual bonuses that sometimes ran into hundreds of millions of dollars.

But even if high prices were necessary for future research and development, it surely couldn't apply in the face of a continent-wide mass emergency. In Africa, tens of millions of the world's poorest people faced death from AIDS. The reason was not because treatment was unavailable. It existed, and was available. The reason was solely drug company patents and pricing policy. That was surely intolerable. The moral emergency of AIDS in Africa required new thinking, and new flexibility, in both business and politics.

In 1998, the activists' arguments were regarded as so far-fetched as to be outlandish. But within a few years, the activists changed the moral framework of the debate on AIDS treatment. Not only on AIDS – more broadly, they revolutionised our understanding that poor people have the right to proper health care. And today their arguments are widely accepted amongst health care planners, governments, international organisations and even drug companies. What changed the moral landscape was the principled, ingenious, high-energy assault the TAC and its allies around the world launched on the drug companies for their immoral exploitation of AIDS drug patents.

A death of a close comrade spurred Zackie to more action. Tseko Simon Nkoli was a brave and outspoken activist against apartheid. Born in 1957, Simon was active in organising the township revolt that engulfed Sebokeng and other Vaal townships in September 1984. For his leadership in these events, he was arrested with other prominent leaders of the internal uprising. They were all put on trial together, in a far-lying town east of Johannesburg, in what became known as the Delmas Trial. Simon was accused number 13. Together with the other accused, he faced trial for treason and murder.

But there was something special, and unusual, about Simon. Simon was not only an anti-apartheid leader from the townships. He was also a proudly and openly gay man. His defiant courage about his sexual orientation helped win over prominent internal leaders in the anti-apartheid resistance to the idea of lesbian and gay equality. The inclusion of sexual orientation in the equality clause of the Constitution was a direct result of Simon's courage.

Barely four years after the Constitution came into effect, in December 1998, Simon died of AIDS. It was a grievous loss. For him, the new drugs hadn't worked. On a rainy night, we gathered for Simon's funeral in inner-city Johannesburg. The sad rite took place in St Mary's Cathedral – the very place where in January 1971 the security police had arrested The Very Reverend Gonville Aubie ffrench-Beytagh for terrorism, and took him off into solitary confinement.

In a stirring speech to Simon's mourners, Zackie took the formation of the Treatment Action Campaign to the public. 'We are not asking everything,' he said: he realised that government had limited funds for treatment. But, he said, we have to do whatever is necessary 'to save the lives of everyone who needs to be saved'.

The campaign gathered momentum. Funders were found. Organisers, field workers, desk administrators and strategists were appointed. Two vital insiders were Mark Heywood and Nathan Geffen. Mark is a savvy Oxford-educated strategist who came to South Africa to commit his life to securing justice for poor people. Nathan Geffen, highly trained in computer science, dedicated ten years of his life to the TAC because of a profound commitment to justice. From the start, Heywood and Geffen provided the steady stream of incisive analysis and ingenious strategy that brought the TAC international recognition as one of the world's most effective civil society movements.

As all this happened, my own silence was becoming unbearable. In the light of Simon's and Zackie's public statements, it was increasingly clear to me that continuing silence was not possible.

Then, just after Simon's death, another death was captured in searing headlines. It was also someone living with HIV. Her name was Gugu Dlamini. She was from KwaMashu, a township near Durban. Unlike Simon, Gugu was not prominent because she campaigned for any cause and, unlike Simon, she did not die of AIDS. She died a violent death because of fear. Only in her death did she become a campaigner – most poignantly so. She has become famous as a symbol of the injury our own ignorance and prejudice and violent hatred can inflict. Gugu Dlamini died because she spoke openly about her HIV. In an interview on 1 December 1998 – the very day of Simon's death – Gugu told Zulu-language radio listeners that she was living with HIV. Her openness in that interview sealed her fate. Three weeks later, fellow residents from

KwaMashu killed her. They beat and stabbed and stoned her to death.

Her death spoke powerfully to me. If Gugu – who enjoyed none of the comforts and protections my life had – could speak out, why not I?

Arthur Chaskalson knew of my illness and of my recovery. Occasionally, I saw him and his beloved wife, Lorraine, for meals. Our conversations would never conclude without touching on my well-being. Setting up the new court required many pressing duties of Arthur, as did helping guide its jurisprudence through its first landmark judgments. Despite these, he took a warm interest in my wellness.

But Gugu's death, coming so soon after Simon's, and in such shockingly different circumstances, made it plain to me that I could no longer be silent. But how to end the silence? And when? Again, Arthur was there. In early 1999, just after Gugu died, I was nominated for a position on the Constitutional Court. Over the Easter weekend of 1999, Arthur invited me to lunch at his home.

Arthur sketched out a plan. I should seize the moment, he said, and the advantage, and make a public statement with maximum effect. I should announce my HIV status, and my successful treatment for AIDS, before the meeting of the JSC that would interview me for the Constitutional Court job.

It was breathtakingly bold, but it was right. And it was perfect Arthur – the hard-headed moralist, the wily legal strategist, and the caring friend.

With close friends and comrades, I carefully crafted my public statement. We aimed to get beyond my profile as a judge and focus instead on the life-and-death issues of stigma and treatment. I emphasised how it was only with the love and support of friends and family that I was able to speak out. And, most importantly of all, that ARV medication had saved my life – but that I had to buy life at a huge cost, one unaffordable to most Africans who, like me, faced death from AIDS.

My statement was very widely carried. It had a significantly beneficial impact, in South Africa, in Africa and elsewhere. That I am still one of the only people in Africa holding public office to speak out about my own HIV status is a mark of the continuing stigma and internalised stigma that beset the disease. For me, speaking publicly was an enormous release. And it garnered me unimaginable resources of endorsement and support. Still today, I am boosted by the public affirmation and affection lavished on me. In all of this, Arthur's timing was perfect.

Meanwhile, Zackie's call at Simon's funeral resounded across the world's circle of global health and treatment activists. In 2000 the massive two-yearly international AIDS conference convened in Africa for the first time, in Durban. The afternoon before the conference opened, the TAC led a big demonstration. It was impressive, vivid and clamant. Drug company executives, physicians, health care planners, and government ministers were confronted with a plain and principled demand: poor people should have access to available medicines. Obstructing this demand was immoral and unacceptable.

The morning after the demonstration, I gave the keynote speech at the conference. I said that I existed as a living embodiment of the iniquity of drug availability and access in Africa. This was despite the fact that I was unlike the typical person living with HIV or AIDS in Africa – a black, heterosexual woman. I was a white gay man.

Yet my presence at the conference embodied the intolerable injustices of AIDS in Africa. This was because, on a continent in which millions of Africans live on less than one US dollar a day, I could afford monthly medication costs of nearly US $400 per month. 'Amidst the poverty of Africa,' I said, 'I stand before you because I am able to purchase health and vigour. I am here because I can afford to pay for life itself.'

V President Mbeki questions the science of AIDS

Within a very few years, the TAC achieved more than its founders could have dreamed possible when it was set up. Its first objective was to challenge the drug companies to make available to poor people in Africa patented drugs that were cheap to manufacture. In this they succeeded. Through a combination of well-directed, principled outrage and masterful tactics, the TAC coaxed and pressured and shamed the drug companies into change.

In a few short years after the Durban AIDS conference, former United States President Bill Clinton and Microsoft founder Bill Gates added their high-level support to the cause. Both started foundations with deep commitment to drug treatments in Africa. Their personal interventions led to breakthroughs in the policies of many pharmaceutical companies.

Some companies radically reduced their prices. Others agreed to grant licences to manufacturers, in South Africa or India or other countries, that could produce and distribute the drugs cheaply. Yet others agreed to allow importers to bring in drugs manufactured elsewhere, which, under strict patent law enforcement, would have been impossible.

But just as the organisers were putting the final touches to the planning for the Durban conference, in late 1999, a new and entirely unexpected hazard emerged. This hazard was even more menacing to the lives at stake than corporate intransigence and high drug prices. And it posed a far greater political danger to the TAC's goal of universal treatment for AIDS. The threat came from an astonishing source. It was from the President, Thabo Mbeki, who in May 1999 succeeded President Nelson Mandela as President of South Africa.

When President Mbeki assumed the presidency, the epidemic was cruelly corroding the country's life and health. In less than ten years, the prevalence among women attending antenatal clinics had soared, from just under 0.8% in 1990 to over 20% in 1999. As the Mbeki era started, the death toll was already frightening. In 1999, perhaps one quarter of a million people died in South Africa from AIDS-related causes.

How would President Mbeki deal with this crisis of death and suffering?

Unlike President Mandela, President Mbeki had not cut his political teeth in the rough-and-tumble world of local emerging activist pro-democracy politics. Going into exile at a young age, in the early 1960s, he had been groomed for high office as part of an ANC elite. This included a period at Sussex University in England, where he acquired an advanced degree. He assumed office with an aura of technocratic expertise. And he had a reputation as an independent thinker, with a self-professed philosophical bent.

These characteristics strengthened some aspects of President Mbeki's leadership. But the President's inclination to self-minded research, and to idiosyncratic reasoning, had consequences for South Africa's management of the AIDS epidemic that can be described with only one word: horrific. Just months after taking office, President Mbeki started giving expression to bizarre views on AIDS. He started signalling that he planned to upend accepted medical and scientific approaches to HIV, the epidemic, and the treatment of AIDS.

In October 1999 the President spoke in the National Council of Provinces, the second house of Parliament. His reference to the impact of AIDS led him directly to AZT, the popular name for Zidovudine or Azidothymidine. AZT was one of the drugs central to life-saving anti-retroviral combination therapies. It was first synthesised in 1964 and used to treat certain cancers. A quarter century later, in the late 1980s, it seemed to show significant promise as an anti-retroviral treatment for people with HIV. But the promise was dashed when studies showed that when the drug was used alone, in monotherapy, the virus adapted itself quickly to find ways around its anti-retroviral properties.

That depressing setback led to the big breakthrough in AIDS treatment – the one that saved my life. It came when doctors started using AZT together with two or more additional anti-retroviral drugs in simultaneous combinations. They found that, while the virus outwitted single and double treatments, combination therapy stopped it in its tracks. And that the new treatments were astonishingly effective – with few side effects. This is what allowed patients dying of AIDS to be restored, amidst vivid and visible drama, to full health.

When President Mbeki took office in 1999, this was already well established. But because of the extremely high cost of treatment, combination therapy had never been tried on a mass scale. And it had never been tried with large groups of poor Africans. Many practical questions remained about the complexities of mass drug administration. We did not know then, as we know now, that anti-retrovirals would be spectacularly successful in all settings. They work for men and women, rich and poor, young and old, rural and urban, black and white, American, European or African.

The TAC foresaw this. It realised that there was no time to waste in dallying with reflective ambiguities. Together with its allies, it demanded action. It knew the drugs worked. They stopped death. Its core objective was to stop the suffering and grief and bereavement of the mass epidemic of AIDS in Africa by extending drug treatments to everyone who needed them.

But President Mbeki's bizarre pronouncements were casting a deep shadow over fulfilment of this dream. In his address to Parliament on AZT, he attacked the core scientific propositions providing the basis for anti-retroviral treatment. He asserted that there was 'a large volume of scientific literature alleging that, among other things, the toxicity of this drug is such that it is in fact a danger to health'. This, he said, was a 'great concern' to government. It would, he claimed, 'be irresponsible for us not to heed the dire warnings which medical researchers have been making'. He said he had therefore urgently commissioned his health minister, Dr Tshabalala-Msimang, 'to go into all these matters' to find out 'where the truth lies'. He urged members of Parliament's upper house to access 'the huge volume of literature on this matter available on the Internet', so that they could inform themselves of the dangers of AZT.

This speech had menace. First, it seemed to suggest that public leaders were under a duty to undertake their own research on the internet. No reliance on experts! This would mean delving into masses of writings on difficult questions. If they did not do as he had done, he implied, their views would be deficient. This was an intimidating challenge. Most public policy is formed relying on knowledge and expertise derived from scientific consensus. Was this no longer to be the case, under an Mbeki presidency?

Second, there was no scientific doubt at all about the effects of AZT. Doctors and scientists had exhaustively studied it over more than three decades, and there was no doubt about its efficacy and importance to people with HIV. It was a highly effective agent that curbed retroviral replication of the deadly virus in their blood. The only mistake doctors made with AZT in the late 1980s was from insufficient knowledge. They had used it as a single drug, or monotherapy. So administered, the virus quickly outwitted AZT and other drugs. But doctors set that right in their breakthrough discovery of triple therapy, or combination treatment.

What about AZT's alleged toxicity? There was equally no doubt that, just like all drug treatments, if AZT is administered in massive and unsuitable quantities, it is bad for the human body. Just like aspirin. The stories of AZT's 'toxicity' were all based on doses that no doctor would dream of giving to any patient, let alone one battling AIDS.

And the 'scientific literature' on the internet to which President Mbeki referred was not scientific at all. It consisted of conspiratorial scare-mongering by discredited fringe researchers and their political backers. Respected mainstream scientists regarded them, with disdain and dismay, as irresponsible loonies.

I knew all this. I knew it from the clear and certain voice in which my own body's vigorous wellness was speaking. After the horror full-blown AIDS had inflicted on it, my body was now vibrant with life and energy. When President Mbeki spoke in Parliament in October 1999, I had been taking anti-retroviral drugs, in appropriate daily doses, for close to two years. It was the reason I was still alive.

Yet from shortly after his October 1999 speech, President Mbeki expressed increasingly outspoken support for views that questioned the science of AIDS. He lent powerful presidential endorsement to discredited dissidents who cast doubt on the medical science of AIDS. He repeatedly questioned the viral aetiology of AIDS, the efficacy and safety of drug treatments for it, and the reliability and meaning of statistics showing that AIDS was having a cataclysmic effect in Africa.

How could it be that these fringe views caught the attention of so impressive and thoughtful a leader in a young African democracy? A man who was now the chief executive in South Africa's new democratic government? One who in many ways was the most powerful person on the African continent – and the most influential African holding power anywhere in the world?

The answer lay in two powerful short words. Race and sex. In North and South America, Europe and Australasia, the AIDS epidemic was largely concentrated amongst men like myself – white men who were gay, or who, even if they didn't identify themselves as gay, had sexual relations with other men. Despite acute fears in the mid-1980s, in countries outside Africa the epidemic never entered the heterosexual population on any significant scale.

And, as the epidemic spread across the world, the same appeared to be the case in South and Southeast Asia. There, low- and middle-income countries had inadequate health care systems, like South Africa. Many thought this put their populations at risk of mass transmission. Yet the virus has never spread widely in countries like India or Thailand.

But Africa was different. The virus spread with frightening ferocity amongst heterosexual Africans. A compelling set of statistics illustrates the difference. In 1990 both Thailand and South Africa had an estimated national prevalence of less than one per cent, but, by 1995, South Africa's prevalence amongst pregnant women attending public antenatal clinics had skyrocketed to over 10%. By contrast, that of Thailand had stabilised, and even decreased.

The only continent where a mass epidemic of AIDS took fire and spread amongst the heterosexual population was Africa. From Uganda southwards, country after country – mass epidemics of AIDS occurred, caused by a sexually transmitted virus. What could the difference be? Was it because Africa was black? Was it because black people had sex differently?

Of course not. Many theories have sought to explain the particular course and shape of the AIDS epidemic in Africa. Some rest on poor health care provision. Others suggest that unique patterns of concurrent sexual partners have caused the high rates of HIV transmission. Experts contest them all. And none seem satisfactory to me. Most of them point to environmental or behavioural phenomena that exist also in other societies that have not experienced mass epidemics of AIDS.

My own view – that of a lawyer, without training in medical science, virology or epidemiology – is that current explanations take too little account of the fact that the epidemic in Africa is not continent-wide. It is sub-continental. The mass epidemic of AIDS in Africa is almost entirely confined to the heterosexual populations of Central and Southern Africa. In West Africa, thirty years after the epidemic ravaged Uganda, no country has yet registered a national prevalence of higher than three or four per cent. Most prevalences in West Africa are 2.3 or 4%, or even lower. This makes AIDS a serious public health problem, but not on a mass scale. The search for an epidemiological key must therefore focus not on Africa but on the peoples of Central and Southern Africa, those who are sometimes referred to as the continent's Bantu-language speakers, because of the vast language grouping they share.

It is my surmise that further research may eventually pinpoint a physiological, not behavioural or environmental, key. Scientists will identify susceptibility to HIV transmission that is peculiar to the peoples of Central and Southern Africa. In short, a genetic co-factor – something in the bodies of the people of this region, that makes them devastatingly vulnerable to infection by HIV. This will explain why a massive epidemic of HIV took place in this region and nowhere else in the world.

President Mbeki himself missed this point. He regarded the epidemic as African – and he thought the implications of its sexual transmission applied to all black Africans. This led him to castigate AIDS scientists and doctors and epidemiologists for inflicting demeaning racial stereotypes on all Africans.

He was desperately wrong. But, beyond his dire error, the real point is that it almost doesn't matter. That the mass epidemic of HIV is sexually transmitted, and that it exists in Central and Southern Africa and nowhere else, cannot matter one jot to whether we should offer treatment for the disease. The fact that HIV is overwhelmingly transmitted through sex is of course crucial to how we urge people to take preventive measures. And if the particular vulnerability of the peoples of Central and Southern Africa to the virus *is* genetic, then this will of course affect research priorities.

The fact that the virus is sexually transmitted, however, cannot matter to our understanding of the virus itself, or of the effects of the disease, and to whether medical science can alleviate them. The mode of transmission in Africa matters only if you consider sexual transmission something embarrassing. An accusation. Something shameful. In other words, if you brand those who have HIV as sexual sinners. If that is what you think, you would resent scientific findings that point out that only your continent, and no other, has a mass sexually transmitted epidemic of disease.

And this seemed to be how President Mbeki saw things. Shortly after his speech in Parliament, he established a 'Presidential AIDS Advisory Panel'. Almost half its number were discredited but stridently loud AIDS denialists. One of the key jobs President Mbeki assigned to the panel was 'to determine if HIV was the cause of AIDS'. The question was absurd. Scientifically verified evidence had long established that HIV was the cause. It was like asking if the earth was round.

Despite this, President Mbeki responded vehemently to criticisms of his panel. He wrote to world leaders, saying that his critics were mounting an orchestrated 'campaign of intellectual intimidation and terrorism' against him. He lionised AIDS denialists as martyrs to true intellectual inquiry. 'At an earlier period in human history,' he told President Clinton and other leaders, 'these would be heretics that would be burnt at the stake!'

Shortly before the world's AIDS experts gathered in Durban in July 2000, President Mbeki wrote to an opposition leader, Mr Tony Leon, denouncing those who said that HIV originated in Africa. This claim, the President said, was 'wild and insulting'. Why would the physical location of a virus be insulting, unless you thought that the virus itself was shameful?

And, if not a virus, what was the cause of the epidemic of death and illness afflicting the continent from Uganda southwards? President Mbeki's views emerged most clearly when he officially opened the AIDS conference in Durban. Speaking just hours after the TAC's big demonstration, Mbeki sought to attribute the ravages of AIDS not to a virus, but to poverty. He was addressing nearly 15 000 scientists, doctors, health care workers and activists from across the world. To this audience, the President noted that the world's 'biggest killer and the greatest cause of ill health and suffering across the globe, including South Africa, is extreme poverty'.

For the President to say this was not in itself disturbing. What was disturbing was the inference he plainly sought to draw – that AIDS was not virally caused, but was instead an environmental phenomenon. He said that 'the deeply disturbing phenomenon of the collapse of immune systems among millions of our people' could not be blamed on HIV alone. 'It seemed to me,' President Mbeki stated, 'that we could not blame everything on a single virus.'

But the President's most searing attack on those who accepted scientific learning on AIDS was to a university audience in October 2001. His target was treatment activists. Amidst the rising death toll from AIDS, TAC marches in townships and cities were demanding anti-retrovirals for all. President Mbeki took aim directly at those 'carrying their placards'. They considered black

Africans 'germ carriers, and human beings of a lower order', he said, who cannot subject their 'passions to reason'.

Scientists and treatment activists, he said, insisted that Africans must 'adopt strange opinions, to save a depraved and diseased people from perishing from self-inflicted disease'. He added that the conventional explanation of AIDS branded Africans as 'natural-born, promiscuous carriers of germs, unique in the world', and that those adhering to science proclaimed that Africa was 'doomed to an inevitable mortal end because of our unconquerable devotion to the sin of lust'.

These views were breathtaking in their unscientific ferocity. Worse, though, was their frightening consequence for practical policy. If AIDS was not caused by a virus, then anti-retroviral drugs should not be used to treat it. If poverty caused AIDS, then medicines would not work against it. AIDS would have to be addressed by anti-poverty projects, not anti-retroviral treatments.

This reasoning led the President to refuse to allow government to distribute the only known treatment for AIDS – anti-retroviral drugs. The cost in lives and in human suffering was anguishingly high. As hundreds of thousands in South Africa fell ill and died, the mists of an absurd debate delayed decisive government action. Conservative calculations show that more than 330 000 lives (or what epidemiologists call 2.2 million 'person-years') were lost because President Mbeki thwarted a feasible and timely ARV treatment programme.

VI The courts, presidential policy-making and the new Constitution

President Mbeki's policies on AIDS did not stand unchallenged. As the death toll from the deadly disease mounted, the activists turned to the courts. That the courts were available for the activists' challenge was one of the central achievements of the new constitutional dispensation. And in securing that achievement, President Mbeki had himself played a pivotal role.

In 1994 South Africans achieved democracy under an interim Constitution. This represented a deal negotiated between the outgoing apartheid government, the ANC and other negotiating parties. None of them had been elected to a constitution-making role, so South Africa's first Parliament, elected by all South Africans in April 1994, was charged with a double role.

Just like the old Parliament, it was a legislative body. And in the wake of apartheid it immediately set about enacting important reforming statutes. One of the first legislative acts of the new Parliament was to enact the Restitution of Land Rights Act. This statute started a process by which black South Africans, dispossessed of their land by the notorious Native Land Act of 1913, could claim restitution.

But the new Parliament had a second function. It was in addition a constitutional assembly. For this purpose, the two chambers of the Parliament had to sit together. This carried some historical resonance. The entrenched procedure designed to protect the coloured voters on the common roll, which the apartheid government had circumvented by a legislative fraud, explained in chapter 1, also required both houses of Parliament to sit together.

Constituted as the Constitutional Assembly, the new democracy's lawmakers were charged with drafting the final Constitution. In one of its early judgments, the Constitutional Court explained that, instead of an outright transmission of power from the old order to the new, there was a two-stage, programmed transition. An interim government, established and functioning under the interim Constitution agreed to at the end of 1993, would govern the country on a coalition basis while a final constitution was being drafted. A national legislature, elected by universal adult suffrage in South Africa's very first national democratic elections, would double as the constitution-making body and would draft the new Constitution within a given time.

But the new Constitution would have to comply with guidelines the negotiating parties agreed on in advance. There were 34 Constitutional Principles. They laid down the main framework of the new Constitution.

It had to provide for a common South African citizenship and a democratic system of government committed to achieving equality. The new Constitution had to entrench fundamental rights for all. These included equality and a ban on discrimination. And these rights had to be justiciable – in other words, someone complaining of a rights violation had to be able to turn to the courts.

Importantly, Parliament was no longer supreme. Instead, the Constitution was to be supreme. There had to be separation of powers between the legislature, the executive and the judiciary, with checks and balances to ensure accountability, responsiveness and openness. Diversity of language and culture had to be acknowledged and protected, and conditions for their promotion encouraged.

Finally, the parties agreed on a radical innovation, one previously unknown to the field of constitutional development. They agreed that, before the new Constitution could come into effect, an independent body would have to determine whether its provisions did indeed comply with the Constitutional Principles the negotiators had previously agreed. So the interim Constitution itself provided that the new constitutional text, passed by the Constitutional Assembly, would be of no force or effect unless the Constitutional Court certified that all provisions of the new constitutional text complied with the Constitutional Principles.

That body had to have legal expertise. And it had to be respected by all sides. Its rulings would have to have the stature necessary to survive potentially stormy disagreements.

That independent body was the new Constitutional Court. One of its first and most burdensome tasks – after it delivered its historic judgment declaring that the death penalty was incompatible with the Constitution – was to certify the final Constitution. On 8 May 1996 the Constitutional Assembly adopted the first version of the new Constitution. The court sprang into action immediately. It invited objections not just from political parties, but from anyone interested in the constitutional process and its outcome.

Five opposition political parties and a further 84 private entities – including business and employers' organisations – lodged objections to the new Constitution. The political parties, the Constitutional Assembly itself, as well as 27 of the other bodies or persons, were permitted to address the court. The process had to be as inclusive and respectful as possible.

Even so, the court's task was immensely delicate. It was careful to explain that its job was judicial, not political. It had to certify a constitution. The difficulty was that in its very nature a constitution deals with political power. Despite this, the court's task was not to say that the political choices made by the Constitutional Assembly were right or wrong. The court emphasised that the political wisdom of the provisions of the final Constitution was 'not this court's business'. Rather, its business was to ensure that the final Constitution faithfully reflected the negotiated Constitutional Principles.

Within this carefully delineated, but delicate framework, the court heard oral argument over nine gruelling days. On 11 July 1996, it reserved its judgment. All the judges worked on the judgment. Instead of it coming out in any individual judge's name, the judges pooled their expertise and writing skills and produced a single judgment. This is called a judgment of the court, and is not attributed to any individual judge. Instead, all members of the court sign onto it.

It is the most powerful way a court can express itself and, apart from largely procedural matters, it is usually reserved for only the most important disputes.

The court handed down its judgment on 6 September 1996. It found that the proposed Constitution was a monumental achievement. The overwhelming majority of its provisions complied with the predetermined principles. Yet it found that in various lesser respects, the proposed Constitution fell short.

The right of individual employers to engage in collective bargaining had to be recognised and protected. Parts of the draft Constitution that shielded ordinary legislation from constitutional review had to go. To amend the new Constitution had to require special procedures involving special majorities. The fundamental rights, freedoms and civil liberties protected in the text had to be properly entrenched. The independence and impartiality of the Public Protector, the Auditor-General and the Public Service Commission had to be properly protected. Better provision had to be made for local government.

The powers and functions of the provinces were substantially less than and inferior to those in the interim Constitution. This had to be fixed.

The court nevertheless sent a reassuring message to the constitution makers. It said the instances of non-compliance it had found, although important, should not serve to prevent the formulation of a text that did fully comply.

In the wake of the court's refusal to certify the first draft, the Constitutional Assembly had to reconvene. Changes had to be agreed. Further compromises had to be made. The changes the court required were indeed made. And on 11 October 1996, the Constitutional Assembly adopted a revised constitutional text.

Even so, some parties persisted in their objections. The court convened a further sitting. In November it heard the objections over three days of argument. Then it reserved judgment. Finally, the court decided that none of the remaining objections were sound. It delivered its judgment on 4 December 1996. It issued the following order:

'We certify that all the provisions of the amended constitutional text, the Constitution of the Republic of South Africa, 1996, passed by the Constitutional Assembly on 11 October 1996, comply with the Constitutional Principles.'

The Constitution was finally certified. Six days after the court granted certification, on International Human Rights Day, 10 December 1996, President Mandela signed the new Constitution. It took effect on 4 February 1997.

VII The new Constitution and the fundamental right to health care

There was one significant difference between the interim Constitution and the final Constitution. This was to prove momentous to the AIDS activists' challenge to President Mbeki's policies.

Unlike the interim Constitution, the final Constitution enshrined rights to social and economic goods. The inclusion of this bundle of rights set the South African Constitution far apart from the constitutions of the United States or Canada, or even the European Convention on Human Rights. The South African Constitution explicitly acknowledges that it is impossible to enjoy rights like equality, freedom, free speech and religion, and freedom of association, without a minimum level of social benefits. You had to have education, social security, food, water, housing and health care to be able to enjoy the other constitutional rights.

The new Constitution therefore included two kinds of social and economic rights. First, it included the right to basic education. It also included a provision that no one may be refused emergency medical treatment. The Constitution does not define these two rights. But they are absolute.

By contrast, the Constitution also includes a larger category of social and economic rights that are not absolute or immediate. These are expressed as rights 'to have access' to various social goods. These include adequate housing, health care services, sufficient food and water, social security and further education.

Government is not required to realise these rights immediately. The Constitution obligates the state to 'take reasonable legislative and other measures, within its available resources, to achieve the progressive realisation' of each right.

As one of the chief ANC participants in the transitional negotiation, President Mbeki had fought for a system of constitutional supremacy. Parliament and the executive would not exercise untouchable power as it had previously done under apartheid. Instead, the Constitution would be supreme. This idea – that there would be constitutional review of legislative and executive action – lay at the heart of the new Constitution. President Mbeki's own deep scepticism about what caused AIDS, and his consequent reluctance to authorise anti-retroviral treatments, would now be subjected to that very process.

The stage was thus set for an immense drama: one that would determine whether millions of South Africans with HIV faced only death, or whether they would be offered life.

Chapter Four

The Rule of Law, Supremacy of the Constitution and AIDS

I Pretoria High Court, Monday morning, 26 November 2001

If you stepped off the street into the spacious foyer of the Pretoria High Court on the summer's morning of Monday 26 November 2001, and studied the daily roll pinned up on the public notice board, you would have found listed amongst the cases set down for hearing that day one of the most momentous ever brought before the court. The Judge-President, Judge Bernard Ngoepe, had assigned a court to hear case number 21182 of 2001 that morning. It was the application brought by the Treatment Action Campaign against the Minister of Health.

The imposing court building, elegantly dominating the capital city's Church Square, had seen many significant legal clashes. In 1964, it was before a judge of this court that Nelson Mandela stood trial for his life. Before Mandela's epoch, the Pretoria court's judges had tried many momentous cases. These included life-and-death issues arising from the Afrikaner rebellion in 1914, the mineworkers' strike in 1922, the World War II Nazi sympathisers (it was in this same court that Judge Schreiner, the courageous dissentient in the coloured voters' case, sentenced the pro-Nazi ringleader Robey Leibbrandt to death for treason), and the Defiance Campaign of 1952.

And throughout the 1980s, my colleagues and I, working from the LRC and CALS, together with other public interest lawyers, brought many cases to the Pretoria High Court. We crossed its foyer to demand justice in its courtrooms for activists being held in police detention, for communities government was trying to force from their land in pursuit of the grand scheme of apartheid separation, for religious and conscientious objectors defying conscription into apartheid's army, and for fighters charged with treason for opposing that army.

And the first employer challenges – mostly unavailing – to the rising power of the industrial court, which after the labour reforms of 1979 and 1980 was granting more and more muscular rights to unions, and affording more and more employment protections to workers, were brought before the judges of the Pretoria High Court.

All these cases were momentous. Many of them dealt in matters of life and death. But none concerned the lives and deaths of so many people as case number 21182 of 2001.

II The law, the Constitution and the crisis of death from AIDS

In the ten years since February 1990, when President De Klerk committed the apartheid government to negotiations, the HIV prevalence in South Africa had risen astronomically. Amongst pregnant women attending antenatal clinics it had spiked dramatically. It was 0.76% in 1990. Five years later, it had risen nearly fifteen-fold. In 1995, it was 10.44%. And in 2000, the last year the epidemiological experts who testified in the case described, it had risen to 24.2%. Twenty-four point two per cent! Nearly one-quarter of all pregnant women visiting public health facilities in South Africa had HIV.

Some provinces were worse affected than others. KwaZulu-Natal was the most severely burdened. There, the figures indicated a province-wide prevalence of 36.2%. But in Gauteng, the urban and industrial heartland of the country – the province in which both Johannesburg and Pretoria are situated – the position was hardly better. The 2000 survey found an average prevalence of 29.4%. And pregnant women in Gauteng between the ages of 25 and 29 were particularly hard hit - 30.6% of them were found to have HIV. Nearly one-third.

These figures were staggering. They were worse than any of us could ever have believed conceivable in the dire years before 1990, as the epidemic insidiously seeped southwards. Worse even, there was no indication that the rise in infections was levelling off. On the contrary, South Africa was in the grip of one of the fastest growing epidemics anywhere in the world.

The evidence led epidemiologists to estimate that, by 2001, when the Pretoria High Court sat to hear the case, five million South Africans had HIV. The epidemic was exploding. And too, too many of the people who had been infected with HIV in this explosive growth started dying. By 2000 it was estimated that the yearly death toll from AIDS in South Africa was 270 000.

That was nearly 750 people dying every day.

I knew some of them. To say this involves no special claim. Every South African knew some of them. They were our husbands and wives and lovers, our parents, siblings, cousins, aunts and uncles, our colleagues, our neighbours, our fellow congregants and employees. By 2000, death from AIDS was marking our country heavily, cutting deep scars of grief and loss across the faces of our people.

And there was a racial tinge to all this. HIV infection was found amongst all races. I knew this, because I was white. But it was spreading about ten times more quickly amongst black people than in other groups. The racial pointedness President Mbeki saw in the AIDS statistics was exactly right. This was a largely black epidemic of disease and death. And in Southern Africa its sexual profile, uniquely, was overwhelmingly heterosexual.

President Mbeki's response to the African shape of the epidemic was indignation. He questioned whether HIV existed. He cast doubt on whether it was sexually transmitted. He queried the value of HIV testing. And he scoffed at suggestions that HIV was the cause of AIDS ('Can a virus cause a syndrome?' he asked in Parliament: but he already knew the answer, because he gave it – 'It can't,' he said, 'because a syndrome is a group of diseases resulting from acquired immune deficiency.'). About all these issues, in the face of overwhelming scientific and medical proof, he fostered scepticism.

Some praised what the President was doing. They said his questions were a justified and even welcome philosophical inquiry. At the height of the crisis, the Vice-Chancellor of the University of Cape Town lauded the President's 'steadfast and intelligent refusal to be trapped in a web of assumptions' about AIDS.

But behind the abstract questions lay chillingly practical issues. Who would live? And who would die? Would life-saving medications be made available to South Africans dying of AIDS? And, most practically and immediately in 2001, would doctors at public health facilities be allowed to prescribe the drugs to pregnant mothers with HIV who wished to protect their infants from getting HIV?

As the death toll rose, and hundreds of thousands of South Africans died, these questions became more and more achingly urgent. And behind them lay an even more profound question, one which went to the heart of South Africa's democratic and constitutional transition. Did the law and the Constitution have a part to play in providing answers?

Over a few momentous months, the courts told South Africans the answer was Yes.

III The crisis of infants and HIV

What drove the crisis of death into the courts was a particularly anguishing aspect of the epidemic – the number of babies being born with HIV. Most new infections were amongst young, sexually active people – the child-bearing population. And as happens when young people have sex, babies were conceived. Without medical intervention, about one-third of women who have HIV transmit the virus to their babies. This happens either during the birth process, which always involves exposure to the mother's blood, or when the mother breastfeeds her newborn infant afterwards.

In South Africa, shortly before the court case, it was estimated that more than 60 000 new HIV infections each year resulted from mother-to-child transmission. By the time the case was argued in court, it was undisputed that 70 000 babies were being born with HIV every year.

A baby born with HIV at that time had little chance in life. HIV attacks the infant's immune system, which never has a chance to develop. The baby is chronically sick. A doctor working in a paediatric ward at the Cecilia Makiwane Hospital in East London, in the Eastern Cape province, described the babies' torment in these words:

'Wards are full of human suffering, both physical and mental. Wasted little infants, struggling to breathe despite oxygen, broad spectrum of antibiotics, nebulisations, refusing to feed as swallowing is too painful because of extensive candidiasis requiring parenteral antifungals, with itchy, uncomfortable skin rashes; some with incurable diarrhoea often with painful perineal rashes.'

IV The breakthrough of hope – anti-retroviral protection for babies

A significant proportion of this grievous suffering was unnecessary. Science was showing the way to decisively reducing transmission of HIV from mothers to their babies. In fact, science had
already shown the way. And it had done so conclusively, and decisively.

In the middle of the decade preceding the court case, in 1994,
a paediatric AIDS study group published breakthrough findings.
They reported the first ray of significant hope for babies of mothers
with HIV. The study involved AZT, President Mbeki's bugbear,
which he had attacked in the upper house of Parliament in October 1999. But the group's findings established beyond doubt that
giving a pregnant mother regular doses of AZT from quite early
on in her pregnancy – after the first fourteen weeks – significantly
reduced the risk that she would transmit HIV to her child. This
simple procedure could save the baby from lifelong disease.

Coming after the previous dismal findings that long-term use
of AZT did not save adults with AIDS from dying, this new study
represented a gleaming shaft of light in a dank landscape. It gave
enormous hope to women with HIV/AIDS, to doctors and to those
managing the epidemic. It showed that short-term – as opposed
to long-term – use of AZT could well be medically very important.

In many developed countries, the study's findings quickly established a new minimum standard of care for pregnant women
with HIV. They had to be given AZT from fourteen weeks into
their pregnancy – not for their own sakes, but for the sakes of their
unborn infants.

There was one problem. AZT was still very expensive. In 1994
the TAC did not yet exist, and its campaign of outrage and principle
had not yet succeeded in bringing drug prices down. That all lay

ahead, in the late 1990s and early 2000s. For now, to give a pregnant woman 100mg of AZT five times daily, from fourteen weeks into her pregnancy, was exorbitantly expensive. It would bankrupt the health budgets of most African countries. It was beyond the reach of the vast majority of developing countries.

But science was offering more and more hope. In 1996 scientists reported the astonishing benefits of combination therapy for adults with AIDS. Surely there was more good news to come? And indeed there was. In 1998 the results of a study in Thailand showed that a short course of AZT was also very safe and very effective to reduce mother-to-child transmission. The study showed that much smaller doses, administered later in pregnancy, also cut mother-to-child transmission by half.

This study was particularly important for a developing country like South Africa. It offered hope because the shorter-course AZT was much cheaper and could be incorporated easily into existing prevention programmes.

Thailand, a country with resources and health infrastructure comparable to South Africa's, promptly implemented these findings. It lost no time in introducing a country-wide mother-to-child HIV prevention programme in 1999. It quickly succeeded in halving HIV infection in newborn children. Suffering was lessened immediately.

But what about Africa? Were things not different on this continent? No. The very next year, in 1999, studies in Côte d'Ivoire and Burkina Faso showed significant reductions even where mothers with HIV continued to breastfeed their infants, as was common on our continent. These results were extremely hopeful. They showed that, despite breastfeeding, a short course of AZT, administered before birth, cut HIV transmission by well over a third.

But that was West Africa. Would it be the same in South Africa?

Yes. Results were no different in this country. In Khayelitsha, near Cape Town, doctors showed that short-course AZT cut HIV transmission by about half. This programme was particularly promising for our country, with its health care system creaking from the post-apartheid difficulties. It showed that even a fairly complex anti-retroviral regimen was feasible in a township setting – and that the benefits in lives and health were significant.

But the breakthrough that proved to be crucial to the court case was a scientific study not on AZT, but on the drug Nevirapine. Nevirapine belongs to a class of anti-HIV drugs called non-nucleoside reverse transcriptase inhibitors (NNRTIs). They use a different mechanism from AZT to stop HIV from replicating, although both classes target the same step in the virus's reproduction cycle.

Nevirapine is fast-acting and potent. And it has a long 'half-life'. This means that the human body takes a long time to eliminate it through the kidneys or the bowels, so its pharmacological properties keep working in the body. Doctors immediately saw that it was a vital additional weapon in their armoury against HIV – particularly to reduce the risk of mother-to-child transmission. The body absorbs it quickly, and, most importantly, it passes easily through the placenta. This is the barrier in the womb that joins the foetus to the mother, and protects it from harmful agents in her blood. It allows Nevirapine to pass readily through.

The drug is much cheaper and easier to use than AZT. To prevent transmission of HIV from a mother to her infant, Nevirapine is used alone as a single oral dose of 200mg to the mother during labour, followed by a single oral dose to the infant within 48 to 72 hours after birth.

A carefully supervised and administered drug trial in Uganda shortly before the court case compared this regimen of Nevirapine with an oral dose of AZT at onset of labour and further doses every three hours during labour, plus a dose of AZT to the infant twice daily for seven days after birth. The results were exciting. They showed that just over one in ten infants in the Nevirapine group had HIV – whereas just over double that number in the AZT group were infected. Short-term Nevirapine worked extremely well in preventing HIV transmission.

Researchers and doctors sang the praises of Nevirapine. It is true that a single dose was not the best treatment available. Putting all pregnant women on full ARV treatment, as opposed to a short course of a single drug, would be better for their babies, and better for them. There was also some question about whether giving a woman a single dose of Nevirapine might make her resistant to the drug if she took it later as part of full-course ARV treatment. Despite this, doctors at the time were enthusiastic about the drug's simplicity, low cost and potential for widespread use. Compared with other anti-retroviral treatments, it achieved a comparable reduction of transmission but with just a single dose.

The Medicines Control Council (MCC) had already registered Nevirapine to treat HIV in adults, adolescents and children with HIV/AIDS. In April 2001 the MCC expanded this registration. It allowed the drug to be used to reduce the risk of transmission of HIV from mother to child in pregnant women not taking antiretroviral therapy at the time of labour. The registration was subject to the condition that its manufacturers continue to provide data on how the drug was performing. And patients had to be informed that breastfeeding was not a good idea.

The evidence in these studies was so overwhelming that it led to a rapid scientific and medical consensus: mothers with HIV had to be offered anti-retroviral treatment to reduce the risk of transmitting the virus to their babies.

In 2000 the World Health Organisation and UNAIDS, the joint United Nations agency dealing with the worldwide epidemic, convened an important meeting of experts from across the globe in Geneva. The experts unanimously concluded that anti-retroviral treatments for preventing mother-to-child transmission are safe and effective and that they had to be included in a minimum standard of care for women and children with HIV.

So effective was Nevirapine that its German manufacturers, Boehringer Ingelheim, made a smart move. In July 2000, immediately after the Durban conference – which turned up the flames of international moral opinion under the feet of the international pharmaceutical industry – they made an extraordinary offer. They undertook to make Nevirapine available to the South African government, free of charge, for five years, to prevent mother-to-child transmission. Astonishingly, President Mbeki's government refused the offer. Even so, the estimated cost of the required dosage was negligible – only R10 per baby.

V Combivir, plus Nevirapine – my own drug combination in 2000

The public debate raging about AZT and Nevirapine engrossed me. This was because both these drugs were coursing through my bloodstream. Their anti-retroviral properties were keeping me alive. They were enabling me to lead a fit, healthy and vigorous life. At the end of 2000, I had been a high court judge for six years. The Judicial Service Commission then recommended me for appointment to the appeal court in Bloemfontein. Despite my outspoken public criticism of his stance on AIDS, President Mbeki accepted the Commission's recommendation. He signed my certificate of appointment. It still hangs on the wall of my court chambers.

But I was well enough to do my job so vigorously only because of anti-retroviral treatment – including both AZT and Nevirapine.

Since 2000 I had been taking both drugs. In that year, my doctor, Dr David Johnson, changed me to Combivir. This meant that I had to take one tablet of Combivir, together with one tablet of Nevirapine, twice a day. Combivir contains both AZT and 3TC, which is also known as Lamivudine. I switched to Combivir because it was much cheaper than the combination of drugs I had been taking.

My new drug combination gave me a dramatic front-row interest in the doubts President Mbeki was trying to cast on AZT. And it made me intensely interested in the important new findings about Nevirapine. I spoke at TAC meetings, and at a special conference the TAC convened in Durban with the national trade union federation COSATU. I bore witness to my wellness, and the horror and folly of President Mbeki's scepticism. I could not remain silent. My own life – the fact that I was living at all – afforded daily evidence of the efficacy of two of the drugs whose usefulness and safety were in dispute before the court.

VI Infants born with HIV – government digs in its heels

Despite the heavy weight of the accumulating evidence, government still refused to act decisively to make anti-retroviral treatment available to pregnant mothers with HIV.

Most pointedly for South Africa, the Geneva experts in 2000 had concluded that there was no justification for restricting any of the available anti-retroviral treatments to pilot projects (research and training sites) or to research settings. In other words, the international medical and scientific consensus was clear. Anti-retrovirals for preventing transmission to infants should go public, this should happen immediately, and it should happen big.

Yet South Africa was dragging its feet. It was doing so in precisely the way the experts had authoritatively discountenanced. It was limiting anti-retrovirals to pilot sites.

Instead of accepting Boehringer Ingelheim's extraordinary offer, and making Nevirapine unconditionally available to all mothers with HIV wanting to protect their babies from infection, President Mbeki's government decided to make Nevirapine available only at a limited number of pilot sites. These numbered only two per province – making eighteen in total. In Gauteng, the country's most populous province, apart from a previously existing research site at the Chris Hani Baragwanath Hospital, the designated sites were Natalspruit and Kalafong hospitals.

After the litigation started, programmes to prevent transmission to babies were later (by 17 October 2001) available also at the Leratong, Carletonville, Coronation and Johannesburg hospitals. Additional programmes were due to start at hospitals in Sebokeng in November 2001, and Ga-Rankuwa in Pretoria by February 2002. But this was still pitifully small. The pilot sites themselves reached only about 10% of the population. The result was that doctors at public health clinics not selected as pilot sites could not give pregnant mothers and their newborn babies Nevirapine – even though the manufacturer was offering it to government at no cost.

In addition to refusing to make Nevirapine generally available at public clinics, government was patently dragging its feet over a major and obvious policy imperative – the development and implementation of a comprehensive national programme to prevent mother-to-child transmission of HIV.

Over an extended period, activists and child specialists pleaded with health minister Tshabalala-Msimang and with President Mbeki to implement a programme. Their pleas were all ignored.

VII The activists consider the courts – the legacy of *Soobramoney* and *Grootboom*

By late 2000, six months after the Durban conference, doctors in the field and their activist allies had come to a reluctant decision. They would have to turn to the courts. But they did so with hearts of stone, and with feet that were heavy.

Why were the doctors and activists reluctant? There were varying reasons. Many of them supported the ANC, some as paid-up members. They were loath to take legal action against a government they thought embodied their ideals – one they had fought to put in power. Many had long-standing associations with former activists who now served in government. Legal action risked putting these associations and loyalties on the line.

What was more, litigation is in its nature oppositional. A court case is between two sets of adversaries. It pits one view, one party, one set of interests against the other. It risks driving two parties who are already in conflict even further apart. Most cases require a judge to say that one party is right, and the other wrong. It requires the court to decide who wins, and who loses. It is set up to see one party walking away triumphant, and the other disgraced.

The activists and their supporters in the health professions wanted to work with government, not against it. They did not want the courts to have to force the government to do what it was obvious it should do.

There was a further, powerful reason. Any court action would venture into legal terrain that was as yet largely unexplored. And the part that had been explored had not proved hospitable to the explorers. They had been defeated. The applicants in any court case would be asking the courts to rule on government's responsibility to provide health care rights – a deeply controversial area of law and policy.

The Constitutional Court had at that time given only one judgment on the right of access to health care. The final Constitution, which added social and economic rights to the Bill of Rights, came into effect on 4 February 1997. Just nine months later, in November the court issued its first ruling on the right of access to health care. The judgment concerned a 41-year-old man, Mr Thiagaraj Soobramoney. He was in the final stages of chronic renal failure.

The court's decision denied Mr Soobramoney the dialysis he sought. He died soon afterwards.

The decision attracted extensive criticism, but the court's ruling was undoubtedly correct. The health policy Mr Soobramoney challenged limited dialysis to patients with acute renal failure who could be successfully treated. But Mr Soobramoney's condition was irreversible: he was in the final stages of severe kidney failure. Dialysis would prolong his life, but allowing him to have it would deny treatment to others, who had a better chance of surviving.

The court's decision was agonising, but clear. It could not have ruled that government was failing to take reasonable steps to realise Mr Soobramoney's right of access to health care. It could not tell the health care administrators that their distributional policy of rationing dialysis for those who at least had a chance of surviving was wrong. Even though the court's decision was correct, it sent a clear signal to litigants: the court would not readily interfere to set aside the policy decisions of health care administrators.

A second decision in the area of social and economic rights sent a similar signal. This decision was three years after Mr Soobramoney's case. It proved not much less controversial.

Mrs Irene Grootboom was one of a group of desperately poor people who lived in Delft, a poor area near Cape Town. To create informal homes for themselves, they moved onto private land to erect shacks, but the land had already been set aside for formal development into low-cost housing. So government evicted Mrs Grootboom. She and her fellow dwellers now had nowhere to go.

It was the middle of an exceptionally wet and cold Cape winter. Emergency accommodation was provided, but what did government have to do beyond that?

Mrs Grootboom argued that government had not done enough to furnish her with housing. In a unanimous judgment, the court refused to grant an order giving concrete effect to Mrs Grootboom's right of access to housing. Instead, it made a broader order. It declared government's housing policy, as a whole, invalid. But the order had no specific bite in it.

The court's judgment faulted government's housing programme generally for making no express provision for those in desperate need. The order declared that government housing programmes were obliged to provide for people like Mrs Grootboom. These were people 'who have no access to land, no roof over their heads, and who are living in intolerable conditions or crisis situations'. Because government's programme failed to do so, the court declared the policy invalid.

But to Mrs Grootboom, it gave no specific relief. When she died a few years after the court's judgment, she was still living in a shack. Some commentators taunted the court's socio-economic rights rulings. They pointed to the fact that, despite all the legal fanfare, Mrs Grootboom died without a home. All the lawyers and all the evidence and all the arguments and all the judges – fourteen, in all, who heard the case – failed to provide her with a house.

That is true, and Mrs Grootboom's death, still in a shack, is a humbling reminder of the limits of what lawyers and judges can achieve for the poor. But history has judged the judgment in Mrs Grootboom's case better than those who scoffed at the ruling. Many commentators have praised the judgment. They note the court's order that government had to reshape its entire policy so that it included provision for the poorest of the poor. They note how the court demanded that government rigorously rethink its entire plan for housing. They note that, because the poorest were not covered, the court ruled government's entire housing policy unlawful and unconstitutional. That order has led to significant shifts in housing policy. These have benefited many poor people.

That is the judgment of informed opinion and of history. But in 2001, when the doctors and the activists had to decide what to do about babies suffering and dying unnecessarily because of AIDS, the *Grootboom* decision was less than a year old. Its limits, and the caution the Constitutional Court showed in issuing its ruling, were still fresh. The lesson from both Mr Soobramoney's and Mrs Grootboom's cases was this: move very carefully indeed.

VIII The Biko case in medical memory

But despite all these doubts, by the middle of 2001 the paediatricians and the activists knew they could wait no longer. Their pleas to President Mbeki's government had gone unheeded. The death toll from AIDS was rising. The number of young women with HIV was increasing. The number of pregnant mothers with HIV was growing. And the number of babies born unnecessarily with HIV was reaching new heights.

One particular memory haunted many of the paediatricians and other doctors who decided to take a stand. It impelled them to action. It was the case of Steven Bantu Biko, the charismatic and articulate black consciousness leader. The police found him so threatening to the apartheid order that they bludgeoned him to death in September 1977. When this happened, medical professionals failed to do anything to prevent his death.

The security police arrested Steve Biko near Grahamstown on 18 August 1977. They took him to Port Elizabeth and detained him in solitary confinement. Three weeks later, on 12 September, he died in Pretoria. An inquest into his death found that the cause of his death was a head injury with associated extensive brain injury, followed by contusion of the blood circulation, disseminated intravascular coagulation, as well as renal failure with uraemia.

District surgeons – state-appointed official doctors – had the power under the detention statute to visit detainees in police custody. They exercised immense power. This was because, apart from their security police inquisitors, they were almost the only persons who saw detainees.

While Biko was in the hands of the security police in Port Elizabeth, the local district surgeons were Dr Ivor Ralph Lang and Dr Benjamin Tucker. Between 7 and 11 September 1977, they saw Biko. He was their patient. Biko was also seen by Dr Hersch, a specialist physician. But it was Drs Lang and Tucker who bore primary responsibility for Biko's medical well-being while he was in detention.

These doctors found Biko in leg-irons, semi-comatose, lying on blankets wet with urine, and in a grievous state of injury. They repeatedly examined him while he lay on a mat, manacled to a metal grille. None of them reported what they saw. And none of them intervened to save Biko. On the contrary, during Biko's detention Dr Lang signed a certificate at the behest of the security police, which stated that he had 'examined Steve Biko as a result of a request from Colonel Goosen of the Security Police, who complained that the abovementioned will not speak. I have found no evidence of any abnormality or pathology on the detainee.'

And Dr Tucker gave the police permission to transport Biko, despite his terrible injuries, to Pretoria. They threw him onto the back of a Land Rover, naked, critically ill, and with no medical supervision. Biko was already suffering a brain lesion as a result of trauma-induced injuries, and had by then collapsed. The arduous journey, in grotesque circumstances of exposure, almost certainly contributed to his death.

At the inquest that followed, as the world watched, Sydney Kentridge for the family subjected the doctors who should have cared for Biko to devastating cross-examination. Dr Lang conceded that the certificate he had issued was incorrect. It was, in fact, 'highly inaccurate'. But he claimed he was not aware of its significance or that the police might use it as a cover in case of later allegations of assault. Both he and Dr Tucker denied medical incompetence, negligence or malpractice.

The inquest documented distressing details of the horrific injuries Biko suffered while in the power of the security police. Despite this evidence, the inquest magistrate exempted the police from blame. He found that Biko's head injury was probably sustained 'in a scuffle' with security police members.

A *scuffle*! At least the magistrate thought that Drs Lang and Tucker had to answer for a seeming case of improper or disgraceful conduct. He acted under a statute that empowered a court of law to alert the Medical Council if there was a *prima facie* case (a case at first glance, or one that appears, unless rebutted, to provide proof) of unprofessional conduct. He sent the doctors' evidence to the Medical Council for it to consider.

But most of the members of the Medical Council were appointed by the apartheid government. It refused to act. On 17 June 1980, it took a majority decision, by eighteen votes to nine. The majority decided that there was no evidence of improper conduct on the part of the two doctors. The Council would take no further action against them.

Many doctors across the country were outraged. The medical school at Wits University adopted an impassioned resolution denouncing the decision. The statement condemning the Council was published worldwide under the name of its Dean, the renowned palaeo-anthropologist Professor Phillip Tobias.

Eventually a group of doctors, including many from Wits and other medical schools, took the Council to court. They asked for an order overturning the decision that exonerated the doctors. They felt soiled by what they saw as their profession's official condonation of shameful neglect on the part of Drs Lang and Tucker.

Five years later the Judge-President in Pretoria, Mr Justice Boshoff, presiding over a full bench, upheld the professors' challenge. He ruled that there was a *prima facie* case of misconduct for which the two doctors had to answer. He set aside the Medical Council's decision that there should be no inquiry against them. The court directed the Council to act against them.

The Council considered appealing, but decided against it. Eventually, after years of foot-dragging, it did take action against the doctors. Dr Lang was found guilty of improper conduct. He was given a warning and reprimand. Dr Tucker was found guilty of improper as well as disgraceful conduct. The disciplinary committee recommended that he be suspended from the medical register for three months – but this sentence was itself suspended for two years. During that time Dr Tucker retired.

But a full meeting of the Council decided Dr Tucker should be struck off the roll of practitioners. Dr Tucker later publicly repented. Fourteen years after Biko's death, in 1991, he apologised for his role in neglecting to treat and to protect Steven Bantu Biko. His licence to practise was reinstated.

The Biko tragedy left deep marks of shame and sorrow over much of the medical profession in South Africa. Many doctors considered that members of their profession had remained disgracefully silent in the face of cruelty and misconduct. This was at two levels. First, individual doctors had folded their hands when they had power to intervene to avoid suffering. The doctors involved in treating Biko should have spoken out. They should have intervened. If they had done so, a great human tragedy could have been avoided.

At a second level, the organised medical profession through its Council had shamed all doctors by initially refusing to take action against the individual doctors.

During the TRC proceedings, a senior and respected doctor, Professor Peter Folb of UCT, apologised to the Biko family for the medical profession's disgraceful treatment of Biko and of his case. Testifying at a TRC session in June 1997, he said the Biko case illustrated 'an abject acceptance by individual doctors and the medical profession of interference in their duties by the state'. He added that the medical profession 'continued to address' the ethical issues the Biko case raised.

His words proved prophetic. Though the circumstances now were different, many doctors thought that government's refusal to make anti-retroviral treatment available to pregnant mothers with HIV at public health facilities was as shameful as the mistreatment Steve Biko had suffered at the hands of the apartheid police. This memory called the medical profession to action. Their oath committing themselves to providing beneficent treatment, and to avoiding evil, obliged them to intervene.

Many doctors felt determined: there would be no repeat of history. A strong group of paediatricians and other specialists involved in HIV care made themselves available to advise the lawyers and the activists who now planned to act against government. One of them was Professor Peter Cooper, the head of child care at Johannesburg's general hospital. In defiance of President Mbeki's ban on Nevirapine outside the handful of pilot sites, he offered mothers with HIV the choice of taking it. The drugs were donated by the Anglican Church. For this, government threatened him with disciplinary action. He nevertheless went on oath for the applicants in their case against government. He was one of the doctors who understood and heeded the lessons of history.

IX The claimants decide to act

On 17 July 2001 the attorneys for the applicants wrote to the Minister of Health and to each of the provincial government executives (MECs) responsible for health. They set out their case, and demanded action within fourteen days. The letter of demand required the Minister and MECs to provide reasons why they refused to make Nevirapine available to patients in the public health sector, except at the designated pilot sites. And it required an undertaking to put in place a programme for medical practitioners working at public clinics to decide whether to prescribe Nevirapine for their pregnant patients who wanted it.

Government refused to give any undertakings. Legal action had become unavoidable.

On Tuesday, 21 August 2001 the applicants lodged their claim with the high court in Pretoria. They sought two orders. One, a declaratory order, would spell out government's responsibilities. The applicants wanted the court to say that, under the law, government was obliged to make Nevirapine available to pregnant women with HIV who give birth at public hospitals and clinics. Second, they sought an order that gave the declaration teeth. The court should also issue an order compelling government to make Nevirapine available to pregnant women at public health facilities.

The relief the applicants sought was narrowly crafted. It focused on pregnant women at public health facilities only. And it sought only a very slender use of judicial power – that doctors working at these facilities should be free to offer mothers with HIV Nevirapine should they want it. This was astute, since the manufacturer's offer to give government Nevirapine free was on record.

But behind the narrow order the applicants sought lay a much bigger issue. Anti-retroviral treatment was becoming cheaper and cheaper. Proof of its efficacy in restoring life and health was becoming stronger and stronger. Deaths from AIDS were climbing steeply. This was not evident only to me, and people like me, who owed their lives to ARV treatment. It was becoming obvious to everyone. Could government continue to refuse to make life-saving treatment available to poor people in South Africa?

The country's legal system, and its Constitution, would now be the arbiter of who would live and who would die from AIDS.

X The TAC claimants make their case for court intervention

The TAC put together an eloquent founding affidavit, deposed to by its deputy chair, Ms Siphokazi Mthathi. In addition, it welded a strong coalition of experts. The second applicant was Dr Haroon Saloojee, a child care specialist who headed up community paediatrics at the University of the Witwatersrand medical school. He spoke with particular authority. In November 2000, along with a number of child specialists, Dr Saloojee had started a campaign called 'Save Our Babies'. The purpose was to take a stand on ARV treatment for infants. Dr Saloojee and his colleagues considered that although they most vividly witnessed the effects of AIDS on the life and health of children, the Ministry of Health was ignoring them.

So, in November 2000, 'Save Our Babies' gathered 273 signatures from other medical specialists and child health practitioners around the country. The petition pleaded for a programme to reduce mother-to-child transmission. In December 2000 they sent this to the Minister, Dr Tshabalala-Msimang. Nine months later, when the case was launched, she had still not responded.

Dr Saloojee said it was 'imperative' to make Nevirapine available as soon as possible to women relying on the public health system. Why? He gave the reason simply in the concluding paragraph of his affidavit: 'Children's lives matter.'

The Durban-based Children's Rights Centre was also an applicant. Its director, Katy Vawda, testified that one of the most heart-breaking parts of the Centre's work was dealing with mothers whose children were very ill or dying, even though this could be avoided. She described these mothers as 'often very angry and confused by the failure of the government to provide them and their children with treatment which would have prevented this'.

Dr Quarraisha Abdool Karim provided an affidavit supplying expert evidence on the epidemiology of AIDS. A mother of young children herself, she depicted the agony of the epidemic's 'increasing morbidity and mortality'. These are specialist terms for the increasing cost in suffering and lives. The virus, she said, was spreading disproportionately in the economically active age group – in other words, among young people between 15 and 49. People in the prime of their lives.

Professor Robin Wood of UCT provided evidence on the medical science of HIV and its treatment. He based his affidavit on clinical trials and international findings and expert consensus. He told the court that these demonstrated 'conclusively' that prevention of mother-to-child HIV transmission should be part of the minimum standard of care for women known to have HIV.

Professor Nicoli Nattrass, a distinguished UCT economist, gave detailed evidence that controverted a popular misconception about the cost of ARVs. Far from a national programme to prevent mother-to-child transmission being too expensive, she explained, it would actually save the state money. She pointed out that children with HIV need health care for dreadful opportunistic infections over their short lives. Fewer children with HIV reduces these costs. Her detailed analysis showed how the total cost to the health sector of prevention programmes (including the costs of voluntary counselling and testing, the costs of the drugs, and the costs of treating children born with HIV despite the programme) would be less than the cost of treating all children born with HIV without any programme.

The TAC did not restrict the founding papers to experts. On the contrary, young mothers who themselves saw that agony of the virus delivered powerful personal testimony, both positive and negative. They included Ms Bongiwe Mkhutyukelwa, a 25-year-old mother from Khayelitsha township outside Cape Town. She recounted how, after she volunteered to be tested when she was pregnant in 1999, anti-retroviral treatment had saved her baby from infection with HIV. Ms Busisiwe Maqungo, a mother from Mfuleni, also in Khayelitsha, related an anguishing story. She testified that she had herself tested for HIV in 1999. This was because her one-month-old daughter Nomazizi was desperately sick from pneumonia, diarrhoea and dehydration, and was found to be HIV positive. Her child died on 31 January 2000, when she was only nine months old. Ms Maqungo then had to face the painful task of telling her nine-year-old son that she herself had HIV. It was beyond question that the Maqungo family's anguish, and the life of their baby Nomazizi, would have been spared if government had made anti-retrovirals available.

Sarah Hlalele, volunteer counsellor for a support group in the Vaal area, volunteered to provide an affidavit when she heard about the court case. At the time she was very ill with AIDS. Her son had been born prematurely, failed to receive Nevirapine and remained in hospital for the first month of his life. She described how she had obtained a Nevirapine tablet from Chris Hani Baragwanath Hospital, 60 kilometres from her home in Sebokeng. Unfortunately, she went into premature labour and left the tablet at home. Sebokeng Hospital, where she gave birth to her son, had neither Nevirapine tablets nor syrup.

Tragically, Sarah Hlalele died of a rare side-effect of HIV treatment, lactic acidosis, on 14 April 2002. I attended a memorial service for her in Yeoville, Johannesburg. Mourners were devastated by her death, particularly because we feared that her adverse reaction to ARVs might signal a rash of similar cases. To our relief it did not, but Sarah Hlalele's death was a stark moment in the struggle for treatment.

Ms Tshidi Mahlonoko brought her skills as a nurse. She worked in Boipatong – the township where the massacre of June 1992 had imperilled the negotiations for democracy. She spoke about how anti-retrovirals and other treatments for AIDS and opportunistic infections – including Fluconazole or Diflucan, the drug that alleviated my thrush when I had AIDS – had brought hope to her work and to her patients. But government's refusal to help prevent transmission of HIV from mother to child was thwarting this. Sister Mahlonoko added a strategic punch to her nursing expertise. 'If we make drugs available to manage HIV then we would not be wasting time and money with court cases. We will be improving the lifespan of poor people, and at the same time strengthening the confidence of the community in the government and the health sector.'

The applicants' concluding affidavit was from Nurse Vivienne Nokuzola Matebula. She had worked in the Vaal township hospital of Kopanong, but government policy confined Nevirapine to the largest hospital in the province, Soweto's Chris Hani Baragwanath Hospital. Nurse Matebula gave a shocking instance of how this constriction in the availability of Nevirapine affected pregnant mothers. She told of a pregnant mother in her care who in the last week of June 2000 went into labour, but she was told she had to travel to Chris Hani Baragwanath to receive life-saving treatment for her baby. The woman had to undertake the rigours of an arduous journey while cramping from the pains of labour. She did so, in order to save her child from HIV.

XI Government's response in the court case

In response, government's witnesses did not deny much of this powerful evidence. Instead, it filed affidavits explaining its approach to the pilot sites where Nevirapine was permitted. Its argument in essence was that it needed more time. And it objected that the TAC wanted the courts to make a choice that lay deep within the realm of governmental, not judicial, power: the power to choose the policy with which to respond to the AIDS crisis. Government's decision to embark on a research and training programme at selected sites was responsible and correct. To allow doctors to prescribe Nevirapine would throw the system into disarray, cause budgetary distortions, and set a precedent for patients to demand expensive drugs for obscure conditions.

Dr Ayanda Ntsaluba, the head of the department of health, filed an affidavit on behalf of the Minister of Health. In addition, Dr Nono Simelela, the head of government's AIDS programme, Dr Jonathan Bernhard Levin, a senior statistician at the MCC, and Dr Philip Chukwuka Onyebujoh, a member of the MCC, deposed on behalf of government.

Dr Ntsaluba levelled a surprising personal accusation. In response to Sarah Hlalele's anguished tale of trying to get ARVs to protect her infant, but failing to do so, he accused her of being 'neglectful of her health and the health of her baby'. He also said the applicants ignored infrastructural and operational complexities in making Nevirapine available. And they were asking the court to make what amounted to a policy choice for government. Nevirapine, he said, had not yet been shown to reduce transmission of HIV even with breastfeeding. Its registration was still conditional. The research and training sites had still to provide additional data on its efficacy and safety. There were questions about resistance in mothers given a single dose of Nevirapine. It was not safe to expose a largely breastfeeding population to Nevirapine unless stringent measures were taken.

He alleged that it was the practice all over the world to test drugs that may be used in the public sector. To allow doctors in the public sector to prescribe any drug would cause chaos. Budgets would be strained. Government could also be exposed to claims for damages if Nevirapine were given without support services.

Government policy, he said, was not irrational and unconstitutional. Government had to balance all the factors. It had decided on a research and training programme before making Nevirapine generally available at public health facilities. It could cause a public health crisis if Nevirapine was administered without the necessary support. Hence Nevirapine should be made available gradually – an incrementalist approach.

Dr Ntsaluba conceded that maternal transmission programmes might be cost effective, but to use Nevirapine would entail other costs. The point of the pilot projects was to gather data on the cost issue. Government, he assured the court, did envisage that a national programme would be extended as lessons were learnt from the pilot sites.

Dr Simelela's affidavit underscored many of these points. She accepted the WHO's conclusion that the benefit of prevention programmes greatly outweighed concerns about them, but pointed out that it recommended further research. Dr Levin's affidavit emphasised that more time was needed to devise a fully informed long-term strategy to control mother-to-child transmission of HIV.

He concluded that Nevirapine does reduce maternal transmission, though probably by considerably less than the 50% the applicants claimed.

Dr Onyebujoh, a clinical immunologist employed by the WHO in Geneva, also gave evidence for government. He was careful to say that he did so as a member of South Africa's Medicines Control Council. His evidence did not reflect any WHO endorsement. Dr Onyebujoh pointed out that the MCC had granted Nevirapine only conditional registration. This was because data was obtained from only one clinical trial conducted in Uganda. Hence, he said, there was a 'need for more information regarding safety, efficacy and resistance' of Nevirapine. And, Dr Onyebujoh added, there was 'the possible impact of ecological differences on the overall public health impact of the intervention on HIV transmission vertically'. It was not clear what this meant.

Government added extensive evidence concerning its national and provincial health budgets, and available personnel and resources. A recurring theme was operational difficulties – the complexities anti-retroviral provision entailed. Another was budgetary constraints.

XII The TAC rejoins to government's response

The TAC submitted affidavits in response (called a rejoinder) to government. Ms Mthathi pointed out that the TAC did not claim that Nevirapine should be provided immediately to every pregnant woman with HIV. The point was government's programmatic response. It had failed to design a programme to offer prevention to mothers with HIV on a comprehensive and nationwide basis.

One of the affidavits in the TAC's reply came from Professor Folb, who had apologised to the Biko family at the TRC for the medical profession's ethical failings. He was a former member of the MCC. He explained that the registration of Nevirapine implied that the MCC thought the drug was safe and effective. And there was nothing sinister or extraordinary about the condition the MCC imposed. Nevirapine could be used.

Two potent elements in the TAC's reply came from the director of the Public Service Accountability Monitor at Rhodes University, Mr Colm Allan, and from Dr Fareed Abdullah, a brave health official in the Western Cape province.

Mr Allan's evidence was directed at government's claims that it had no money. He pointed out that the Eastern Cape province, for the 2000-2001 year, had allocated R33 million to HIV/AIDS, yet the Auditor-General's report showed that this money was not spent on AIDS at all. In fact, it had been transferred to the official foundation of the University of Fort Hare. This evidence was damning. So far from lacking money for AIDS programmes, government's lax budgeting and lack of focus meant that available money was not being spent where it was urgently needed in AIDS. In response, government lodged affidavits explaining that the Eastern Cape's R33 million for AIDS had had to be returned to the Treasury. The failure to use the money was not deliberate.

Dr Abdullah's evidence recounted that the Western Cape province, bucking the national restriction, had made Nevirapine generally available. The result was very successful. There had been no disruption.

XIII The Pretoria High Court hears the TAC case

With full sets of affidavits on record, the case was ready to be heard. On that summer's Monday outside the Pretoria High Court, activists sang and waved banners. Many of them were wearing T-shirts boldly emblazoned with the sign 'HIV POSITIVE'. Former president Nelson Mandela later made these T-shirts famous when he visited TAC founder Zackie Achmat at his home in Muizenberg, and donned one himself.

Members of the public jammed the public gallery. Tensions were high. The TAC lawyers were Gilbert Marcus, a highly regarded senior counsel, Geoff Budlender – who in the 1980s helped Arthur Chaskalson argue many of the cases that stymied apartheid – together with another well-regarded lawyer from the Legal Resources Centre, Bongani Majola. To them, the atmosphere in court, with hostile government lawyers seeking to defend the indefensible, called to mind the toughest court battles they had fought against the apartheid government. But the activists jamming the court were determinedly hopeful. They had to be. Many of them were living with HIV themselves. Or they had loved ones or friends who were positive, or who were dying of AIDS.

The Judge-President had assigned Mr Justice Chris Botha to hear the case. Though his legal profile was not prominent – he seldom marked his judgments up for publication in the law reports – he was known as an unassuming but studious man, with a depth of reading and learning. He had a reputation as a humanist and a philosopher. In his judicial duties, he was known to be scrupulous and diligent.

The lawyers appearing for government were Marumo Moerane, a highly experienced senior counsel, who happened to have a family connection to President Mbeki, together with Kgomotso Moroka, Bashir Vally and Philip Coppen.

Over two days, on Monday 26 and Tuesday 27 November, the opposing legal teams strenuously advanced their positions before the judge. At the end of argument on the second day, he reserved his judgment.

XIV The Pretoria High Court decides the TAC case

The judge was known to work quickly. Despite the difficult nature of the matter, the heavy bulk of the evidence, the successive sets of multiple affidavits, and all the pages of written argument, his registrar informed the parties after barely more than a fortnight that the judge was ready to deliver his judgment. The date set was Friday, 14 December 2001.

That morning at 10, to a packed and expectant courtroom, Judge Botha handed down his judgment. The TAC had won. He accepted most of the arguments it put forward. The claimants, he said, had established that they were entitled to the orders they claimed. The question, he said, was whether government had taken reasonable legislative and other measures within its available resources to achieve the progressive realisation of the right to health care services, including reproductive health care. This was what section 27(2) of the Bill of Rights required of government.

The real issue was thus whether government's steps in establishing pilot sites and confining Nevirapine to these sites complied with its obligations under section 27(2). It was wrong, Judge Botha said, to claim that the TAC wanted the court to make policy choices. 'The court does not assume the task of the executive when it pronounces on the reasonableness of steps taken by the executive in the fulfilment of a constitutional obligation.'

Over Judge Botha's decision hung both *Soobramoney* and *Grootboom*. *Soobramoney*, he said, was quite different – it dealt not with a right of access to a social service, but with the right not to be refused emergency medical treatment. This case, he said, was closer to *Grootboom*. In both, the state had a duty to take reasonable measures to realise the right at issue progressively, within its available resources.

Quoting heavily from *Grootboom*, Judge Botha concluded that

169

government had not done this. Government could not be faulted for establishing pilot sites in each province. With a recently registered drug it was a 'prudent precaution' to have centres where performance could be tracked, and to pick up counter-indications. Nevertheless, the evidence was that government could go further than only the eighteen pilot sites. The cost was minimal. There was no evidence of disarray or chaos.

Judge Botha agreed with government's argument that doctors should not be allowed to prescribe Nevirapine indiscriminately or irresponsibly, but that was not what the TAC had asked. It should be prescribed only after proper testing and counselling. Access to Nevirapine was a vital element lacking in government's programme. It would add an element of flexibility and pragmatism. It need not in any way detract from the pilot sites. It merely provided another means of access, less structured, less perfect, 'but infinitely to be preferred', the judge found, 'to the choice between all or nothing'.

Government policy in prohibiting the use of Nevirapine outside the pilot sites in the public health sector was therefore not reasonable. Dr Simelela had given no particulars of a clear plan for a comprehensive roll-out to prevent mother-to-child transmission. This was not reasonable.

Hence, the judge granted both orders the TAC sought. He granted a declaratory order, which said what government's duties and pregnant women's rights were. And he also granted more detailed orders that gave the declarator teeth. These required government to make Nevirapine available generally to pregnant women with HIV in the public sector. The order required government immediately ('forthwith', in the language beloved of lawyers) to set about planning an effective comprehensive national programme. He also mandated government to report back to the court by 31 March 2002 on what it had achieved.

The judge finished reading his order. He then adjourned the court. Pandemonium erupted. There were tears of joy and relief. The TAC had got what it had set out to obtain – an order that would require government to start making anti-retroviral treatment available. So many lives at stake. So much suffering. But a long and arduous battle still lay ahead.

XV Government appeals to the Constitutional Court – the spectre of Castro Hlongwane

Government decided to appeal against the judgment. Some activists were bitterly disappointed. It meant that the operation of the judge's order would be delayed. It meant more HIV infections, more suffering, and more deaths. This is because the effect of an appeal is to suspend the order the judge has granted. So Judge Botha's orders would remain in limbo. While the cumbersome appeal processes were pending, thousands, perhaps tens of thousands, more babies would be born unnecessarily with HIV.

But government's decision to challenge the judgment was hardly surprising. President Mbeki had staked his international reputation on the questions he was posing about AIDS. His standing not only as an intellectual, but as an African leader, was at stake. What was more, the question of anti-retroviral provision wasn't simply a fringe issue. It lay at the very heart of the dissidents' beliefs about the AIDS epidemic. Their claim that anti-retroviral drugs were toxic and harmful, and that profit-driven drug companies were peddling them unnecessarily to populations in Africa, lay at the very heart of the denialist movement.

At the most crucial part of the court battle, in early 2002, after the high court had given its ruling, and when government had announced it was appealing, a shocking document appeared. It was widely distributed to members of the ANC. Titled 'Castro

Hlongwane, Caravans, Cats, Geese, Foot & Mouth and Statistics: HIV/Aids and the Struggle for the Humanisation of the African', it had no author attribution. Written in a heavily conspiratorialist style, it claimed that two well-known figures who had died of AIDS had in fact died because they had taken ARVs. They were President Mbeki's own spokesperson, Parks Mankahlana, who died in October 2000, and Nkosi Johnson, the young boy with HIV who achieved international renown for his courage and eloquence before dying of AIDS in June 2001.

In 2007 President Mbeki's biographer, Mark Gevisser, recorded that the President had confirmed to him that this document reflected his, the President's, views. The document claimed that pharmaceutical companies were marketing anti-retrovirals to make profits, and that they were peddling them in Africa because their markets in wealthy countries had diminished. In truth, these drugs, the document asserted, were highly toxic and wholly unnecessary, since AIDS was not caused by a virus. It was an environmentally caused condition. Poverty, not HIV, was the cause.

To the extent that these views reflected those of President Mbeki and other members of his government, it was impossible for them to accept the court's order. No. Resisting the distribution of anti-retrovirals by every means possible was profoundly important. The appeal was obvious.

But the TAC fought back. Because the pending appeal suspended the implementation of Judge Botha's order, it applied to the judge for a ruling that the most important part of his order should take effect immediately anyhow. This was the order that government had to allow public service doctors, where appropriate circumstances existed, to make Nevirapine available immediately to mothers with HIV. To obtain an immediate-implementation order, a litigant must show the court that it will suffer irreparable harm pending the appeal. It was not difficult for the TAC to show this. Every baby born unnecessarily with HIV proved exactly that harm. On 11 March 2002 Judge Botha granted the TAC the immediate-implementation order it sought.

Government now engaged in complicated legal manoeuvring. It applied for leave to appeal against the immediate-implementation order itself. So, on 25 March 2002, Judge Botha reinforced his order by dismissing this application. Government was undaunted. So deeply embedded was anti-ARV feeling in President Mbeki's administration, that it now decided to appeal urgently to the Constitutional Court against the immediate-implementation order. This showed the measure of its determination to resist expansion of anti-retroviral drug treatments.

The Constitutional Court convened specially during its recess, on 3 April 2002, to hear government's argument on the interim order allowing Nevirapine. The very next day, the court issued an order. It dismissed government's attempt to appeal the immediate-implementation order. The court later explained that the actual effect of the order Judge Botha granted for interim implementation was quite narrow. 'There can be no doubt,' it held, 'that requiring government to provide Nevirapine where attending doctors consider it medically indicated, superintendents consider it appropriate and where facilities for testing and counselling already exist, can cause no serious harm to the public health services.' Hence, pending the full appeal hearing, interim implementation could go ahead.

The big question now was: what would the Constitutional Court decide on the main merits of the appeal?

XVI The Constitutional Court and the perils of the Nevirapine case

The Constitutional Court heard government's challenge to the Nevirapine ruling a month after it allowed interim implementation of Nevirapine to go ahead. It heard counsel's argument over three days, on Thursday 2 May, Friday 3 May and Monday 6 May 2002.

The court was then not quite eight years old. Its eleven judges had convened for the first time on 31 October 1994. They heard their first case just more than three months later, on 15 February 1995. The judges who sat on that day were the court's President, Arthur Chaskalson, together with Justices Ackermann, Didcott, Kriegler, Langa, Madala, Mahomed, Mokgoro, O'Regan and Sachs. In addition, because Justice Goldstone was abroad, a distinguished acting justice was appointed in his place. He was Sydney Kent-ridge – the lawyer who had defended the Dean and helped un-cover the truth in the Biko inquest. The court's very first case presented a tough issue – the death penalty. But the court had no difficulty in dealing with it. In a unanimous ruling nearly four months later, on 6 June 1995, it declared the death penalty in-compatible with the Constitution.

The form the judgment took was unusual. This was because each one of the eleven judges wrote a separate judgment ex-plaining why he or she considered the death penalty unconsti-tutional. The variety of the judgments, and the strength of their diverse reasoning, made a powerful impact. The unusual proce-dure showed how every judge, from every background, despite differences in reasoning and approach, came to the same end point: democratic South Africa would not tolerate death sen-tences.

The Nevirapine case also concerned life and death, though not execution at the hands of the state. At the height of the hang-man's activities under apartheid, the highest number of execu-tions in a single year occurred in 1987. In that year, 164 people were executed on death row in Pretoria. The Nevirapine case did not involve the horror of official execution, yet it concerned many more thousands of lives than were ever at risk of Pretoria's hangman.

The problem at the core of the TAC's case was that it involved a government decision in a controversial area of health policy. The epidemic itself was frightening and new – and anti-retroviral treatment for AIDS, notwithstanding the electrifying promise it had clearly shown, was brand new.

How would the court approach the enormous challenges the case presented to it?

The court's judgments in its first eight years had shown two things. The first was that the judges were well attuned to the crucial project of transforming society. The Constitution made the judiciary an integral part of this task. South Africa at the end of apartheid was a deeply unjust society, riven by inequality and exclusion and dispossession. The Constitution was designed to change this. It was clear that the court whole-heartedly embraced its role. Its judgments showed a commitment to finding judicial mechanisms to enhance social justice and to reduce inequality and to outlaw unfair discrimination.

There was a second feature of the court's mettle. Where the Constitution required it to do so, it would not hesitate to rule against government. The Constitution provided in express terms that the Constitution itself was supreme. The legislature, the executive, and the courts themselves, were subject to its provisions. The Constitutional Court took the doctrine of constitutional supremacy into its vigorous embrace. If either Parliament or government strayed from it, the court showed no hesitation in ruling against them.

Soon after taking office, the court was put to its first big test. The country's first democratic local government elections were scheduled for 1 November 1995. But a dispute arose between national government, controlled by the ANC, and the Western Cape province, controlled by the opposition National Party – the governing party under apartheid. Although the National Party was now part of the transitional government of national unity, its provincial government in the Western Cape took its case against President Mandela to the Constitutional Court.

On 7 June 1995 President Mandela issued a proclamation in which he amended provisions of the statute under which the local elections were to be held. At issue was the power to appoint members of a provincial committee that would be influential during the local elections. The President's proclamation took that power away from the Western Cape, and gave it to national government.

President Mandela acted under powers the statute expressly gave to him as President. During the process of restructuring local government, Parliament in November 1994 amended the statute to give the President power to amend the Act by proclamation. The Western Cape disputed this power. It did so by invoking a fundamental constitutional principle – the separation of powers. It said that Parliament could not give the President power to amend a statute of Parliament by issuing a proclamation.

To understand the extent of the challenge facing the Constitutional Court in this case, and even more starkly in the Nevirapine case, requires a short digression to explain the supremacy of the Constitution, the separation of powers and the rule of law.

XVII Constitutional supremacy, the rule of law and the separation of powers

Unlike that of the United States, which has rather skeletal constitutional provisions, our Constitution is fully detailed and amply expressed. After the Preamble, it is divided into fourteen chapters (the Bill of Rights, Parliament, the President and National Executive, the provinces, local government, the courts and administration of justice, independent institutions supporting democracy, public administration, finance and so on).

Symbolically the first chapter is the most important. It is titled 'Founding Provisions'. It contains six sections, as lawyers call the separate numbered segments of an enacted text. The very first section sets out the values on which the Republic of South Africa, as one, sovereign, democratic state, is founded. These are the express foundational values of South Africa's constitutional settlement.

The section lists these values as, first, human dignity, the achievement of equality, and the advancement of human rights and freedoms; second, non-racialism and non-sexism; third, supremacy of the Constitution and the rule of law; and, fourth, universal adult voting rights (suffrage), a national common voters' roll, regular elections and a multi-party system of democratic government, to ensure accountability, responsiveness and openness.

But perhaps the Constitution's most pivotal provision, both symbolically and practically, is its second provision. It is titled 'Supremacy of the Constitution'. It gives a hard-toothed bite to the founding value that enshrines the supremacy of the Constitution and the rule of law. It repeats, for emphasis, that 'This Constitution is the supreme law of the Republic'. But it adds two important operational consequences. Negatively, it provides that law or conduct inconsistent with the Constitution is invalid. And, positively, it provides that the obligations imposed by the Constitution must be fulfilled.

Through this provision, the Constitution creates an ideal legal world. The Constitution makes it the task of all three arms of government – lawmakers in Parliament, executive government and judges – to translate that ideal into reality.

And by stipulating that the Constitution is the supreme law, and spelling out the two-sided practical implications of constitutional supremacy, section 2 encapsulates the most profound part of the doctrine of the rule of law. The rule of law is the notion that all power, especially state power, must be exercised under law and according to the dictates of law. In short, power is subject to law.

From this foundation, significant consequences flow for how laws have to be adjudicated. For if law governs the exercise of power, then the law must be capable of guiding those who are subject to it. As a leading legal philosopher has recently explained, people should not be ambushed by the law. They should be able to anticipate the legal consequences of their actions, and to avoid adverse results (whether in steering clear of taxes or criminal prosecutions) by following the law. And this means that laws should not be secret, retroactive, unclear, impossible to conform to, or forever in a state of flux; and particular legal rulings should be applications of general and recognisable legal norms (rules).

Unless laws live up to these standards, people subject to the law cannot truly follow them.

Sections 1 and 2 of the Constitution enshrine these high ideals for South Africa. But section 2 of the Constitution does something even more dramatic and practical. It encapsulates a particularly oppressive part of our history, and puts it behind us.

Under apartheid, Parliament was supreme. The model of parliamentary sovereignty was one South Africa inherited in 1910 from the Westminster Parliament, in London. Any enactment it passed constituted law. In a true democracy, the system may be acceptable, because if the legislature passes an evil law, the electorate can vote it out of office. But in apartheid South Africa, only whites could vote. From 1948, the apartheid Parliament exploited its electorally unaccountable Westminster-type powers aggressively to enforce separation of black and white, and to subordinate black beneath white.

The apartheid legislature could enact any law, no matter how hateful or oppressive or demeaning. And it often did. No provision of the Roman-Dutch common law, no court ruling, no principle of fairness could make the slightest difference. What Parliament enacted was supreme law, and had to be enforced. The only hope for mitigation was to soften the edges of the law through interpretation, and to defeat its application in a particular case through court manoeuvres. This was the space in which human rights lawyers worked under apartheid.

Outside that narrow space, Parliament was supreme. And if it didn't like what judges did, it simply passed another statute that changed the law. And the apartheid Parliament regularly did so. In 1963 it went so far as to pass a law that violated every precept of the rule of law. The law was dubbed the 'Sobukwe clause' and it enabled the apartheid minister of justice to issue a yearly decree to prohibit the release of Pan Africanist Congress founder Robert Sobukwe from Robben Island, even after he had served the prison sentence to which the courts had sentenced him.

Section 2 of the Constitution puts that behind us. It makes a 'Sobukwe clause' unthinkable. It provides that the Constitution itself, and the values in it, stand supreme – above the legislature, above the executive, including the President, and above the judges and the courts. Instead of the colonial legacy of Westminster parliamentary supremacy, the Constitution creates a thoroughly home-grown mix of institutions and concepts, with respect for the rule of law at its very centre. The courts can now strike down legislation as incompatible with the Constitution (though the Constitutional Court must always confirm an order of legislative invalidity, and one striking down an act of the President), though Parliament is then free to re-enact the legislation in a constitutionally compliant fashion. In this way, the courts and Parliament engage in a dialogue about the Constitution.

This dialogue is a beneficial result of the negotiations that led to the Constitution. Apartheid's offences against the rule of law were so deep-going and so odious that, during the entire constitution-drafting process, there was unanimity that the Constitution and its values had to be supreme. All parties to the pre-democracy negotiations that led to the interim Constitution, and all parties in the Constitutional Assembly that drafted the final Constitution, agreed on this.

The supremacy of the Constitution does not make it inflexible. It is not written in tablets of stone. It can be amended. Section 74 provides that Parliament may amend the Constitution. But there are special safeguards, and special procedures have to be followed. For normal legislation, a simple majority of votes cast in the legislature is enough. Not for a constitutional amendment. For this, a super-majority is needed.

For even the simplest amendment to the Constitution, there must be a two-thirds majority of votes in the National Assembly. And in the National Council of Provinces (NCOP), six of the nine provinces must support the amendment.

For some amendments, even more is required. To amend section 1– the provision setting out the founding values of dignity, equality and the supremacy of the Constitution and the rule of law – even more is required. To change them, a majority of 75% of the members of the National Assembly is required, plus the support of six of the nine provinces in the NCOP. And the amendment provision itself is entrenched. The same three-quarters super-majority is required to change it.

There have indeed been amendments to the Constitution, although not many. In contrast to ordinary statutes, which are often amended, constitutional amendments happen rarely. The Revenue Act, which empowers collection of taxes, undergoes multiple amendments every year. Not the Constitution. This is the correct approach. Even though the Constitution is not cast in stone, changing it is a serious business, to be approached soberly. It is the country's founding instrument, describing its path to its own future, and should not be tinkered with lightly.

In the eighteen years since the end of 1996, when the Constitutional Assembly replaced the interim Constitution, and President Mandela put his historic signature to the final Constitution, the document has been amended only seventeen times. The latest amendment, the seventeenth, was adopted in late 2012. It received presidential assent on 1 February 2013. One of its two main changes was a provision making explicit that the Chief Justice is the head of the judiciary and that it is the Chief Justice, and no one else, who has responsibility to establish and monitor norms and standards for all courts. The Amendment gives the courts full authority over their own administration and standards.

The Seventeenth Amendment took a second important step. In a provision that came into effect on 23 August 2013, the Constitutional Court was finally clothed with general jurisdiction. Until the Amendment, the court could hear constitutional cases only. In practice, this was not a severe restriction. This is because the Constitution is the supreme law, and all law is subject to it. In effect, therefore, every legal question inevitably in some form becomes also a constitutional question. Hence it was never difficult for litigants to clothe their disputes in constitutional terms. And the court never struggled to find a legitimate constitutional ground on which to hear a case, if it thought it had to intervene to set right an injustice.

But the amendment puts the court hierarchy beyond doubt. It stipulates that the Constitutional Court is the country's apex court in all matters. It provides that the Constitutional Court can hear even a non-constitutional case, provided it raises an arguable point of law of general public importance, which ought to be considered by the court.

XVIII The rule of law and the power of judges

The Constitutional Court's position at the head of the country's judicial system underscores another important feature of the rule of law. It is the role of judges. You cannot have a legal system without entrusting the task of declaring what the law is to some person or body. Under religious systems of law, including Jewish or Islamic law, spiritual leaders declare the law. The authority of their pronouncements claims a source beyond humankind.

But the Romans pioneered something more exclusively human, and therefore more humanly complex. It was the idea of a system of law rooted in non-religious, or secular, precepts. It was the extraordinary and liberating notion of authority rooted in human reason. The precepts on which that authority was based would be tabulated in public form. General principles would guide particular cases. And decisions could not be arbitrary. They had to be supported by reasons.

Four hundred and fifty years before the Christian era, Roman law was codified, in the law of the Twelve Tables. The Roman Praetor declared what the law was, and civilian judges – not priests – decided disputes. The modern conception of law was born. The system of civilian judges that is now common throughout the world is, together with our alphabet, paved roads and aqueducts, part of the heritage the ancient civilisation of Rome bequeathed to us.

Our legal system in South Africa derives directly from this lineage. Dutch law in the mid-1600s was based on Roman law, as interpreted and developed by Renaissance jurists. So the legal principles and processes the white settlers brought to the southern point of Africa in 1652 were Roman-Dutch. Through the 1950s to the 1980s, anti-apartheid lawyers tried to invoke this heritage of rational principles of fairness to stem the degrading intrusion of apartheid ideology.

When the British occupied the Cape in 1806, they decided not to abolish Roman-Dutch law. They did so to minimise the disruption their conquest caused. Instead, they grafted onto it their own rules of evidence, criminal procedure and court process. In addition, English law institutions like the trust, and the modern-day corporation and company law, became part of our law.

But, even in the face of the English overlay, Afrikaner jurists were very protective of their Roman-derived system of law. So, when I studied law, you still had to be able to read Latin to earn a law degree. This was a strenuous requirement, demanding long hours of study. I relished it. I started learning Latin when I entered Pretoria Boys' High in my second year at high school. For me, the subject became a symbol of my entry into a world of intellectual challenge and attainment that, from the children's home, had seemed unimaginably remote.

For four years I continued Latin at Stellenbosch. I even abandoned my law studies to specialise in Latin and classical culture for my honours year. At Oxford I initially wanted to study Latin and ancient Greek, but in a moment of transcendent clarity, in the icy northern winter of January 1977, after three months of dejected grappling with Greek texts, I saw that my life demanded something different. I wanted to undertake a skill that would enable me to play a practical remedial part in people's lives. Academic studies in classics would take me far from that. The shocking memory of my father's encounter with the criminal justice system was seldom consciously in my mind. But it was also never hidden very far away.

In contrast to my idiosyncratic delight in Latin, most law students suffered heavily under the obligation to learn it. Increasingly it became obvious that the Latin requirement for practising law was archaic and untenable. One of the earliest acts of the first Minister of Justice in President Mandela's Cabinet, Dullah Omar, was to steer legislation through Parliament in 1994 to abolish Latin as a prerequisite.

So with its Roman, Roman-Dutch and English components, South African law in the twentieth century was truly a uniquely hybrid institution. The Constitution has continued this opulent tradition of fusion. It has further enriched and hybridised South African law. The Constitution retained the Roman and Roman-Dutch common law, but made it subject to the Constitution. And it charged judges with the duty to develop the common law so as to promote the spirit, purport and objects of the Bill of Rights.

To ensure compliance, the rule of law requires an institution or body that can resolve inevitable disputes about what the law and the Constitution mean. So the judiciary wields immense power. And the Constitution underscores this, by entrusting judges with particular responsibilities. They, together with the legislature and the executive, are one of three arms of state. Parliament can pass statutes, but it is the judiciary, and the judiciary alone, that has power to state the law, and say what the Constitution means. The powers of the arms of government are separate.

When the appeal court ruled in 1952 that the High Court of Parliament, which set Parliament above the judiciary in declaring the law, was invalid, it was invoking this principle – that Parliament and the executive cannot pronounce the law. Only the judiciary can.

But the judiciary's power is not power exercised for the judiciary's own sake, or in the judiciary's own interests. It is power that must always be exercised subject to and for the advancement of the Constitution. And there is something unusual about the power a judge exercises. It must always be accompanied by reasons. Unlike state officials and even parliamentarians, judges must always give reasons for how they decide cases, and for the decisions they make within cases. This is the ultimate safeguard against abuse.

Another safeguard lies in the court hierarchy. Judges are always subject to appeal. A magistrate's ruling can be appealed to the high court. A ruling by a high court judge can be appealed to a full court of three high court judges, or to the Supreme Court of Appeal. And any magistrate's or judge's ruling, including all decisions of the high court and the Supreme Court of Appeal, can be appealed to the Constitutional Court.

It is true that the decisions of the Constitutional Court cannot be overturned. But the Constitutional Court is accountable to the ultimate court of reason. Its reasons, like Supreme Court of Appeal judgments (which in about nine cases out of ten become final), are always rigorously studied and analysed. Any abuse of power by the court, any lapse in logic, any veering from consistency or principle, any betrayal of constitutional values and ideals, would be obvious.

A further safeguard lies in the court's own approach. The Constitutional Court is immensely aware of its position as the guardian of the Constitution. Its judges know all too well that they bear ultimate power to decide what the law and the Constitution mean. This leads to very cautious use of those powers.

A good example is the court's decision in September 2012, magisterially penned by Deputy Chief Justice Moseneke, explaining and enforcing the separation of powers. After spending billions of rands upgrading the roads in Gauteng, South Africa's richest and most populous province, national government tried to recoup its outlay by imposing electronic tolls on road users. This provoked fierce opposition. Opponents challenged the lawfulness of the tolls, arguing that the officials' decision-making process was flawed.

In the high court they obtained an interim interdict that barred government from going ahead with e-tolling. In granting the temporary order, the high court had to weigh many factors. One was a preliminary assessment of how strong the legal case against e-tolling was. Another was who would suffer more harm if the interim interdict were granted – government or the motorists who opposed e-tolling? But in weighing these difficult factors, the high court overlooked an important consideration. It left out the separation of powers. The judge who granted the interdict omitted to consider that the judiciary should be reluctant to intervene in a decision on a matter of policy taken by a different branch of government, the executive.

The question whether electronic tolling should be instituted did not directly concern citizens' rights. It was a matter of policy, namely, how to recoup money invested in public roads. Citizens' rights were of course at stake, for all citizens are entitled to lawful government decision-making, but, apart from this right, the right to administrative justice, there were no rights at stake.

In addition, the harm government was suffering – damage to South Africa's international standing as a debtor nation – was severe, while the harm motorists would suffer if e-tolling went ahead, before the full judicial determination on whether the decision was taken lawfully, was limited to having to pay e-tolls. These might possibly be declared unlawful at the end of the full legal process, but otherwise the motorists' rights were intact.

Deputy Chief Justice Moseneke explained that the Constitution requires courts to ensure that all branches of government act within the law. This means that if the roads agency acted unlawfully in deciding to implement e-tolls, a court would set its decision aside. If there were proof of fraud or corruption, or that the roads agency had acted unlawfully, the courts would step in. But, absent those, the prerogative to formulate and implement policy on how to finance public projects was in the exclusive domain of the executive. Courts must thus refrain from entering the exclusive terrain of the executive and legislative branches unless the Constitution demands that they do. The duty of determining how public resources are to be drawn upon and re-ordered lies in the heartland of the executive's function and domain.

Justice Moseneke pointed out that how to collect and spend public resources entails many complex and competing factors. Courts are not well suited for making decisions in this area. They are well suited to deciding right and wrong, not how to put together a budget.

So the court set aside the temporary interdict. At the full court hearing, later, the opponents of e-tolling would get a chance to prove that the decision to impose e-tolls flouted administrative justice. In the meanwhile, government policy had to be freed of an untenable judicial clog. So the rights and wrongs of e-tolling as public policy reverted to where they belonged – in the domain of politics and public debate, and not inside the courts. Politicians, accountable to the public and their constituencies, and not judges, accountable to the Constitution, had responsibility for the decision. (In October 2013, the Supreme Court of Appeal confirmed a high court decision dismissing the substantive administrative law challenges to e-tolling.)

Another way in which the Constitutional Court is sensitive to the separation of powers is the way in which it crafts its orders. It often does so in the form of dialogue with government. When a statute is declared invalid because it is incompatible with the Constitution, the court almost always allows Parliament time to set matters right, before the court's declaration of invalidity takes effect.

And, often, when the court orders a government agency, like a municipality, to take action, it includes in its order a requirement that the municipality and those subject to its power engage in meaningful dialogue with each other so as to try to find a solution. The first time the court gave an order that parties 'meaningfully engage' with each other was in an eviction dispute in February 2008. It required the Johannesburg metro to negotiate with occupiers whom it planned to evict from an unsafe building. The court said the city could not do so without engaging the occupants about the best way of doing so. It has issued similar orders on many occasions since. By requiring state officials to engage with those subject to them, they have proved to be a successful use of judicial power.

The separation of powers itself is the biggest reason why judges exercise power with extreme care. This doctrine differentiates modern states from top-down, single-line ways of governing like monarchies or dictatorships. The world, and our continent, have seen many authoritarian regimes. Almost universally, they are an evil. In one of our neighbours, Swaziland, there is an autocracy in the form of a ruling monarch. In another, Zimbabwe, there is a government that has repeatedly and defiantly refused to respect rulings of its own courts.

Our Constitution renounces these law-less ways of exercising power. Intrinsic to its structure is that the power of the state can never be exercised by a single person or entity. Instead, power is distributed between three separate branches of the state – the legislature, the executive and the judiciary.

A profound corollary of splitting political power in this way is that each of the three branches must respect the other, and not intrude on the others' roles. The 'Sobukwe clause' violated the rule of law, because it was legislation directed at one single individual, instead of creating a rule applying generally to all people. But it violated also the separation of powers. This was because it took from the courts their task of determining how long a particular individual offender should be incarcerated, and gave that power instead to a member of the executive, the minister of justice.

XIX President Mandela, the rule of law and the separation of powers

In the Western Cape case, the first case that challenged executive and legislative conduct on the basis of the separation of powers, the Constitutional Court split.

The majority upheld the Western Cape's argument. Justice Chaskalson gave the majority ruling. He pointed out that Parliament 'can no longer claim supreme power subject to limitations imposed by the Constitution'. Instead, the legislature was now 'subject in all respects to the provisions of the Constitution and has only the powers vested in it by the Constitution'. The Constitution itself spelled out Parliament's powers. It provided that the legislative authority of the Republic vested in Parliament, and in Parliament alone. This meant, Justice Chaskalson ruled, that Parliament could not delegate its legislative powers to the President.

The provision of the statute under which President Mandela was given power to amend the statute was therefore invalid, and his proclamation purporting to amend the statute was invalid. The argument of the National Party government in the Western Cape was victorious.

The court announced its ruling on 22 September 1995. In legal terms, it was a public rebuff for President Mandela and his government. President Mandela did not take it so. He used the opportunity to educate South Africans about the power of the law. He went onto public television to explain that the court had ruled against him – and to emphasise that he fully accepted the court's judgment, and that the Constitution and the rule of law required him to do so. The rule of law had prevailed.

Since 1995, the court had given many important rulings against government. It had ruled that terror suspects could not without proper procedures and assurances be handed over to the United States authorities to face the death sentence. It had invalidated laws prohibiting consensual sex between same-sex partners. In *Grootboom* it set aside government's entire housing policy. And it had ruled that only Parliament itself, and not the Electoral Commission, could take away prisoners' right to vote; unless Parliament did so, prisoners retained that right.

But now, in 2002, the court faced undoubtedly the most momentous issue since the birth of democracy eight years before had confronted the court's skills and authority.

Over the seven years since it heard its first case in 1995, the court's membership had changed. Chaskalson still headed the court, though he now held the office of Chief Justice. His deputy, Pius Langa, was Deputy Chief Justice. Sitting together with them in the Nevirapine case were Justices Ackermann, Goldstone, Kriegler, Madala, Ngcobo, O'Regan, and Sachs. In the temporary absence of two members of the court, Justices Mokgoro and Yacoob, two acting justices sat. They were Justice Ben du Plessis, an Afrikaans-speaking high court judge from Pretoria, and Justice Thembile Skweyiya, who shortly afterwards was appointed permanently to the court.

Some of these judges had associations with the ANC before their appointment. Arthur Chaskalson was never a member of the ANC, or any party associated with it. But he had defended Mr Mandela and the other accused in the Rivonia Trial. And his commitment to the general kind of social justice the ANC aimed to achieve in South Africa could not be doubted.

During the ANC's years in exile, I saw Arthur on one occasion interact with its leaders. In June 1989, the distinguished legal philosopher Ronald Dworkin organised a meeting at Nuneham Park near Oxford between the ANC's legal and constitutional committee and South African judges and lawyers. One evening Arthur led a small group of us to meet ANC leaders who were not part of the legal negotiations. We travelled to the nearby country home of British philanthropist David Astor. Present was the charismatic Thabo Mbeki, and we also met the ANC's leader in exile, Oliver Tambo – who in the years before his exile had been Mandela's law partner in the justly famous partnership of Mandela and Tambo.

It was Arthur who spoke on behalf of our group, and who introduced us to the ANC leaders. When he did so, I was struck by the deferent way in which he referred to Mr Tambo. He did not say 'Mr Tambo'. He certainly did not use his first name, 'Oliver'. He addressed him respectfully as 'Mr President'. It was as though he was foretelling a time when Tambo would be President of South Africa. Tambo's premature death forestalled that, and Nelson Mandela became President, but of Arthur's respect for Mr Tambo and the ideals for which he stood there could equally be no doubt.

XX The Constitutional Court decides the Nevirapine case

Now Arthur, Chief Justice Chaskalson, presided over a court that had the power to overturn a central plank of government's health policy – its refusal to expand anti-retroviral coverage.

The atmosphere was tense, and the three days of argument gruelling. But if, as in the appeal court in Bloemfontein, the judges' interventions are some indication of which side has the harder case to argue, the advocates for government had a distinctly tougher time. Lead counsel for the TAC, Gilbert Marcus, recalls that though the TAC's argument was by no means plain sailing, he had one of the longest uninterrupted periods of argument he had ever experienced before an appellate court. This was when he described to the court the horrific effects of government policy denying Nevirapine to women with HIV.

The court issued its judgment in less than two months. On 5 July 2002 it announced to the world that it had rejected government's appeal. While it fine-tuned the order Judge Botha had granted, and used a different legal route to get there, in all essential details the TAC had won the case.

As with the judgment that certified the Constitution, the Nevirapine ruling was a 'judgment of the court' – the strongest way a court can express itself. The judges all contributed to writing the judgment. No single judge was credited with the opinion or any part of it. Instead, every judge took equal responsibility for every part of it. The court was speaking with the closest unanimous authority its individual judges and their public position made possible.

The judgment opened with striking words. The court quoted a document speaking in direst terms about the AIDS epidemic. The epidemic in South Africa has been described, it said, as 'an incomprehensible calamity' and 'the most important challenge facing South Africa since the birth of our new democracy'. Government's fight to contain AIDS was 'a top priority'. The epidemic 'has claimed millions of lives, inflicting pain and grief, causing fear and uncertainty, and threatening the economy'.

Who said that? In a deft touch, the court revealed the source. The quotations came from government's own documents.

The court then spent time sketching government's commitment

to action in the epidemic, and to explaining why government wanted to study the effects of Nevirapine by setting up pilot sites. But the court soon came to what it described as the crux of the problem. This, it said, lay not with the programme of research and pilot sites, but elsewhere: 'What is to happen to those mothers and their babies who cannot afford access to private health care and do not have access to the research and training sites?' With damning understatement, the court noted that it was not clear how long government planned to take before Nevirapine would be made available elsewhere.

Once the court posed the question in this way, it was clear that the TAC had to be granted the relief it sought. But the court did not shrink from recognising the charged political face-off that led to the litigation. It noted that debate about AIDS has been 'fraught with an unusual degree of political, ideological and emotional contention'. While this was perhaps unavoidable, given the magnitude of the catastrophe, it said, it was nevertheless 'regrettable that some of this contention and emotion has spilt over into this case'. Not only did this 'bedevil future relations between government and non-governmental agencies that will perforce have to join in combating the common enemy, but it could also have rendered the resolution of this case more difficult'.

Ultimately, though, the court said, 'we have found it possible to cut through the overlay of contention and arrive at a straightforward and unanimous conclusion'. And that conclusion was against government. The court dealt with the four reasons government advanced for refusing to expand access to Nevirapine – efficacy; drug resistance; drug safety; and the capacity of the public health system.

On each, it found that government's case lacked any credible or persuasive basis in the evidence. The minister's concerns about efficacy were 'not supported' by the data on which she relied.

Resistance? The risk was 'small in comparison with the potential benefit' – the court pointed out that 'the prospects of the child surviving if infected are so slim and the nature of the suffering so grave that the risk of some resistance' was 'well worth running'.

Safety, the court said, was 'no more than a hypothetical issue'. And since the TAC asked for Nevirapine to be made available only where facilities were already adequate, capacity was not in question.

Government's policy to confine Nevirapine to pilot sites was inflexible and denied a potentially life-saving drug to mothers and their babies. The court endorsed the high court's finding that this was not reasonable. This meant that government's entire approach to preventing mother-to-child transmission of HIV would have to be reviewed.

What order should the court grant? It rejected a contention by government that it should issue only a declaratory order, as it did in *Grootboom*. A declaratory order says what each party's duties and rights are, but without giving practical bite to them. Here, the court saw its duty differently. Its duty was to ensure that effective relief was granted. In the circumstances of this case, that demanded a detailed concrete order. In doing so, the court was not stepping onto government's terrain, so its order involved no violation of the doctrine of separation of powers.

The court gave a wide-ranging order. It ordered government to remove the restrictions on the availability of Nevirapine and to permit doctors to prescribe it where needed.

Importantly, the order specified that the fact that it mentioned Nevirapine 'did not preclude government from adapting its policy' if better methods of preventing mothers from transmitting HIV to their babies were to become available.

XXI A historically momentous judgment and order

The Constitutional Court issued its order two days before the start of the two-yearly international AIDS conference. Two years before, in 2000, the conference was held in Durban. That meeting led to a breakthrough in international thinking about how anti-retroviral drugs should be made available to those caught in the mass epidemic of AIDS in Africa. The question on everyone's minds over the next two years was: how will the impetus of Durban 2000 find practical effect in the lives of Africans living with HIV?

In 2002 the conference was held in the Spanish city of Barcelona. More than 18 000 scientists, executives, government officials, health workers and activists jammed the halls of the lovely Mediterranean port's international convention centre. The news of the court's order spread quickly to those who, like me, were attending one of the many pre-meetings. The court's judgment provided a partial, but significant answer to the momentous question the Durban meeting had posed. Drug availability would be expanded to poor people in Africa. There would be less suffering. And less death. The judgment was a breakthrough.

There was elation about it. And acclaim for it. The court's decision, available immediately on many websites, was studied, analysed and quoted in countless sessions. It was one of the few unequivocally good pieces of news to emanate from the epidemic in Africa for nearly thirty years. It boosted South Africa's reputation. And enhanced international respect for law.

And rightly so. Even after more than a decade, it is hard to overstate the importance of the Nevirapine judgment. The TAC, founded to tackle the evils of unaffordably expensive drugs, was forced to turn its attention to presidential denialism instead. It did so with courage and ingenuity, and with great strategic skill. It carefully selected its campaign partners. They included the

195

Congress of South African Trade Unions (COSATU), the South African Council of Churches (SACC), and women's and children's groups. These, together with other organisations, joined the TAC in challenging the President and in campaigning for rational policies and treatments.

Some journalists and political analysts in South Africa spoke out against President Mbeki's questions about AIDS science, but their courage was isolated. Large sectors of society were cowed into silence. President Mbeki was a forbidding man who headed a governing party with an illustrious history and a massive electoral majority. Many felt fearful of crossing him. The issue – a mass epidemic of sexually transmitted disease on a continent oppressed by centuries of racism – was explosive.

As a result, many prominent members of South Africa's intellectual elite stayed silent. Business leaders were mute. Some actively kowtowed to the President. Members of his party and Cabinet, even those regarded as forceful, for more than a year dared not state openly that HIV caused AIDS. Even international diplomats were cowed. Out of fear, conformity, deference or sycophancy, many in the establishment maintained an appalled silence, while the TAC and other activists, together with their allies in COSATU and the media, struggled to persuade the President that his stance was ruinous. Their struggle was in vain. President Mbeki did not budge.

In this gloomiest hour, the activists were able to turn to the courts. They were forced to do so. And they did so with extreme reluctance. But when they resolved to take legal action, they did so with the skill and foresight they had brought to their war against extortionate drug prices. And the Constitution, which enshrined the rule of law, meant that the courts had the power to consider the evidence and the arguments. The courts had the power to rule in their favour.

The judgment the activists obtained was a ringing victory for treatment access as well as for rationality. But it was also a pivotal victory for the rule of law and for constitutionalism itself. More than the Western Cape case or any other case that preceded it, the Nevirapine case was a test of law's power when government behaved irrationally. And it was a test that the Constitution, and the court created to guard it, passed with honour.

XXII The rule of law and life-saving treatment for AIDS

As a matter of political history, the court's decision was the pivot that eventually forced government to take decisive action in the epidemic. Although it responded grudgingly at first, government eventually gave effect to the ruling. Large-scale provision of ARVs began 30 months later, in December 2004.

Today, well over two million people in South Africa are living because of ARV treatment. I am one of them. I receive my medications with the assistance of the medical insurance scheme that covers judges and parliamentarians. The cost of my medications today is minimal. But no one, rich or poor, employed or unemployed, is denied treatment for AIDS because they cannot afford it.

The South African government programme to provide antiretroviral medications is the largest publicly provided AIDS treatment programme in the world. This is the most significant practical outcome of the court's decision. Although too many people are still dying of AIDS, the decision saved many lives. More even than *Grootboom*, the Nevirapine case materially changed the lives of hundreds of thousands and ultimately millions of people: it enabled them to not die. In this way, the court's decision had dramatic practical force.

But it also had a profound effect on public ideas and public discussion. Twenty-one months before the TAC ruling, the court, in a stirring judgment by Justice Sandile Ngcobo, had outlawed job discrimination against those living with HIV. In 1996, Jacques Charl Hoffmann applied for a job as a cabin attendant at SAA. He was one of nearly 200 applicants. He got through a rigorous four-stage test that only eleven other applicants passed. This showed his fitness for the job. He then took a medical examination. This showed he was healthy and well. But his employment was made subject to an HIV test. When his results came back, they showed that he was HIV positive. He had the virus that causes AIDS. SAA, the national airline, refused to employ him.

Hoffmann was devastated. He consulted lawyers at the AIDS Law Project and they took his case to the high court. A judge ruled that SAA was entitled to discriminate on the ground of HIV status. So the ALP took the case on appeal to the Constitutional Court. There they scored a ringing victory when the court overturned the high court's decision. It ruled that SAA could not refuse to employ Hoffmann.

In his judgment, Justice Ngcobo included a long section setting out the medical facts of AIDS. He did this even though SAA did not dispute the basic medical science of AIDS. The judgment was delivered on 28 September 2000, eleven months after President Mbeki had publicly started expressing scepticism about the causes and treatments of AIDS. The judgment seemed a courteous but pointed rejoinder to the President's scepticism.

However, Justice Ngcobo's endorsement of the science of AIDS went largely unnoticed. His judgment was noted mainly for its effect in barring discrimination in employment.

But 21 months after the SAA judgment, the Nevirapine judgment left no room for ambiguity at all. It was a rebuke not only for government inaction on AIDS drugs, but for the anguished and utterly unnecessary debate that led to that inaction. That poor women had a legal right to use anti-retroviral drugs to protect their babies from HIV transmission, and that government was constitutionally obliged to offer them the choice to do so, dealt a blow that would eventually prove fatal to the presidential discourse of denialism.

President Mbeki had made his stand on AIDS an article of faith of his administration. He had proved impervious to activist pressure, international scientific entreaty, and impassioned condemnation by commentators. But large sectors of the established elite, including members of his own party and government, had maintained a cowed silence.

By contrast, when its moment came, the court unflinchingly committed its moral capital to the issue. Its judgment was courteous, understated and respectful of the President. But its stand affirming medical science was unmistakable. And it proved pivotal.

Presidentially licensed denialism continued to dog government's response to the epidemic. In March 2002, when the case was pending before the Constitutional Court, the health minister, Dr Tshabalala-Msimang, threatened that government would refuse to enforce an adverse judgment.

This attitude, if maintained, could have provoked a crisis for the rule of law and the Constitution, but fortunately sounder judgments prevailed. The Minister of Justice, Dr Penuell Maduna, assured the country that government would abide by the court's order.

Dr Maduna came to the court in December 2012 to attend the farewell ceremony for my colleague Justice Zak Yacoob, who had to retire when he reached his fifteen-year term limit. On his way to the ceremony, Dr Maduna stopped briefly by my court chambers. I asked him if it was President Mbeki himself who had mandated him to state that government would abide by the court's decision. He confirmed that it was. In bowing to the courts when they disclaimed his own dogma, President Mbeki, more signally even than President Nelson Mandela, ensured a victory for the rule of law in South Africa. When history assesses his legacy, this must weigh substantially on the credit side.

The court's authoritative assertion of reason proved vital. It shifted public and governmental discourse in ways that eventually forced President Mbeki's government into broader action. The judgment constituted an authoritative, morally cogent and politically irrefutable assertion of the science of AIDS, and of the necessity for public action in accordance with it.

It showed the court as a source not merely of institutional decision-making power, but of unparalleled moral and intellectual authority. My retired colleague Justice Kate O'Regan has spoken of the court as a 'forum for reason'. The court's Nevirapine judgment powerfully supports this assessment. The court spoke with a depth of authority that vindicated reason. But it also saved many tens of thousands of lives, and avoided unquantifiable depths of human suffering.

The rule of law cannot speak more powerfully.

Chapter Five

Diversity and Constitutionalism

I First intimations of difference

I was barely beyond my toddler years when I first realised I was gay. I was three or four years old. My father had found employment as an electrician at the municipality in Pietermaritzburg, KwaZulu-Natal's provincial capital and its second-largest city. It was the longest he ever held a job. For nearly four years, apart from intermittently destructive bouts of drinking, we lived just as we thought a normal family did, in a newly built council house at 11A Wallace Road, on the fringes of the city – my mother and father and Laura and Jeanie and me. An open tract of veld separated the row of tiny, snug dwellings from the swift-flowing Msunduzi River. On its banks and in its thick brown waters we played with the neighbours' children, innocently unsupervised.

The Msunduzi in turn separated our white working-class neighbourhood from a crowded Indian residential area even further from the city's edges. The road from the city centre to the Indian quarter passed over a bridge close to Wallace Road. My first intense awareness of cultural otherness came one Saturday afternoon – it must have been Saturday, for my father was home. A richly decorated parade of colourful carriages, accompanied by flower-garlanded crowds, and music and crackers and sparkles, proceeded boisterously from town along the road towards the bridge.

It was tantalisingly close. I think now it must have been a celebration of the annual Hindu festival of chariots, Rath Yatra, during which images of gods are carried out from their temples and conveyed through public thoroughfares on festooned and decorated carriages. It looked strange and intriguing and colourful and animated and – to a young child in a white, Calvinist home – quite fantastically exotic.

I remember feeling fascinated and drawn. Could we run across and get a closer look? No. We could not. The prohibition was emphatic. Those were Indians, and that was their culture. They worshipped strange idols. Alien. The inescapable implication was: inferior. With a keen sense of retrospectively imported mortification, I remember the stock, racially derogatory terms my mother sometimes used of Indians. Her language was of course conditioned by racist attitudes common amongst white people generally, and it was given a particular edge by our menial social standing within that community. The loftiest employment rung on Wallace Road was occupied by a policeman. In authority and stature my father, a municipal electrician, was far beneath. What was more, we were poor. We didn't own our house. We struggled to make ends meet. My father, with regularly shaming alcoholic episodes, could barely keep his job (and eventually he lost it, precipitating our catastrophic move, further down, to the children's home in Queenstown).

But, despite all of this, there was one surpassing social feature about us. We were white. Thank goodness. White, and not black. Not Indian. Not coloured. White. More tellingly, in the term then widely used, 'European'. Not non-European. Better. At least.

This propelling sense, that whiteness was valuable, superior, virtuous, clean and desirable, blanketed my formative childhood and adolescent and even early adult years. As a child, I remember reflecting with pity how it must feel to be black. Imagine! It was really only at Oxford, after Steve Biko was murdered in September 1977, and I read some of what he wrote, that I came to a fully mortifying sense of the stupidity and horror of racism.

Soon after, also at Oxford, I met someone who was to become my first intensely close black friend, Loyiso Nongxa, with whom I later worked when he was Vice-Chancellor of Wits University, and I chaired the governing council. This and other friendships helped me to realise that, apart from its ignorant errors, the greatest folly of racism is to impoverish – by imprisoning in a foolhardy superior cocoon, enforcing famine amidst the riches of a sumptuous feast of otherness, differentness and diversity.

But even in a society in which I bore that potent marker of privilege, a white skin, I knew from very early on that I was different. Perilously, perhaps shamefully, different. This differentness was present to me before I went to school, before I thought about Indian people as alien, and long before I realised that as a white person I was a minority in an overwhelmingly black land.

The insight came with urination. When the boys who lived across the road, Barry and Garth, stood at the toilet bowl to pee – we were just barely old enough to stand beside it – they stood with their legs sturdily apart, confidently releasing their bodily water. I stood with my legs pressed primly together. And I *wanted* to stand that way – not the way Barry and Garth stood. Why? I couldn't say. But the difference felt important. It constituted a mysterious divide separating me from them. And I knew I had to keep it secret. It was not something to share. I could not vaunt it. It must be hidden.

Why the sense that this difference might be shameful and should be closeted? I think I remember. Two incidents from that early time stand engraved in my memory. The first involved a teddy bear. It was a gift, perhaps from Aunt Laura, after whom my elder sister was named. She was my father's unmarried cousin from the branch of his family who left Scotland for Canada, when his parents came to South Africa, where he was born. She visited us once in Pietermaritzburg, glamorously, leaving a sense of North American sophistication and prosperity in her wake.

My mother offered to sew some miniature clothes for my bear. This seemed a good idea, since the furry beast was naked. She asked me what she should make. I told her I wanted a bearish skirt or dress. This did not please. Why girls' clothes, my mother inquired. She looked bemused, even slightly embarrassed. My preference seemed to have struck an awkward note. Shouldn't the bear wear pants, like Garth's and Barry's, she asked? No, I said. I want a dress. This was definitely the wrong answer. A boy should not want his teddy to wear girls' clothes.

So she made boys' clothes instead – a cute pair of miniature pants, and a short-sleeved shirt. I was puzzled, but hid my disappointment. It was my first explicit instruction in how gender roles are created and imposed.

The next incident was somewhat more traumatising. I was, I think, a wilful child. I could be a brat. I was after all the first boy, after three girls (before my birth, my parents, having had Laura, Jean and Daphne, felt forced by circumstances to give Daphne away in adoption – almost immediately after, my conception and birth re-augmented the family). So, quite apart from not being given away in adoption, I received special boy-treatment and privileges – a further lesson in gender formation.

One day, as a very young child, I provoked my father's displeasure, screaming in protest at some perceived injustice of treatment or circumstance. His response was stern. That was not surprising from a man who enlisted in the Union Defence Force in 1939 when barely older than seventeen, and saw service against fascist forces in North Africa, where he was wounded, and later taken prisoner. He spent a good part of the war years in a prisoner of war camp in Italy, where, a lover of words and language, he learned to speak Italian. On his return from the war, he never spoke about his experiences, but his sisters, my aunts, told us later that his alcohol dependency stemmed from that time.

Now the ex-soldier, no doubt wondering how to deal with a shrieking toddler, decided on firm action. He spoke sternly. If you scream like a girl, you will have to be dressed like a girl. This elicited even more protest. But, despite my anguished tears, and kicking and screaming, he forcibly arrayed me in one of my sisters' dresses. And, to complete the humiliation, he carried me out into the garden for the neighbours to see. There he deposited me, struggling tearfully, to absorb in public the lesson that a boy should not scream like a girl. As quickly as I could, I rushed inside to rid my body of the shamefully imposed fabric of femininity.

So I received an early double lesson in gender politics. First was a lesson in hierarchy. Girls were definitely down the scale. For why should putting a boy into girls' clothes be so humiliating a punishment, unless girls, and everything associated with them, were inferior? And, second, it was a lesson in the perils of not conforming. There were ways a man had to behave. If you deviated, dishonour and public shame would follow.

The way I wanted to stand when peeing, in contrast to Garth and Barry, felt exactly right for me. But it also felt girlish. It sprang from the part of me that wanted girl-clothes for my teddy. That was why it had to be secret. Wanting girlish things, and wanting to be with girls, and to play with them rather than with boys – an inner hankering that increased as our family fractured, and our circumstances shifted downwards with giddying insecurity – must at all costs be cloaked under conformity.

I spent the next decades covering my difference, hiding the fact that my experiences, and my sense of who I was, diverged from those of others. Through my school years I was terrified of being called a 'sissy'. My fear was the guilty dread of one who knew that, because it belonged, the shameful label would stick. For of course, beneath the covers, I really was a sissy, and wanted to be a sissy. But to be true to myself and actually *be* a sissy in life and deed was unthinkable. For me, the price of non-conformity seemed far too high.

I have always secretly admired queens – gay men whose behaviour is extravagantly and unapologetically feminine. They have a courage I have always lacked. Instead, I deliberately coached myself to act with mannerisms and gestures I reckoned were more masculine. Stood squarely. Dropped my voice. Eschewed flamboyant gestures and speech. Played rugby. Dated girls.

Of course I did not know then that my apartness from other boys was because I was 'gay', in the sense of having a pronounced erotic and emotional disposition towards my own rather than the opposite sex. Gayness both as a category, and as a conscious act of political self-identification, arrived only later. But from my very earliest years I knew with complete certainty that my own way of wanting to be was in an opaque but important – and shameful – way a challenge to the rigidity of the boy/girl divide.

The realisation that my inner feelings placed me in a differently labelled category from most of humanity came only after the onset of adolescence, when I was in my second year at Pretoria Boys' High, contriving strenuously, and mostly succeeding, to be as much like the other boys as possible.

In late 1968, when I was fifteen, the national radio broadcaster's English-language service ran a provocative series of programmes on Sunday evenings. Called 'The Broken Link', it explored controversial social issues – drug use, student protests, counter-culture. It had a large audience, and rightly so. I recall the programmes as deeply researched, thought-provoking, and enthralling but mostly unsensational.

Then, one Sunday evening, as I listened with my ear pressed close to my portable radio in my compact balcony room three floors above the traffic on the corner of Sunnyside's busy Esselen and Troye streets, I heard a Broken Link programme that changed my consciousness forever. The subject was homosexuality – a word I probably hadn't heard until then. The programme interviewed people who identified themselves as homosexual. It spoke about clubs in Johannesburg where homosexuals congregated. It broadcast a tale about a lesbian called Mandy. It was understated, factual, sympathetic and gripping.

What was most disquieting to me was that the programme presented homosexuality as a fact. It occurred. Some men and women were homosexual. Simple as that.

I listened, fascinated and horrified. Could this be me? Surely not. Yet this accounted for the sexual fantasies that with urgent adolescent intensity were intruding on my consciousness. It explained the near-obsessive tender feelings I sometimes developed for older boys or male teachers. It explained why from my earliest consciousness I wanted girlie things!

But one thing I knew for sure. With my whole being, I did not want to be homosexual. I did not want to belong to a stigmatised, isolated, reviled minority whose sexuality was shamefully different – whose conduct was so despised and ungodly and immoral that it was a crime. I solemnly and seriously pledged, if it turned out I really was homosexual, to commit suicide – though fortunately, with a survivor's prudence, from time to time I postponed the final decision.

Yet with increasing clarity, as my adolescent feelings cooled and hardened, and I grew into young adulthood, it became unavoidably clear that what the Broken Link programmes portrayed, as I listened, my ear to my radio, heart beating intently, was more than just an alien cult in the big bad city of Johannesburg. They were portraying me.

The next fifteen years, until I was almost thirty, I spent fighting that realisation – every minute of the conscious day, with every fibre of my will.

II The Constitution and national diversity

But of course we are all different. That is the beauty of humanity, and of nature. It is infinitely diverse. Each of us is singular, unique and incapable of being copied. And many of us experience intense intimations of being different from other people in early childhood, just as I did, but without turning out to be gay.

And, joyfully, our individual singularities are reflected in the singularities of the groups to which by birth or circumstance or choice we are affiliated – reflecting differences of language, dialect, belief, culture, religion, ethnicity, social class and race.

Why should we not respect and value difference? And why should we not rejoice in it? The South African Constitution does. It starts with an inspirational Preamble:

> *We, the people of South Africa,*
> *Recognise the injustices of our past;*
> *Honour those who suffered for justice and freedom in our land;*
> *Respect those who have worked to build and develop our country; and*
> *Believe that South Africa belongs to all who live in it, united in our diversity.*
> *We therefore, through our freely elected representatives, adopt this Constitution as the supreme law of the Republic so as to-*
> *Heal the divisions of the past and establish a society based on democratic values, social justice and fundamental human rights;*

*Lay the foundations for a democratic and open society in which
government is based on the will of the people and every citizen is equally protected by law;*

*Improve the quality of life of all citizens and free the potential
of each person; and*

*Build a united and democratic South Africa able to take its
rightful place as a sovereign state in the family of nations.*

May God protect our people.

Nkosi Sikelel' iAfrika. Morena boloka setjhaba sa heso.

God seën Suid-Afrika. God bless South Africa.

Mudzimu fhatutshedza Afurika. Hosi katekisa Afrika.

The only place the Constitution expressly mentions the word
'diversity' is right here, in this lovely Preamble. It pledges that
South Africa belongs to all who live in it, 'united in our diversity'.
But though the word appears nowhere else, diversity is one of
the most fundamental underlying premises of the country's founding charter. And rightly so.

We are a gloriously diverse country. Though black African people are numerically overwhelmingly predominant (79%, with
coloureds and whites constituting 9% each, and Indian/Asian
South Africans 2.5%), the 2011 census indicates, according to how
people gave their mother tongues, that no one language or cultural grouping is predominant (rounded off, the figures are isi-
Zulu 23%; isiXhosa 16%; Afrikaans 14%; English 10%; Sepedi
(Sesotho sa Leboa) 9%; Setswana 8%; Sesotho 8%; Xitsonga 5%;
siSwati 3%; Tshivenda 2% and isiNdebele 2%).

Nor is there any predominant religion. Amongst those who
identified a religious affiliation, the census lists the two biggest
groupings as the Zion Church of Christ (ZCC) and 'other Apostolic groupings'. They have respectively five and five and a half
million adherents – not much more than about 10% of the population each.

Alongside the founding values, set out in the first provision immediately after the Preamble, the entire Constitution is rooted in the notion that our differences are valuable in themselves, and enriching for us as South Africans. The promise of our differentness is the cherished basis of our whole constitutional settlement. It is the unstated 'founding value' of our Constitution.

III Constitutional diversity – citizenship, national flag and language

The 'founding provisions' in the first chapter of the Constitution establish a common South African citizenship. This was of particular historical significance because apartheid ideology tried to keep South Africa 'white' by hiving off black South Africans into separate quasi-'independent' homelands, or Bantustans. That is what the apartheid government sought to do with Moutse and KwaNdebele in the 1980s. Never again. The citizenship provision asserts that all citizens are equally entitled to the rights, privileges and benefits of citizenship, and equally subject to its duties and responsibilities.

A further founding provision provides that the President determines the national anthem by proclamation, while the fifth describes the colours of the national flag, and alludes to its depiction in a sketch contained in the first schedule to the Constitution.

Yet another founding provision is most lavish in its commitment to diversity. It deals with the vexed question of the country's official language. And it resolves the question by stipulating that there is not one official language, but eleven official languages – Sepedi (Sesotho sa Leboa), Sesotho, Setswana, siSwati, Tshivenda, Xitsonga, Afrikaans, English, isiNdebele, isiXhosa and isiZulu.

It also provides that the state must take 'practical and positive measures' to raise the status and encourage the use of these languages. Official languages must 'enjoy parity of esteem and must be treated equitably'. The Pan South African Language Board (PanSALB), which the Constitution obliges Parliament to create, must promote and develop the use of the official and other languages, including Khoi, Nama and San languages, and sign language. PanSALB must also promote and ensure respect for languages commonly used by communities in South Africa, including German, Greek, Gujarati, Hindi, Portuguese, Tamil, Telegu and Urdu, and languages used for religious purposes, including Arabic, Hebrew and Sanskrit.

Although the 2011 census found that English is the mother tongue of only 9.6% of the population, it is the language most widely understood in South Africa, and the second language of the majority of South Africans. In effect, in South Africa, as in other multilingual countries, English has become the language of business. It is the language most spoken in Parliament, in the world of business and in courtrooms.

But the importance of the official languages provision is more than symbolic. Any person doing business with government, and any litigant, is entitled to engage and be responded to in any official language. A party may address the Constitutional Court in any official language. The court supplies the interpreter for the judges who don't understand the language to be used. The only requirement is that the person must give the court notice. Should a person wish to address the court in an official language other than the language of his or her written argument, he or she must let the Registrar know, so that arrangements can be made.

Again, this provision of the Constitution has created an ideal world – a world in which there is not, in effect, only one language of business, namely English, but truly eleven official languages. That ideal world is very far from reality. Our daily debate in South Africa reflects disgruntled minorities complaining of broken promises and discrimination. As with other constitutional promises, translation into reality is a far distant prospect.

The Constitution takes a further step in recognition of South Africa's diversity. It recognises the country's indigenous legal heritage. It gives formal recognition to traditional systems of customary law. It provides that the courts must apply customary law when it is applicable, subject to the Constitution and any legislation. The Constitution remains supreme, and its values prevail. So our system of law, though richly diverse in its elements and origins, is now unitary. The Constitution commands authority over all of it. All common law and customary law is subject to the Constitution and must conform with it, just as legislation and executive and administrative conduct must.

IV Diversity – sexual orientation and the rich harvest of history

The Constitution's extraordinary commitment to diversity sprang from our history. Apartheid left a suffocating legacy. That was a constant and humbling reminder to the negotiators to go wide. Be generous. Open up an inclusive concept of constitutional citizenship.

Apartheid valued conformity. Above everything else, it prized so-called racial purity. It treasured whiteness and European culture. Its entire edifice of separation, of exclusion, of subordination, of pass laws and body searches – the degrading systems Pius Langa, later Chief Justice, described in his submission to the TRC – was built on the premise that one culture, one race, one skin colour, was superior, valuable above all others. That shameful history was constantly present during the constitutional negotiations. It told the drafters that every provision of the Constitution should resonate with appreciation of our country's diversity.

The negotiators heeded the call. The high energy of their commitment carried me and other lobbyists on behalf of the gay and lesbian community through the negotiating process. It meant we could argue that, though apartheid most shamefully focused on race, and though discrimination against women, and against black women in particular, were our most pressing legacies, apartheid's oppressions were multiple. Protection of difference should therefore not be afforded only on racial grounds. It should not be limited to gender discrimination. It should cover as many conditions as possible.

It enabled us to argue that gender domination should be understood as a widely pervasive evil. It would be wrong, we said, to see it as involving men subordinating women only. Gender oppression encompasses also discrimination against persecuted sexual minorities. And I was able to contend that protection on the grounds of race, gender, age, culture, and religion were relatively 'easy cases' for constitutional drafting. No one disputed them. The hard case was lesbian, gay, bisexual, transgender and intersex (LGBTI) people. As a group, they had been reviled and stigmatised under apartheid, as in most modern political systems. And they were a minority who needed constitutional protection more even, I argued, than numerically powerful groups.

Behind the technical structure of our legal and constitutional arguments lay a less tangible and more emotional issue. It was the pervasive atmosphere of transition-era generosity. Our arguments sought to invoke this. We urged that lesbians and gays should be included as beneficiaries of the new era of embracing constitutional openness and inclusiveness.

Crucial to all our arguments, both technical and emotional, was the fact that people known to be lesbian or gay had participated in the struggle for freedom. When Nelson Mandela was arrested in KwaZulu-Natal in 1962, after returning from abroad, where he had travelled to help get uMkhonto weSizwe (MK) off the ground, he was operating under a cover. His pose was as a chauffeur to a white companion called Cecil Williams. Williams was known within the ANC to be a gay man.

The most important and outspoken apartheid-era gay activist was Tseko Simon Nkoli. Simon was arrested and put on trial for his part in the Vaal uprising in September 1984. Even earlier, when he was in his mid-twenties, Simon had become active in gay and lesbian politics. His arrest on political charges meant that there could be no stepping back from his fight against oppression as a gay man. Simon was black. He was born and bred in the townships. But he was also gay. Sexual-orientation politics were not an optional extra. They were central to his being, and to his entire political commitment.

Once in prison, Simon took astonishingly fearless action. He unflinchingly came out to his fellow accused. He insisted that they treat him with full human dignity and acceptance. The trigger was a matter as mundane, and as deeply important, as the awaiting-trial prisoners' food. Who would dish it up? When it was discovered that Simon was gay, he was excluded from the roster, but he would have none of it. He harangued his fellow prisoners intrepidly about their prejudices. He insisted that he be allowed to take his turn in serving the food.

And his fellow accused responded well. Led by Popo Molefe and Mosiuoa 'Terror' Lekota, both later political leaders in democratic South Africa, and his close friend Gcinumuzi Malindi, accused number 5, later a senior counsel and acting judge, Simon's fellow Delmas trialists accepted his entire person. They embraced him as a gay man.

It is not overdramatic to see what happened in prison between Simon and his fellow trialists as a watershed in South African political consciousness.

Simon's story is as inspiring as it is practically instructive. The greatest ally of gay and lesbian persecution, and the greatest enemy of acceptance, is invisibility. Unlike most racial and gender differences, sexual orientation is generally invisible, unless people choose to come out. Once families, neighbourhoods, communities, congregations, or co-workers know that gayness is not an alien phenomenon, once they know they have lesbian and gay sisters, brothers, neighbours, colleagues, or friends, attitudes quickly change. From suspicion, ignorance and prejudice, most people move quickly to acceptance.

How can they not? Once recognised, same-sex orientation is as natural and human as opposite-sex orientation. It is the same as left-handedness – a natural though minority variant of humanness. Both left-handedness and some measure of same-sex orientation occur in between 5 and 10% of people. They occur in people across all societies, cultures, religions, races and continents. Both should be accepted.

Left-handedness, also, used to be subjected to ignorant abuse. When my sister Jeanie started school in Pietermaritzburg in the 1950s, she attended a convent school near our Wallace Road home. When the nuns discovered she wanted to write using her left hand, they beat her. To this day, Jeanie remembers the nuns caning her on her left hand. They did so because their pedagogical ethics were benighted and misguided and because they didn't know better. My mother promptly took Jeanie out of the nuns' care. In her new school, left-handedness was accepted as natural to Jeanie, as indeed it is – as natural, and ineradicable, as my homosexuality is to me.

No teacher would dream of caning a child for writing left-handedly today. Nor should anyone in any position of authority dream of reproving or punishing anyone for identifying themselves as gay, lesbian, bisexual, transgender or intersex. The sexual variant is as natural to our humanness as the distribution of left- and right-handed people.

Much less bravely or spectacularly than Simon, when I came out as a gay man, I was a professional white man in a suit. I was making my career as an advocate at the Johannesburg Bar. Just as I was starting legal practice, at the age of thirty, I took a firm resolution. I would put my heart-rending struggles against my own inner self behind me. In the same month I started my practice at the Bar, I moved into a small rented house in Westdene with my first male lover, Wilhelm Hahn, an architect teaching at Wits University.

Less than two years later, Wilhelm relocated to America for a teaching job in Houston, Texas. Not long after he left, I became infected with HIV. Wilhelm returned to South Africa after twenty years. He died in his home country, of prostate cancer, in March 2008. I felt privileged to be at his side until just two days before his death. We were able to express how deeply we cared for each other, and how important to our lives our love for each other had been, and still was.

My relationship with Wilhelm, after a brief failed heterosexual marriage, and the long years of agony, gave me the strength and pride to say, Never again. I resolved that I would never again apologise for something so deeply intrinsic to my nature that it makes me what I am as a human. I would never again say sorry for being gay. I started speaking on public platforms about lesbian and gay equality. Together with my legal work defending guerrilla fighters and conscientious objectors and anti-apartheid organisations and communities dispossessed of their land, I spoke out for gay and lesbian equality.

After Wilhelm left for the United States, Simon and I became friends. He was in prison at the time. Simon knew of me from my political work as a lawyer, but he also knew I was proudly and openly gay. He asked to see me when the Delmas accused were released from isolated detention, and were allowed to apply for bail. I visited him in prison immediately before their first appearance in court.

We shared a political philosophy about gayness. We were both clamantly outspoken that our sexual orientation had unavoidable political implications. And we both saw our commitment to equality, justice and dignity in South Africa as all-embracing. It included a struggle for justice for all – including full equality for sexual minorities.

I knew then already that Simon was a remarkable man. He died, tragically, of AIDS in December 1998, after the ARV treatments that saved my life failed him. But his impact on South African constitutionalism – not just on sexual orientation within it, but on the extraordinary depth of our Constitution's commitment to equality – was momentous.

From his arrest in 1985, until the court delivered its main verdict acquitting him of all charges in 1988, Simon Nkoli was unapologetically vocal. His visibility and his firm voice during the Delmas Trial were historically crucial to our search for equality and dignity in South Africa. With the work of other progressive activists, including the women and men in Cape Town's Organisation of Lesbian and Gay Activists (OLGA), who reached out to Albie Sachs and others on the ANC's constitutional and legal drafting committee, Simon's stand proved critical. It created simple awareness and solidarity and acceptance. It allowed us to argue convincingly to the constitutional negotiators that our journey to a just society would not be complete if it excluded lesbians and gays and other sexual minorities.

And so the equality clause in the interim Constitution made history. It was extraordinarily generous and ample in the protections it extended. It prohibited unfair discrimination on any ground. But fourteen grounds it named expressly. They included race, gender, sex, ethnic or social origin, colour, age, disability, religion, conscience, belief, culture or language. But the most astonishing ground set out in the clause was sexual orientation. No other national constitution anywhere in the world expressly mentioned those two words. In affording express protection to gays, lesbians, bisexual, intersex and transgender people, South Africa achieved a world first.

I benefited from that generous-spirited protection when, at the end of 1994, President Mandela accepted the recommendation of the Judicial Service Commission, and appointed me as a judge of the high court. I was an openly and proudly gay man. But I was equally a South African committed to our new project of democratic constitutionalism. Rightly, my sexual orientation did not stand in the way of the contribution I offered to make. On the contrary, I believe being gay enhanced my understanding of oppression wherever it occurs. It enabled me to bring to the task of judging my subjective awareness of discrimination in all its forms.

And this sense is not unique to black people in racist societies, or to women in gender-oppressed societies, or to lesbians and gays. It is available to everyone. We can all appreciate the importance of otherness and difference, simply because each of us is uniquely different. We have only to listen carefully, and to reach out to embrace its richness.

V Diversity – the sharp lessons of history

It would be wrong to credit solely the suffocating ethos of apartheid for our vibrant national commitment to inclusiveness. The constitutional negotiators also had grimmer practical instruction in the importance of inclusivity. The grievous history of the rest of our continent gave them ample warning that celebrating diversity was a pragmatic necessity.

Our continent has been riven by bloody ethnic conflict and debilitating wars. In the Nigerian civil war of 1967-1970 as many as three million Biafrans died, mostly of famine and disease. In South Sudan, between 1983 and 2005, perhaps two million people died as a result of war, famine and disease. The genocide in Burundi in 1972 slaughtered 100 000 people. And in Rwanda, in the first months of 1994 – just as South Africa was taking its final steps away from apartheid towards democracy – nearly 900 000 people were clubbed and pangaed to death. This happened in just 90 days: an almost unimaginable tally, in a small country, of 10 000 people murdered, every day, for three unspeakably long and horrific months.

The causes of the various conflicts were complex. Some had their roots in divisions it suited the various colonial powers to exploit. But in each case the signal factor was a failure or inability to commit to an inclusive national polity, in which linguistic, ethnic and racial diversity were recognised as a source of strength, rather than as weaknesses.

That is the commitment that has so richly distinguished South Africa's constitutional project. The events from our own continent exhorted us imperatively to choose the path of tolerance and inclusivity. In addition, closer to home, hard-headed prudential considerations counselled inclusivity. It made sense for all parties to support constitutional provisions that encouraged minorities to vest their futures in South Africa. In 1972, the brutal dictator Idi Amin expelled tens of thousands of Asians and Indians from Uganda, on just 90 days' notice. They fled leaving everything – and impoverishing Uganda in the process. Rich skills and expertise were lost. Businesses that were thriving, collapsed. Capital for investment vanished.

Soon after, white people fled in their hundreds of thousands from Mozambique and Angola. A successful coup in 1974 put an end to authoritarian rule in Portugal – and dramatically also ended colonial rule in the country's African colonies. In exile, the ANC supported the radical transformation of post-colonial Angola and Mozambique, but the flight of most white Portuguese speakers from the two former colonies taught the ANC a sobering lesson: processes that seemed to bring the greatest rewards to poor and oppressed peoples in the short term might cause much greater hardship in the longer run.

The events that our Southern African neighbours experienced convinced the ANC to support moderating policies, policies that celebrated diversity, but allowed a constitutionally mandated process of affirmative action. The ANC wanted democracy to be associated with a better life and with peace – not with poorer living standards and civil war.

There was a further factor. There had always been prominent South Africans of both white and Indian descent in the anti-apartheid struggle. It was thus unthinkable that South Africa would follow Uganda's path of expelling minorities, or allow the flight of skilled citizens as occurred in Mozambique and Angola.

The result was a Constitution that made the greatest allowance possible for linguistic, cultural, religious and racial minorities. A Constitution that barred abuse of power by distributing it between three separate arms of state. A Constitution that entrenched constitutional supremacy and the rule of law, and subordinated all exercise of power to its norms and values. A Constitution that entrenched property rights, but expressly provided for affirmative action.

A Constitution that expressly pledged to transform South Africa from a country built on racist triumphalism into one in which racial discrimination was prohibited, and in which the human dignity of all was fostered. A country in which the poor are guaranteed minimum social benefits, and in which equal protection and benefit of the law is promised to all.

The Constitution's commitment to diversity is not rooted in sentimentality. It is based in sound political and social calculation. It is true that tolerance and acceptance foster human well-being. They create good feelings. But diversity is not only about warm feelings. It is rooted in hard-nosed conceptions of essential public interest. We have to tolerate and celebrate our differences as people so that we can thrive economically and culturally and intellectually. Both materially and spiritually, diversity is good for us.

That is the most fundamental lesson of South Africa's commitment to the rule of law and constitutionalism.

VI The Constitutional Court rules on how far diversity must be protected

In February 2007 the Constitutional Court confronted a case that took me back to my earliest childhood, to when I had watched, fascinated, the colourful Rath Yatra parade passing near our home in Pietermaritzburg.

This case truly tested the stretch available within the constitutional promise of diversity. At stake were the rules adopted, for all learners, by a top-rate publicly funded government school, Durban Girls' High (DGHS). Formerly, like Pretoria Boys' High, for whites only, DGHS had long admitted learners of all races. A young girl of South Indian, Tamil descent was admitted in 2002. She was Sunali Pillay. One September holiday, her mother gave her permission to pierce her nose and insert a small gold stud in it.

When she returned to school, the headmistress, Ms Martin,

pointed out a problem to Sunali. Her nose-stud contravened the school's code of conduct. The code had been drawn up carefully, in consultation with learners' representatives, parents and the school's governing body. When Sunali was admitted, her mother signed an agreement that she and Sunali would be bound by the code.

Apart from plain earrings, simple round studs, one for each ear, the code explicitly barred all jewellery. The nose-stud was forbidden. Sunali would have to give it up.

But Sunali refused to remove her nose-stud. In response to this assertion, the school did not over-react. The next year, it asked her mother to write explaining why Sunali should be allowed to continue wearing the stud. She did so. She explained that she and Sunali came from a South Indian family that maintained its cultural identity by upholding the traditions of the women before them. The nose-stud was part of a time-honoured family tradition. It entailed that a young woman's nose was pierced and a stud inserted when she reached physical maturity. This was an indication that she had become eligible for marriage.

The practice today, Ms Pillay explained, is meant to honour daughters as responsible young adults. When Sunali turned sixteen, her grandmother would replace the gold stud with a diamond stud. Ms Pillay claimed that this was part of a religious-related ritual to honour and bless Sunali. Above all, the nose-stud was not for fashion. Wearing it was a long-standing family tradition and for cultural reasons.

The school's policy was not absolute. The school allowed exemptions from the ban, based on religion. But Sunali's mother did not say the stud was primarily for religious reasons. She invoked culture and tradition.

Nevertheless, the school went about its next steps sensitively. It consulted recognised experts in human rights and Hindu tradition. They advised that the school was not obliged to allow Sunali to wear the nose-stud. But when the school told Sunali and her mother this, the dispute became acrimonious. People started taking sides. The Tamil Vedic cultural authorities backed Sunali's right to wear the nose-stud as part of her Tamil heritage, but the political head of education in the province, the MEC for education in KwaZulu-Natal, took a different view. He sided with the school.

So the school scheduled a disciplinary hearing for Sunali. But Sunali's mother refused to budge. She pre-empted the disciplinary process by taking the school to the equality court. This is an institution the Equality Act created in 2000 inside existing magistrates' and high courts. Presiding officers are specially designated from amongst existing judges and magistrates. They hear complaints claiming unfair discrimination in breach of the Equality Act and the Constitution's promise of equality.

The equality court heard evidence from Hindu experts that the nose-stud was an expression of Hindu culture. It was not obligatory. Though it was difficult to separate Hindu culture and Hindu religion, it was not a religious rite. On this evidence, the equality court ruled against Sunali. It found in favour of the school. Although the code discriminated against Sunali, the equality court found, this was justified. The code was designed to promote uniformity and acceptable convention amongst learners.

Ms Pillay was not impressed. She appealed to the high court. Two judges there heard the case. They were Judge-President Vuka Tshabalala and Judge Kondile. They reversed the equality court's finding. They found in favour of Sunali. They held that while the code did not discriminate directly against Sunali – because, on its face, it applied equally to all learners – it discriminated indirectly against her. This was because the nose-stud had religious or cultural significance to her. So the impact of the rule was unfairly disproportionate to those in her position. The high court took into account that Sunali was part of a group, Indian South Africans, which historically had experienced adverse discrimination. So the court ruled that the application of the code was unfair.

Now the school dug in its heels. Supported by the MEC, it turned to the Constitutional Court. But the school lost. The Constitutional Court also ruled against it. The main judgment was by Chief Justice Pius Langa – the very judge who had written so movingly to the TRC about his own experiences of being devalued by the apartheid machinery.

The question, Justice Langa said, was whether Sunali's religious or cultural beliefs or practices had been impaired. Despite uncertainty about the exact boundaries and definition of Hindu and Tamil culture, she undoubtedly belonged to an identifiable culture. It was true the stud was not compulsory. It was a voluntary expression of South Indian, Tamil or Hindu culture, but that culture was intimately intertwined with the Hindu religion.

While wearing the stud was to Sunali a voluntary religious and cultural practice, this did not mean that it was not protected under the equality legislation. On the contrary, Chief Justice Langa said, the code was discriminatory on both religious and cultural grounds. And the discrimination was unfair because the school had not taken reasonable steps to accommodate Sunali. Allowing the stud would pose no undue burden on the school. The school should have exempted her from the code.

The golden heart of the judgment appears where Justice Langa considers the school's argument that allowing Sunali to wear a nose-stud would lead to uncontainable exceptions and excesses, because other learners would claim exemptions. This was a slippery slope argument. Many more learners, the school argued, would come to school with dreadlocks, body piercings, tattoos and loincloths. At the bottom of the slope, it implied, lay chaos and lack of all discipline.

The court dismissed the argument. First, only bona fide religious and cultural practices were covered. The possibility of abuse should not affect the rights of those who genuinely wanted to express themselves. Second, Justice Langa said, 'if there are other learners who hitherto were afraid to express their religions or cultures and who will now be encouraged to do so, that is something to be celebrated, not feared. As a general rule, the more learners feel free to express their religions and cultures in school, the closer we will come to the society envisaged in the Constitution.'

Drawing on a phrase an American judge used to describe the slippery slope argument, Chief Justice Langa drove the point of the judgment home. 'The display of religion and culture in public,' he said, 'is not a "parade of horribles", but a pageant of diversity which will enrich our schools and in turn our country.'

Justice Kate O'Regan wrote separately. She would have given wider protection even than the majority. The question, she considered, was not so much sincerely held religious and cultural beliefs, but rather the need to accommodate diversity in a manner that makes all learners in the school feel that they are equally worthy and respected. She pointed out that religious beliefs had to be sincerely held. Culture, however, was different. Culture was more about associative practices and not individual beliefs. She said that the question was not whether the practice formed part of the sincerely held personal beliefs of an individual, but whether the practice was pursued by a particular cultural community. Sunali's practice qualified, and deserved protection.

VII The nose-stud case and political diversity

The nose-stud judgment was very far-going. To many, the approach of the school, supported by the MEC, did not seem unreasonable.

The school wanted uniformity, but not at any cost. Its approach was flexible, and it sought to give effect to a policy its student body and parents and school governors, including many of Indian origin, had considered and agreed. Since it allowed religious exceptions, its worry about undue proliferation of cultural expressiveness was not wildly misplaced.

Nevertheless, the judgment of Chief Justice Langa carefully unpicks each of its arguments. He explains how, in a society seriously committed to inclusiveness, conformity must yield in favour of the richness of otherness. His judgment shows how seriously the judiciary takes the Constitution's promise of diversity protection. It shows that a commitment to inclusiveness requires us to value diversity even at the cost of our own comfort and the convenience of conformity. But the judgment does more than admonish and instruct. It invites us to join the journey joyfully. As Chief Justice Langa said, the expression of diversity is 'something to be celebrated, not feared'.

Despite its generous spirit and clear rationale, the *Pillay* judgment has not been universally implemented. This emerged in May 2013 when a 13-year-old Rastafarian learner from Welkom, Free State, Lerato Hadebe, had to get a court order because her school refused to allow her to wear dreadlocks. The high court ordered the school to permit her to resume classes.

This shows the gap between the constitutional value of diversity and its realisation. Even so, the Constitutional Court has given resonant effect to *Pillay*'s wider implications. Diversity is not only decorative. It is also a constitutional principle with a strong political bite. In a judgment delivered in a very different context five years later, in October 2012, the Constitutional Court upheld the right of individual members of Parliament to introduce legislation as private members' bills, without first getting the approval of a (majority-dominated) sifting committee. The judgment found every private member was entitled to introduce legislation.

To get to this conclusion, Chief Justice Mogoeng, who wrote on behalf of a unanimous court, used a purposive approach. This meant that to understand the provision in the Constitution dealing with private members' bills, he tried to see the point of the provision in the structure of the entire Constitution.

He found that the proper approach to the provision was to recognise that individual legislation accords with the principles of multi-party democracy. This was because the very nature and composition of Parliament renders it a national forum at which even individual members, without majority-party approval, may initiate legislative proposals. Under the Constitution, everyone had a right to be heard and have their views considered. In the legislative process, this meant that individual members ought to have the power to initiate or prepare legislation. This, Justice Mogoeng said, would enrich our representative and participatory democracy.

In the course of this reasoning, Chief Justice Mogoeng issued a powerful statement. His words located exactly the political implications of the constitutional commitment to diversity. He said:

'Ours is a constitutional democracy that is designed to ensure that the voiceless are heard, and that even those of us who would, given a choice, have preferred not to entertain the views of the marginalised or the powerless minorities, listen.'

Diversity is about listening. The Constitution ensures that we hear. It is our choice to do so joyfully.

VIII The broken promises, and the hope, of constitutional diversity

Making the Constitution's promise of equality real for black people, for women and for other formerly oppressed groups, including lesbians and gays, has not been easy. It has in fact proved a rough journey. Sexual violence against women is still rife. Lesbians in particular are vulnerable – especially lesbians living in townships, where a macho violent culture has led to horrific rapes and murders.

This has led some people, including activists in the lesbian and gay community, to question the value of constitutional protection. We have constitutional rights. We have protection against unfair discrimination. Since 2006 we have even had the right to marry. But if the promise of constitutional equality cannot protect lesbians from rape and murder, of what value is it to anyone?

This scepticism is well directed, for it is rooted in a well-warranted scepticism about legal rights and constitutionalism. On their own, they cannot right society. We need far more than rights. To protect women, including lesbians, we need concerted, well-directed and efficient action from police detectives to prosecutors to district surgeons to court officials and judges. In this our administration of justice is grievously failing.

So we also need assertive communities, and independent civil society groups, speaking loudly, and acting strongly.

Yet scepticism about the meaning of our constitutional change is often overstated. Ground-breaking research by Graeme Reid into LGBTI communities in small-town South Africa has shown a new sense of belonging, of citizenship, that comes from 'a new emancipation'. This has resulted from the abolition of laws that were oppressive in terms of race, and equally importantly, sexual orientation. So rights are vitally important, and vitally necessary.

Yet in June 2012, a young man, Thapelo Makhutle, who identified as both gay and as transgender, was horrifically murdered in the remote Northern Cape town of Kuruman. I remember seeing television coverage of Thapelo's alleged killer's appearance in court. Thapelo's friends, neighbours and family turned out in force to express their grief and anger at the unspeakable violence done to his young life. On my television screen during the evening news, an elderly woman appeared. She had a blanket wrapped round her waist, for it was winter. She appeared to be from a working-class, township background. She could have been Thapelo's mother, or his aunt, or his neighbour. Perhaps his grandmother. Or someone who had helped care for him as a baby.

She held up a placard. It read: 'GAY RIGHTS ARE HUMAN RIGHTS'.

Similar placards now appear at the funerals of lesbians murdered because of their sexual orientation, and at the trials of their alleged rapists and killers.

The Constitution failed Thapelo, as it is failing vulnerable lesbians, and many oppressed groups. It has not secured the promise of equality and safety and dignity. But it has brought out the neighbours and families and loved ones of those injured by hatred to protest on their behalf, and to express their commitment to a society that is truly inclusive of difference and truly accepting of minorities.

It has helped all South Africans understand and embrace our diversity as people, and our equal entitlement to rights, if together we are to build a just society. In this way, the Constitution lights the path to that just society. And it has started by giving each one of us, rural and urban, working class or affluent, township or suburban, the knowledge that we are included in the moral project of constitutionalism. In this way, the Constitution has helped all of us to a richer understanding and acceptance of our own complexity as humans. We have a long way to go. But, if only we recognise it, we have started on a vitally important journey.

Chapter Six

Poverty, Social Justice and the Constitution

I A random act of kindness

Two years after Laura's death, when Jeanie and I had returned to the children's home in Queenstown, my mother moved back to Bloemfontein, where she had lived as a child and married my father, and where her daughters were born. She found a job in the municipality's typing pool. She took it to be closer to us. The home provided only one train ticket a year, every December, for children to visit their families. Living in Bloemfontein halved the distance from Pretoria. This made it easier for her to travel down to Queenstown in the middle of the year to see us.

The December holiday after she moved we spent with her, at her lodgings in a boarding house on Kellner Street. This was a few short blocks' walk from where she worked in the city hall, a sandstone edifice on President Brand Street, directly across from the appeal court. That building's monumental pillars and imposing pediment and facade impressed me, but I hardly thought about it. The lawyers who practised there, and the judges who decided cases inside it, seemed to occupy an unimaginably different world – a world of intellectual endeavour and of civic engagement and of respectability and of material abundance. I was not in any position even to dream of one day joining it.

Money was desperately tight. The removal and travel costs had to be repaid. My mother had no formal schooling beyond standard six (grade eight), and the municipality must have started her on the lowest grading for a white worker. Her salary was pitiably small. We spent a straitened Christmas, glad to be at home, away from Queenstown, but with no treats or frills. We went to no shops because there was no shopping to be done.

Jeanie and I played with the Wepeners, Anne and Richard and Martin, also home from Queenstown for December. They lived in a flat in Chembro House on busy Zastron Street. As often as we could, in Bloemfontein's baking summer heat, we visited the municipal swimming baths at the top end of West Burger Street, in the lee of Naval Hill, where admission was two and a half cents. The Wepeners' testy grandfather, who lived with them, would sometimes give us ten cents to see us through.

We lived unburdened by any sense of grievance or self-pity. On the contrary, we knew we were lucky. We had a roof over our heads, as my mother often reminded us, and beds to sleep in. And we ate every day, sparsely, but sufficiently. At the home in Queens-town, too, the ambience our supervisors cultivated was one of respectful gratitude – to the congregants who dropped money into the collection plates in Presbyterian churches across the coun-try, helping to sustain the institution, and to the benefactors who over weekends would sometimes unexpectedly arrive at the gates to deliver cream cakes, or wooden boxes of soda drinks, for us to feast on.

Regularly we were reminded that many were far worse off than we were. And indeed we knew it. Far from decrying our circum-stances, Jeanie and I focused our hopes on the future, in par-ticular on my father. Though my mother had now divorced him a second time (the first was before I was born; they remarried shortly before we moved to Pietermaritzburg, when I was eighteen months old), skilled white artisans were in high demand (job reservation forbad training black artisans). Losing his job in Pieter-maritzburg was surely what precipitated our family catastrophe. If he started work again, he would command a ready wage. If only Dad could keep a steady job, everything would change.

My mother kept us hopeful, too. She spoke of things on which she pinned her dreams. One was getting us out of the children's home. Another was finding Daphne, the third daughter, given away in adoption in Bloemfontein in September 1951, before I was born, when she was just four months old. Where was she now? How was she? In the aftermath of Laura's death, my mother pined unceasingly.

And then there was her dream of getting me into a 'good' school. It had to be one of the elite government boys' high schools – Grey College in Bloemfontein, King Edward School in Johannesburg, which my father had attended until standard eight (grade ten), or Pretoria Boys' High. Getting me a good education would change things. The future would be different.

In the meantime, poverty in itself was no cause for complaint.

Then one day in January, just before Jeanie and I were due to return to Queenstown, something extraordinary happened. It was Jeanie's thirteenth birthday, the twelfth of January, the day after my mother's, the very day on which two years before Laura had met her death. Jeanie and I were at Kellner Street while my mother was at work. There was no money for any form of cele-bration.

There was a knock at the door. Outside, in the hallway of the boarding house, stood a smartly dressed, attractive woman in her thirties or early forties. Expensively dressed and well made up, she exuded an air of polish. I remember her elegant shoes and handbag. I think she was wearing gloves. Her hair was pulled up and tied back in the style of the time.

Her manner belied her polish. It was diffident. She seemed

232

slightly ill at ease, almost nervous. Hurriedly, she addressed me in Afrikaans. Was this where the Camerons lived? Yes, I said. She had something for us. *Dankie*, I said. She handed me a plain un-addressed envelope. Then she took her leave. The envelope in my hand, I watched her walk to the gate and drive off, without glancing back, in an expensive-looking car.

I went inside and handed the envelope to Jeanie. We couldn't contain our curiosity. We looked inside. Its sole content was a ten-rand note. We were amazed. Jubilant. Ten rands! We couldn't believe what had befallen us. The note was crisp and crinkly to our touch. Who was the woman? Where was she from? How did she know us? And why had she done this? What could have led her to see so piercingly into our circumstances?

We had answers to none of these questions. All we knew was that a deliberate act of giving had intruded deep into our lives.

We waited, excited, for my mother to return from work. When she did, she shared our delight at the unexpected windfall, but she could cast no light on our questions. Apart from my account, we had no clues, and my mother could add nothing to the puzzle. So we turned instead to planning how to spend the money. There were many essentials my mother needed, and much that Jeanie and I needed, by way of clothes and toiletries and items for the new school year. For all of these, the money, as my mother put it, was a godsend.

But for now we postponed the practical necessities. Instead, we agreed that first we would visit a cake shop up the road. It closed only at 6, so there was time for Jeanie and me to get there. We chose a lavish cream cake. I still remember the cheer this brought us, carrying the cake delicately home, in its thin white cardboard cake box, and displaying it proudly on the table in the Kellner Street room, before tucking into it. We had a cake for Jeanie's birthday!

The next day, when my mother went to work, she allowed us to go out to make further purchases, for the room and for our return to Queenstown. Jeanie and I walked around Bloemfontein's shops with an air of excited capacitation. We could afford to consider, afford to choose, afford to buy.

I have no accurate notion of what the equivalent today of those ten rands is. But I remember the purchase of the cream cake required less than R2 – under one-fifth of the money. A similar cake at a home enterprise store today costs easily R80. On this calculus, the anonymous woman's gift would today be worth four or five hundred rands. A website that calculates the effect of officially recorded inflation on nominal rand values suggests somewhat more – R686 in current values.

But my imagination jibs at how small both these sums seem. My mind wants the equivalent figure to come out in thousands, for the effect of those ten rands on our lives, and our spirits, was inexpressibly greater. Apart from transforming Jeanie's birthday, and easing our material circumstances in much-needed practical ways, it left a residue that has deeply shaped my political consciousness.

My young life often benefited from charity. Soon after I gained admission to Pretoria Boys' High, early one evening my mother and I received an unexpected visit at our flat in Sunnyside. It was one of the school's administrators. He explained that he was a trustee of a discreet fund the school operated for needy families. I suspect he was directed to us by Hugo Ackermann, the maths and Latin teacher I encountered when I joined Form 2, who took me under his wing and became my guiding mentor, and whose whole family, including that of his older brother Laurie, later my colleague at the Constitutional Court, took me into its bosom.

That evening, the trustee gave my mother and me a small but welcome hand-out. I remember what we did with the money.

We bought a second summer school shirt and a second pair of khaki shorts from the school's officially designated shop in Paul Kruger Street; until then, we'd been rinsing out my only set overnight. From time to time over the next years, that gesture was quietly repeated. It enabled me to attend a school whose boys overwhelmingly came from the affluent upper-middle-class homes of Brooklyn, Lynnwood and Waterkloof, without the potential embarrassment of patent need.

But what remains most deeply imprinted on my mind are not these later hand-outs, whose beneficence touched us through the anonymous mechanism of a fund. What lingers most vividly is the unnamed woman's mysterious act of personal generosity. It left me deeply under the impression of how important acts of interventive kindness are.

I appreciate the argument that, to remedy social injustice, charity is no substitute for political action. In the abstract, this is undeniable, but there is no reason why charity cannot exist alongside political action. Indeed, unless social justice can be realised instantaneously – and we know, sadly, that it cannot – benefaction now is as imperative as political change in due course.

The argument that charity is a diverting balm that soothes the need for change, and must thus be decried because it discourages radical political action, strikes me as absurdly abstract, indeed cruel. Of course we all need a good public education, and not charity, to help us out of poverty. That was my great good fortune, as a poor white youngster: to gain entrance to one of the country's – perhaps one of the world's – best government-funded schools. Of course we all need political and social incentives that provide tertiary education and generate jobs, rather than hand-outs. And I was privileged indeed, on the basis of my skin colour, to have access to education and job opportunities.

But I also got hand-outs – graciously given, most gratefully

235

accepted hand-outs. Distributional interventions that changed my life. Their impact was intense and enduring. Until the practical benefits of good education, good opportunities and good jobs arrive for everyone – and in my case, they did, in time to make a difference to my life – we all need the caring and generosity of others. We all need gestures of the exhilaratingly practical and redemptive kind the nameless woman intruded onto my mother's and Jeanie's and my straitened lives in Bloemfontein in January 1963.

More importantly, we need a government that, on behalf of all of us, expresses that loving care and concern toward our fellows. More specifically, we need a government that is constitutionally obliged to do so.

This is precisely what the Constitution gives us in South Africa.

II Social justice, remedial measures and the Constitution

At the end of apartheid, the lines dividing poor and rich in South Africa were drawn almost entirely along racial lines. Whites were mostly well off, and blacks were mostly poor. It was not difficult to see that massive shifts in the allocation of public resources would be needed to undo the racial segmentation of social opportunity in our country.

That is after all what the apartheid government and its predecessors did for whites. From the 1930s government intervention, sustained over many decades, came close to eradicating the poor white problem. As a poor white, I profited from this. The public resources lavished on Pretoria Boys' High and on Stellenbosch University, both prestige institutions for whites only, gave me a first-rate education that enabled me to get a Rhodes Scholarship, to study at Oxford and to embark on a legal career. My life benefited directly and dramatically from racially directed, racially exclusive social intervention programmes. I was a white beneficiary of affirmative action.

The drafters of our Constitution understood this history acutely. That is why the equality clause in the Bill of Rights, section 9, expressly envisages differential measures to achieve equality in our country.

Section 9 is divided into five sub-sections. The first enshrines a dramatic promise. It says that 'Everyone is equal before the law and has the right to equal protection and benefit of the law'. The second sub-section, section 9(2), elaborates this. It has two parts. The first specifies that 'Equality includes the full and equal enjoyment of all rights and freedoms'. But the second carries a very practical rider. It says that 'To promote the achievement of equality, legislative and other measures designed to protect or advance persons, or categories of persons, disadvantaged by unfair discrimination, may be taken'.

The third sub-section, section 9(3), prohibits unfair discrimination by the state. All forms of unfair discrimination are prohibited. But the provision lists eighteen grounds on which it is explicitly prohibited. Here our Constitution made legal history: we became the first country anywhere expressly to list sexual orientation as a ground protected against discrimination.

Section 9(4) extends the prohibition on discriminating unfairly beyond only the state. It extends the ban to everyone else. It says that 'no person' may unfairly discriminate against anyone on the prohibited grounds. And it directed Parliament to enact legislation to give effect to this prohibition. The Equality Act of 2000 was the result.

The fifth sub-section of the equality clause goes back to the eighteen expressly protected grounds. It creates what lawyers call an onus or burden of proof. This means that one side in a dispute in court carries the burden of proving a fact or a consideration. Cases are often decided simply because one party or another cannot prove some essential fact or issue. So an onus is practically very important.

Section 9(5) is thus vital to the practical impact of unfair discrimination law. It says that discrimination on the grounds expressly listed is unfair 'unless it is established that the discrimination is fair'. This means that if you prove discrimination on the ground of age, race, culture, sexual orientation or any other listed ground, the person responsible for discriminating then bears the duty to show to the court that the discriminatory treatment is fair.

But the most interesting and enigmatic part of the Constitution's equality promises stands in section 9(2). This explains that equality includes full and equal enjoyment of all rights and freedoms. It then specifies that, to promote this vision of equality, special measures may be taken for those who suffered past disadvantage. This provision encapsulates the paradox at the centre of affirmative action. To achieve full and equal enjoyment of the Constitution's rights and freedoms, measures have to be taken to undo the unpalatable inequities of the past. This provision was necessary because the Constitution did not happen onto a virgin landscape. On the contrary. It was designed to bring healing and repair to a very un-virgin landscape – one ravaged by a past that for centuries had deliberately and exclusively privileged whites. Without remedial action, it would be impossible to begin the task to which the Preamble of the Constitution commits us, namely, to 'heal the divisions of the past and establish a society based on democratic values, social justice and fundamental human rights'.

III The Constitutional Court decides its first affirmative action case

Ten years after the start of the constitutional era, the Constitutional Court had a chance to explain the remedial mission of the

Constitution. The case was the first the court heard in its beautiful, light-filled building on Constitution Hill in Braamfontein. The case concerned not broad-based affirmative action, but elite entitlements, so its focus and its impact were limited. Nevertheless, the case gave the court the opportunity to spell out important insights about remedial action and constitutionalism.

The issue was pensions. Those whose pensions were at stake were the members of the first democratic Parliament and other political office-bearers from 1994 to 1999. The political office-bearers' fund Parliament created after 1994 drew a distinction between those who had entered Parliament before 1994, and those who entered after democracy. It provided for higher employer contributions for post-1994 members. It did so because in late 1993, just before it became defunct, the outgoing apartheid Parliament passed a law securing pension benefits for its members, in a closed pension fund. New members of Parliament in the incoming democratic Parliament could not belong and did not enjoy its benefits.

Mr Van Heerden was a National Party MP. He had been elected to the apartheid Parliament during the 1987 election and had remained in office over the transition, becoming an MP in the first democratic Parliament in 1994. As a member of the democratic Parliament, he took exception to the new pension rules. They specially benefited newly elected MPs. He pointed out that this was discriminatory. Under the rules, until 1999, he and other pre-1994 parliamentarians received lower employer contributions to their pensions than new MPs. So their pension payouts would be far smaller. Post-1994 MPs would receive substantially larger payouts for the period 1994-1999 than those who became MPs pre-1994. This, he said, breached the constitutional promise of equality.

Mr Van Heerden went to court to challenge the pension fund

rule. The high court in Cape Town ruled in his favour. The judge found the differentiation impermissible. He invoked the onus in section 9(5). He said it applied to the 'advancement measures' clause, section 9(2). On this approach, government, the party responsible for the differentiation, had the duty to prove that it was not unfair. And government had not done so. In addition, it failed to establish that the differential contributions were designed to promote equality. The court therefore declared the differentiations invalid.

The Minister of Finance, who administered the pension fund, took this on appeal to the Constitutional Court. The court reversed the Cape High Court decision. It found in favour of the Minister. It did so unanimously, though the judges differed in their approach. Some judges, a minority, thought that the matter should not be approached as a question of remedial measures under section 9(2). It was, they considered, a case of discrimination, under section 9(3), which was not, however, unfair.

The majority differed. It considered that the case raised questions about remedial measures. Justice Moseneke wrote the main judgment. He made the important finding that the onus in section 9(5) does not apply to 'advancement measures'. In other words, where government takes measures under section 9(2) to protect or advance persons, or categories of persons, disadvantaged by unfair discrimination, the law does not presume that the measures are unfair unless government succeeds in proving that they are not.

Justice Moseneke's reasoning was succinct. How could the Constitution expressly authorise measures to redress past inequality, but just a few lines later, virtually in the same breath, label them presumptively unfair? That would be illogical. Freed of the onus, the inquiry into the constitutionality of the measures was much narrower. It was simply a question of whether they could properly be slotted in under section 9(2). In other words, there were just three questions: Did the measures target persons or categories disadvantaged by unfair discrimination? Were they designed to protect or advance these persons or categories? And did they promote the achievement of equality? If so, there was no onus resting on government to prove that they were fair.

Justice Moseneke held that the differentiation in the pension fund rules met all three criteria. Clearly, the differentiation targeted post-1994 parliamentarians. These persons were disadvantaged because they could not benefit from the special pension arrangements the outgoing apartheid Parliament had set up in 1993. And, equally clearly, the measures were designed to protect or advance this category of persons. Since the future was hard to predict, government didn't have to prove that they actually would protect or advance this group – it only had to show this was reasonably likely.

Lastly, he found that the pension fund measures did promote the achievement of equality. And here lay the heart of his judgment. The goal of equality, he explained, 'goes to the bedrock of our constitutional architecture'. Achieving equality is not only a practically enforceable right – it is also a core value. It is a standard against which everything else must be tested for constitutional consonance.

Justice Moseneke took time to explain why achieving equality preoccupies our constitutional thinking. When the Constitution took effect, South Africa was deeply divided, vastly unequal and uncaring of human worth. The commitment of the Preamble is to restore and protect the equal worth of everyone, to heal the divisions of the past and to establish a caring and socially just society. The Constitution, he said, explicitly commits us to 'improve the quality of life of all citizens and free the potential of each person'.

Our supreme law, he pointed out, says more about equality than comparable constitutions of other countries. Like those, it confers well-known rights, including equal protection and benefit of the law, and non-discrimination. But our Constitution goes further. It also imposes a positive duty on all organs of state to protect and promote the achievement of equality. And the point is that this obligation rests also on the judiciary. So judges, as much as Parliament and the executive, are constitutionally obliged to promote the achievement of equality.

Commitment to a society based on social justice, Justice Moseneke stated, is as crucial as the very democratic values that underlie the Constitution. In this way, he said, the Constitution 'heralds not only equal protection of the law and non-discrimination but also the start of a credible and abiding process of reparation for past exclusion, dispossession, and indignity within the discipline of our constitutional framework'.

Given our country's history, and the Constitution's broad sweep, the conception of equality it embodies 'goes beyond mere formal equality and mere non-discrimination'. This meant it was wrong-headed to require identical treatment, whatever the starting point or impact. (Justice Moseneke implied, but didn't explicitly say, that the high court judge had gone about it in this wrong way.)

The judgment thus cast wide open the door for redress measures. Government does not bear even the burden of proving that these measures are fair. What then are the limits of constitutional redress? Justice Moseneke's judgment sets important boundaries.

First, he said, it must be accepted that achieving equality may often come at a price for those who were previously advantaged. This meant that pre-1994 MPs serving in the post-1994 Parliament would get less than new MPs. But he sounded a warning about this kind of cost. It should not be blithely accepted. Our long-term goal, he emphasised, is a non-racial, non-sexist society in which everyone is recognised as of equal worth and dignity. Central to this vision, he said, is our diversity as a society, which the Constitution celebrates and protects.

With this in mind, he said, a remedial measure 'should not constitute an abuse of power or impose such substantial and undue harm on those excluded from its benefits that our long-term constitutional goal would be threatened'.

In the light of this assessment, the outcome of the case was not hard to divine. The differentiation was to ameliorate past disadvantage. It was a practically designed and well-focused scheme. It was correct that Mr Van Heerden would receive less pension. But he and his fellow pre-1994 parliamentarians, with the benefit of their exclusive pre-democracy pension benefits, 'remain a privileged class of public pension beneficiaries'. He and those in his position were not vulnerable or marginalised. They had not been excluded or discriminated against in the past. The case therefore had to be dismissed.

The judgment's pronouncement on the limits of redress schemes is important. It entails that if a remedial scheme adversely affects a 'vulnerable or marginalised' group, it may overstep a constitutional limit. It opens the door to remedial schemes to protect disadvantaged groups and to promote equality, but it also signals important limits. If a scheme is an abuse of power, or imposes excessive harm on those excluded from its benefits, the court may strike it down as unconstitutional.

The *Van Heerden* judgment was about a narrow issue. It concerned a very small group of public office-bearers. And it dealt with only their pension rights. This means that the big 'affirmative action' cases have yet to reach the Constitutional Court. The court has not yet spelled out in detail what 'disadvantage' is, what a 'category' of persons is. Is it race? Is it class? Nor has the court spelled out in detail how the design of the measures must tie in with the objective of attaining equality.

Future cases will bring these issues for decision. An exciting and interesting time lies ahead for litigants, and for the judges charged with the responsibility of deciding their cases. What *Van Heerden* makes clear is that the Constitution's overall values, and its fundamental goal of valuing difference while promoting equality, provide a firm framework for clear-headed, just judicial decisions.

IV 'First-order rights', social rights and the promise of equality

The parliamentary pension benefits judgment emphasises how far-going, indeed radical, the Constitution's commitment to equality is. Its conception of equality is not an empty vision, nor is it merely formal. It is a practical goal that must be realised in substantive terms. That means it must be brought about in ways that make an appreciable impact on people's lives.

In this, as *Van Heerden* points out, the South African Constitution goes further than other countries' foundational documents. The Canadian constitution, which provided a helpful template for our Bill of Rights, doesn't go as far as our Constitution in committing government, executive and courts to a practically achievable equality goal.

But our Constitution does even more. The Constitution's drafters saw beyond only grand promises of equality. They saw that it was essential to include a promise of material rights that make it practically possible to enjoy equality. They saw that, in themselves, rights may be empty. A famous aphorism was present to their minds. It was a saying about the majestic equality of the law – which forbids the rich as well as the poor from sleeping under bridges, from begging in the streets, and from stealing bread.

Apartheid cynically hollowed out the rule of law's promises of equality and fairness and dignity. The drafters were determined that the Constitution would be different. It would not give stones where bread was asked. It would nourish where needed.

Hence, to the substantive right to equality, the Constitution adds a raft of social and economic entitlements. This was the biggest shift between the interim Constitution and the final Constitution. The interim Constitution contained no social and economic rights. It contained only what are called 'first-order rights'. These are rights that mostly guard against governmental interference in what we may say or do. They include rights of free speech, religion, conscience, association and movement. They prohibit government from interfering in how we express ourselves and live our lives.

The final Constitution goes further than recognising only these rights. It includes socio-economic or welfare rights. These are not rights that say what government may not do. They are rights that say what it must do.

This followed hard bargaining and much deliberation in the Constitutional Assembly. Negotiators on all sides had misgivings about including this category of rights. One reason was that judges' skills are limited. Are judges properly suited to the job of enforcing social and economic rights? After all, judges have no wisdom or experience in determining how to fulfil people's social needs. They are trained as lawyers. Lawyers fight contested cases. Litigation mostly reaches judges in the form of two-sided disputes, where opposing litigants urge opposite sides of the case before the Bench. Then it falls to the judge or judges to decide who is right, and who is wrong.

Judges have skills in deciding the meaning of language, in

determining right and wrong as between contesting parties, in applying precedents (previous binding decisions) to the case before them. They don't have the skills, and they lack the resources, to take multi-faceted decisions. They do not have the means to consider properly what budgets should prioritise, how budgets should be tweaked, what should be built, or where.

With social rights, a solution either for or against one party will inevitably have consequences for other decisions and priorities. Hence these rights require a broad focus, and not only the rights and wrongs as they emerge from two opposing parties' contradictory contentions.

Another concern about socio-economic rights stemmed from the separation of powers. This is the doctrine we encountered in chapter four, that distributes the power of the state between its three branches, the legislature, the executive and the judiciary. Each branch has its own skills, and its own tasks. Did the separation of powers allow for judges to pass judgment on, and give orders about, the implementation of social and economic rights?

Like the concern about judges' skills, this anxiety flowed from the fact that socio-economic rights require courts to direct the way government allocates state resources. This worry was less about whether judges could do this properly than about whether politically the judiciary is the proper branch of government to do so.

Granting remedies in socio-economic rights litigation always has significant budgetary and policy implications. A case about the right to housing inevitably means that courts exercise power to specify how other branches of government distribute their resources. This makes Parliament's and the executive's budgetary allocations and other policy decisions vulnerable to judicial intervention.

Why is this unacceptable? The answer lies partly in democratic theory. The judiciary is not elected. And its job is not to represent the people. Its job is to decide their rights. Besides, the judges who compose the judiciary are not representative. The argument accordingly was that it is not democratically legitimate for courts to make decisions of this kind.

But those pleading for the inclusion of social and economic rights won the argument. The final Constitution included social and economic entitlements against government. And it gave the courts power to issue rulings about whether government was fulfilling those rights.

And rightly so. The objections to socio-economic rights are not persuasive. The difference critics make between 'first-order rights' – those guaranteeing freedom from government bossiness – and social and economic rights – those demanding that government act – is exaggerated. All rights require government action. And all rights involve budgets.

The most obvious example is the right to vote. The franchise is fundamental to all democratic rights. A rights-based society can barely exist without it. Yet any court order requiring government to hold elections, or directing government to hold them fairly, has immediate budgetary implications. It requires government to take steps and to prepare budgets and to spend money. Yet those opposed to including social and economic rights in rights charters agree that the right to vote is a 'first-order right'. However, if the courts are to be able to enforce this right, we must accept that their orders have budgetary consequences. This shows that the distinction is muddled.

After President Kgalema Motlanthe appointed me permanently to the Constitutional Court at the end of 2008, I saw this clearly in one of the first cases I sat in, in February 2009. The case concerned the rights of registered voters who were staying or travelling abroad. Were they entitled to cast a special vote at a South African embassy or consulate? The electoral legislation said No.

It made very narrow exceptions for those abroad on government service – mainly diplomats – but heavily restricted other categories who could apply for special votes while overseas.

Several voters and political parties challenged the restrictions. The court gave them an expedited ruling. It held unanimously that the restrictions unreasonably limited the right to vote. They were therefore unconstitutional and invalid. Government was obliged to make it possible for all registered voters abroad to vote, provided they signalled that they wished to do so. The narrow, exclusionary categories in the statute were struck down. This judgment entailed significant budgetary outlay. The Electoral Commission's budgets had to be expanded. Government had to provide the extra money. Extra ballot papers had to be printed. They had to be flown overseas, to scores of embassies and consulates – perhaps over a hundred. And at almost every South African legation abroad, diplomats and electoral officials had to be placed on duty to make sure that polling could take place. Voters had to be able to exercise the most fundamental right in a democracy.

So the worry about judges meddling with budgets is real, but over-stated. Every court order affects budgets in some way. First-order rights are no exception.

Much more on point was the concern that judges aren't properly trained, and that the judiciary isn't the right branch of government to decide how to spend public money. In the *TAC* case, the Constitutional Court itself acknowledged the limits of what judges can properly do in the area of social and economic rights. Courts are ill-suited to adjudicate issues, it said, where their orders could have multiple social and economic consequences. Hence, it explained, the Constitution contemplates rather a restrained and focused role for the courts. This is only to evaluate whether the measures government is taking to meet its constitutional obligations are reasonable. Courts' decisions may of course have budgetary implications. But in themselves they are not directed at rearranging budgets. In this way, the court explained, the judicial, legislative and executive functions achieve appropriate constitutional balance.

V Social and economic rights in the South African Constitution

This approach follows from the way in which social and economic rights were included in the Constitution. The rights, and judicial supervision of them, were crafted with particular care.

The rights include adequate housing, health care, food, water and social security, as well as education. In addition, the Bill of Rights provides that everyone has the right to an environment that is not harmful to their health or well-being, and to have the environment protected, for the benefit of present and future generations.

But the rights aren't granted absolutely. They are given as rights of access. Thus, everyone has *a right of access* to adequate housing and other social benefits. Access means the door must be opened. It does not mean that the right must be granted immediately.

Children's rights are different. They are not stated as rights of access. The children's rights provision in the Bill of Rights, section 28, says that children must be provided with certain rights without qualification. It provides, outright, that every child has the right to basic nutrition, shelter, basic health care services and social services. Fulfilment of the right is not offered step-wise or postponed.

In addition, the right to basic education is expressed differently from the other socio-economic rights. Section 29 says simply that everyone has the right to a basic education, including adult basic education. Again, fulfilment of this right is not promised step by step. It is promised immediately. By contrast, the right to education beyond the basic stage – the right to further education – is expressed in the same way as the other social and economic rights. Further education, beyond the basic, is only a graduated entitlement. Section 29 says that everyone has the right to further education, and that the state, through reasonable measures, must make this right progressively available and accessible.

One further right is absolutely expressed. Section 27(3) says flatly that 'No one may be refused emergency medical treatment'. This means that private medical facilities cannot turn emergency cases away. In practice, they give emergency patients sufficient care to stabilise them, then refer them to state hospitals.

But each of the other rights of access to social and economic entitlements is promised only step by step. These are the rights to adequate housing, health care, food, water and social security. In each case, the Bill of Rights couples the right of access with a duty clause that shows how the right must be realised. This explains what government's responsibilities are in fulfilling the right. Each of the duty clauses says that the state must take reasonable legislative and other measures, within its available resources, to achieve the progressive realisation of each of these rights.

The environmental right is somewhat differently phrased. The Bill of Rights provides that everyone has the right to an environment that is not harmful to their health or well-being. This is a very general promise, without visible teeth. But, in addition, the Bill of Rights provides that everyone has the right to have the environment protected, for the benefit of present and future generations, 'through reasonable legislative and other measures'. These measures must prevent pollution and ecological degradation, promote conservation, and secure ecologically sustainable development and use of natural resources while promoting justifiable economic and social development.

These duty clauses in each case require only that government must take reasonable measures. This means that the courts don't determine government's budgets. In this area, as Justice Kate O'Regan explained in a famous ruling about the right of access to water, *Mazibuko*, courts do 'not seek to draft policy or to determine its content'. They decide only whether government, when it drafts its policies and decides on their content, is acting reasonably to fulfil the rights in question.

But how does this work in practice? The first two socio-economic rights cases that came before the Constitutional Court provide vivid answers to the question.

Given the intricate way in which the Bill of Rights qualified the socio-economic rights, and the high hopes everyone in South Africa pinned on democracy, the first rulings were awaited with very high expectation. And the first two judgments both proved controversial.

VI The right to life and the right of access to health care

The Constitutional Court's most famous judgment on the right of access to health care was the Nevirapine case, *Minister of Health v TAC*. There it gave a far-reaching order requiring government to start making anti-retroviral treatment available. Chapter four discussed that dramatic decision and its implications. But more than four years before, the court gave its first ruling on socio-economic rights. It, too, involved the right of access to health care – and it also involved a drama of life and death.

It was a judgment delivered at the end of 1997, not quite ten months after the final Constitution came into effect. The case was brought by a 41-year-old Durban man, Mr Thiagraj Soobramoney.

Mr Soobramoney was severely ill. He was a diabetic who suffered from ischaemic heart disease and cerebro-vascular disease. The previous year this caused him to have a stroke. In 1996 his kidneys also failed. All these health conditions were irreversible.

The court heard Mr Soobramoney's case in early November. By then he was in the final stages of chronic renal failure. His life could be prolonged by means of regular renal dialysis. Dialysis is a technology that removes impurities by passing a patient's blood through a machine that does the work of the kidneys when the kidneys are no longer functioning properly.

Mr Soobramoney needed dialysis, and he needed it badly. He needed it so he could go on living. But government policy on dialysis denied him access to it. He didn't qualify. He then made arrangements to receive dialysis from private hospitals and doctors, but he was unemployed and his finances were soon exhausted. He and his family could no longer afford to pay for private treatment. He needed publicly funded health care to be able to live.

In July 1997 Mr Soobramoney brought an urgent application before the high court in Durban. His claim was based on the brand-new constitutional right to health care, freshly included in the final Constitution, which came into effect on 4 February 1997. More specifically, he based his claim on section 27(3), which provides that 'No one may be refused emergency medical treatment'. Mr Soobramoney also invoked section 11. This stipulates that 'Everyone has the right to life'.

He pointed to Addington Hospital, a public health facility on the Durban beachfront. Addington had dialysis machines. He claimed that under his right to emergency medical treatment, and his right to life, the hospital was obliged to make dialysis available to him. So he asked the high court to order the hospital to do so.

The government health authorities opposed. Dr Saraladevi Naicker testified for the health department. She was a distinguished specialist physician sub-specialising in nephrology (the branch of internal medicine dealing with the kidneys). She had worked at Addington for eighteen years. At the time of the litigation, she was president of the South African Renal Society.

She explained that kidney dialysis is an extremely expensive procedure, so it has to be rationed carefully. The KZN provincial health department carefully formulated a policy to do just this. She explained that Addington did not have enough resources to provide dialysis for all patients suffering from chronic renal failure. Its renal unit had to serve the whole of KZN, and also take patients from parts of the Eastern Cape. Additional dialysis machines and more trained nursing staff were needed to help patients like Mr Soobramoney – but the hospital budget did not provide for this. So he could not be helped.

Addington, Dr Naicker said, wanted a bigger budget. But the provincial health department had said funds were not available. Hence the hospital's policy rationed dialysis. Only patients who suffered from acute renal failure that could be treated and remedied by renal dialysis were given automatic access. Those patients who suffered from chronic renal failure that was irreversible were not admitted automatically to the renal programme.

Mr Soobramoney's kidney failure was irreversible. The question was whether his case fell within the guidelines for patients in his position. Those specified that the primary requirement for patients with irreversible chronic renal failure to get onto the dialysis programme was that they must be eligible for a kidney transplant. A patient so eligible would be given dialysis until an organ donor was found, and a kidney transplant completed.

Under these guidelines, Mr Soobramoney would be eligible for a kidney transplant only if he were free of 'significant vascular or cardiac disease'. The medical criteria in the guidelines also provided that a patient had to be free of significant disease elsewhere. This meant the patient should not have ischaemic heart disease, cerebro-vascular disease, peripheral vascular disease, chronic liver disease or chronic lung disease.

All of this sadly excluded Mr Soobramoney. He was not free of other disease. On the contrary, his body was riven with illnesses. He was not eligible for a kidney transplant and so he could not qualify for dialysis.

On the basis of this detailed explanation, the high court refused Mr Soobramoney's prayer. The court found government had 'conclusively proved' that there were no funds available to provide patients in the position of Mr Soobramoney with treatment.

Mr Soobramoney took his case on urgent appeal to the Constitutional Court and the case was heard on 11 November 1997. Its judgment was delivered sixteen days later, on 27 November. Like the high court, it refused to intervene in Mr Soobramoney's favour. Two days later, on 29 November, Mr Soobramoney died. In the wake of this tragedy, the court's decision was strongly criticised. Many commentators thought the court should have forced the KZN health authorities to help Mr Soobramoney, that the court should have saved his life.

But, despite the critics' strictures, looking back after more than fifteen years, it is hard to see how else the court could have ruled. Before the Constitutional Court, Mr Soobramoney's argument focused on the right not to be refused emergency medical treatment. But the court found against him on this. It held that the purpose of the right was to ensure that treatment be given in an emergency, without being frustrated by bureaucratic requirements or other formalities. A person who suffers a sudden catastrophe that calls for immediate medical attention should not be refused ambulance or other emergency services, and should not be turned away from a hospital that can provide treatment. This did not include Mr Soobramoney's case. He needed ongoing treatment of a chronic illness to prolong his life. That was not an emergency. It was very different. The right did not include claims of this sort.

Mr Soobramoney therefore had to base his claim on the right of access to ordinary, non-emergency health care. And here the difficult issue remained – was the dialysis policy at Addington Hospital reasonable? Mr Soobramoney did not qualify because it limited access to patients with acute renal failure who could be treated. His condition was irreversible and he could not be treated. Dialysis would prolong his life, but to put him on the machine would mean denying life to others, who had a better chance of survival.

The court recognised the anguish of Mr Soobramoney's position. It expressed sympathy for him and his family. It recognised their cruel dilemma. They would have to impoverish themselves to secure the treatment he needed to prolong his life. 'The hard and unpalatable fact', the court's President, Justice Chaskalson, said, is that if Mr Soobramoney were wealthy, 'he would be able to procure such treatment from private sources; he is not and has to look to the state to provide him with the treatment. But the state's resources are limited and the appellant does not meet the criteria for admission to the renal dialysis programme.'

The state, Justice Chaskalson said, has to manage its limited resources to address many competing claims. At times, this means it must adopt a holistic approach to the larger needs of society, rather than focus on the specific needs of particular individuals within society. Here Justice Chaskalson emphasised that it was government that had to make decisions about funding available for health care, and how that funding should be spent.

He said, 'These choices involve difficult decisions to be taken at the political level in fixing the health budget, and at the functional level in deciding upon the priorities to be met. A court will be slow to interfere with rational decisions taken in good faith by the political organs and medical authorities whose responsibility it is to deal with such matters.' In other words, unless Mr Soobramoney could show that the policy was not rational, or was not formulated and adopted in good faith, he could not seek a court's help to overturn it. Though agonising, the court could not tell the KZN health care administrators their dialysis policy was wrong. It had to turn Mr Soobramoney away.

Mr Soobramoney's case shows the sad limitations of constitutional rights. They cannot manufacture facilities and provide budgets to set life right for all. And where government acts reasonably to make socio-economic rights available, it is doing exactly what the Constitution requires it to do. The court will not intervene.

But in sketching the background to Mr Soobramoney's agonising case, the court gave an important explanation of how social rights are indispensable to all other rights. In essence the court said that, unless we change the material conditions in which people live, legal rights are hollow.

Justice Chaskalson noted that we live in a society in which there are great disparities in wealth. Millions of people, he said, are living in deplorable conditions and in great poverty. There are high levels of unemployment, inadequate social security, and many who do not have access to clean water or to adequate health services. The commitment to address these conditions, and to transform our society into one in which there will be human dignity, freedom and equality, lay at the heart of the new constitutional order. 'For as long as these conditions continue to exist,' he said soberly, 'that aspiration will have a hollow ring.'

VII Mrs Grootboom's house and the right of access to adequate housing

The second decision the Constitutional Court gave on socio-economic rights was also highly charged. It concerned the right of access to adequate housing. But in that case, in contrast to *Soobramoney*, the court at least granted some limited relief. Nevertheless, the judgment attracted much criticism.

Mrs Irene Grootboom was one of a group of desperately poor people living in shacks on the eastern fringes of Cape Town. Their dwellings were on waterlogged ground at a settlement called Wallacedene. Mrs Grootboom, like others, had applied for subsidised low-cost housing. She had been on the waiting list for many years. All her many enquiries produced no definite answer. Clearly it was going to be a long wait. Faced with the prospect of remaining in intolerable conditions indefinitely, she and her fellow residents began to move out of Wallacedene at the end of September 1998. They put up their shacks and shelters on vacant land nearby. They called the land 'Nuwe Rust', or New Rest.

Unfortunately, not only was the land privately owned, but it had also been earmarked for development into formal low-cost housing. So, though the residents denied it, the move by Mrs Grootboom and others onto the land seemed very much like a land invasion. In 1999 the landowner, with the support of the Cape Town city government, obtained an eviction order against Mrs Grootboom. But she and her fellow residents had nowhere to go. It was the middle of the exceptionally wet and cold Cape winter of 1999. Emergency accommodation was provided, but Mrs Grootboom rightly pointed out that this left her and her dependants in limbo. She insisted that her right of access to housing meant that government should provide her with housing of some sort while she awaited permanent accommodation.

When we heard Mrs Grootboom's application, I had been appointed to the court for one year as an acting justice, before I received my permanent appointment to the appeal court in Bloemfontein. It was just after my public statement that I was living with HIV, and surviving well on ARVs, so the question of social and economic rights engaged me intensely. I sat in Mrs Grootboom's case, and was part of the judgment.

Justice Yacoob, in a unanimous judgment on behalf of the court, declined to grant an order giving Mrs Grootboom an entitlement to a house or indeed to any specific form of shelter. He noted that Mrs Grootboom's desperate circumstances had driven her to move onto the land set aside for other people's housing, but he warned that this could not be countenanced. This reminds us, he said, of the intolerable conditions under which many people still live. It is also a reminder that unless the plight of these communities is alleviated, people may be tempted to take the law into their own hands to escape these conditions.

'The case,' Justice Yacoob said, 'brings home the harsh reality that the Constitution's promise of dignity and equality for all remains for many a distant dream. People should not be impelled by intolerable living conditions to resort to land invasions. Self-help of this kind cannot be tolerated, for the unavailability of land suitable for housing development is a key factor in the fight against the country's housing shortage.'

Mrs Grootboom asked the court to identify an essential minimum that government had to provide, right away, to comply with its duty to take reasonable measures to realise her right of access to housing. Under international law, there is a strong body of opinion that says that social rights have a 'minimum core component' that domestic courts should identify and declare to be binding.

This the Constitutional Court refused to do. It said that people's needs, and the particular ways of fulfilling the right in question, were too varied. Since *Grootboom*, there has been much criticism of the court's refusal to adopt the 'minimum core' approach, but the court has maintained its stand and had been right to do so. A minimum core is inappropriate to South African conditions, and is unaccommodatingly inflexible. It is incompatible with the Constitution's formula that requires government to take reasonable steps to ensure progressive realisation of the rights at issue within available resources. To pre-empt what may be reasonable by laying down a minimum core would run counter to the process of judicially supervised governmental outlay the Constitution envisages.

So instead of laying down a minimum core content of each right that government is obliged to meet in all cases, unconditionally, the court has focused on developing its socio-economic rights jurisprudence on a case-by-case basis.

In Mrs Grootboom's case, the court examined government's housing programme in detail. It recognised what had been done as a major achievement. Large sums of money had been spent and a significant number of houses built, but the court faulted the programme for not making provision for those in most desperate need. What was missing was 'express provision to facilitate access to temporary relief for people who have no access to land, no roof over their heads, for people who are living in intolerable conditions and for people who are in crisis because of natural disasters such as floods and fires, or because their homes are under threat of demolition'. The court found the absence of this component was not reasonable.

The court appreciated the practical difficulties that devising a comprehensive programme entailed. It said that effective implementation requires adequate funding from national government. This, in turn, requires government to recognise that immediate needs must be met in the nationwide housing programme. This demands that government plan for, budget for and monitor the fulfilment of immediate needs and the management of crises.

The court acknowledged that this entailed a practical balancing act. The programme had to ensure that a significant number of desperate people in need were afforded relief – but it could not be expected to ensure that all of them had to receive it immediately.

Turning back to the case before it, the court refused to grant Mrs Grootboom a concrete order realising her specific entitlement to housing. Instead, it granted only a general, declaratory, order – one that outlined the parties' rights and entitlements in general terms. It declared that government housing programmes were obliged to provide for people in Mrs Grootboom's position – people in intolerable conditions or crisis situations, with no roof over their heads and no access to land. People, in short, in desperate need.

Their need, the court held, could be met by solutions that might fall short of the standards of durability, habitability and stability that formal housing usually demands.

The court's order declared government's programme invalid because it failed to do so. But the order did not mention Mrs Grootboom or her fellow residents. On the morning the court's order was handed down, Wednesday, 4 October 2000, they left court without any specific order realising their need for longer-term housing. The court has been heavily criticised for this. Eight years after the judgment, in August 2008, Mrs Grootboom died. She was still living in a shack. Many commentators taunt the court's socio-economic rights rulings by pointing out that she died without a home. The litigation failed to secure her a house.

The taunt is justified. It is a humbling reminder to those of us practising law and who engage in high-flown constitutional rhetoric that what we do has limits. But even though Mrs Grootboom did not secure a house before her death, the *Grootboom* litigation did not achieve nothing. On the contrary, it made a very big impact on government housing delivery. And it is now recognised as providing a strong basis for the court's entire jurisprudence on socio-economic rights.

The *Grootboom* judgment is widely cited internationally as one of the court's most finely tuned and effective rulings. This is because, without telling government directly how to run its housing programme, the court said that the existing programme failed to pass constitutional muster. The result of the decision was direct and material in many people's lives – perhaps many millions of lives. The nub of the judgment was to require the state to take active steps to create access to social services and economic resources for the poorest and most vulnerable in our country.

And government proved responsive to the court's order. In direct response, it enacted Chapter 12 of the National Housing Code. This is an obligatory guide that requires national, provincial and municipal government to plan for and act where people are in desperate need.

The Code itself refers to *Grootboom* as a 'landmark' in its development. And it puts on record that, a year after the judgment, the court's decision impelled national and provincial ministers responsible for housing to take action. They authorised a national programme for quick action 'to relieve the plight of persons in emergency situations with exceptional housing needs'.

These words in the Code make it clear that without Mrs Grootboom's challenge to government's housing programme, and without the declaratory order the court granted, the country's housing programme would have continued to limp. It would not have included provision for the needs of the poorest and most vulnerable.

Rights are not only written on paper in the Constitution. They have practical bite.

VIII From *Grootboom* to *Blue Moonlight*

Eleven years later, the practical implications of *Grootboom* still grew. In 2011 the court gave a decision expanding housing rights for poor people who lose their homes in urban areas. The case concerned 81 adults and five children, all very poor. They were living in a property called 'Saratoga Avenue' in Berea, a crowded inner-city suburb next to Hillbrow on the fringes of Johannesburg's central business district. The owner had never agreed to their stay, so they were all there unlawfully.

Saratoga Avenue was an old and dilapidated commercial building with office space, a factory building and garages. It was not suitable to live in. After the unlawful occupiers moved in, an enterprising property company, Blue Moonlight, bought up the property with a plan to redevelop it. Its plans accorded with the City of Johannesburg's overall housing vision. This was to formalise informal settlements and to provide 100 000 additional housing units by the end of the year 2011. These ambitious objectives depended on private-sector investment. This would help create a property market in historically disadvantaged areas, and rejuvenate the inner city. To achieve these ambitious goals, the City needed the co-operation not only of national and provincial government – it also needed investment from private companies like Blue Moonlight.

Before it could redevelop Saratoga Avenue, Blue Moonlight needed the occupiers to leave. But the Constitution provides in section 26(3) that no one may be evicted from their home, or have their home demolished, without an order of court. And before a court may grant an order that makes someone homeless, the Constitution says it must consider 'all the relevant circumstances'. Section 26(3) also prohibits arbitrary evictions. No legislation may permit them.

Hence, even though the people living in the property were there without permission and therefore unlawfully, Blue Moonlight had to go to court to obtain an eviction order. That is where its travails started. From the very outset, everyone agreed that Blue Moonlight was entitled to evict the occupants, but on what terms? The major dispute was what help the evictees should receive from City government. The residents, assisted by the Social and Economic Rights Institute (SERI), claimed that the City should provide them with emergency accommodation until they could be housed under its longer-term housing programme. This claim meant that Blue Moonlight had to journey all the way through the high court and the appeal court to the Constitutional Court, for there was a problem.

The City's housing policy didn't cover people in the position of the Saratoga evictees. The City's housing programme differentiated between those relocated by the City itself, and those evicted at the hands of private landowners. Persons relocated at the instance of the City were housed in temporary accommodation in City-controlled buildings. Persons evicted by private landowners were not covered. They had to fend for themselves.

It was this dispute that unwarily ensnared Blue Moonlight. The company conceded that the occupiers' eviction could be delayed for reasons of fairness – but it argued that an indefinite delay would amount to an arbitrary deprivation of its property. This would violate the Constitution's property clause, section 25(1). This provision stipulates that no one may be deprived of property except in terms of law of general application, and that no law may permit arbitrary deprivation of property.

Blue Moonlight complained, entirely reasonably, that a private owner has no obligation to provide free housing to unlawful occupiers. It wanted the court to take account of the expense and inconvenience it was suffering, and issue a prompt eviction. The court was sympathetic to its plight, but it noted that Blue Moonlight had purchased the land for commercial purposes. And when it did, it knew full well about the building's unlawful occupants. In these cases, Justice Van der Westhuizen said on behalf of the court, the owner may have to endure the unlawful occupation for a while. Of course a property owner cannot be expected to provide free housing for the homeless indefinitely, but sometimes, as here, he said, 'an owner may have to be somewhat patient'.

Hence the first question was this: what was the City obliged to do to help the occupiers? Chapter 12 of the National Housing Code, enacted in response to *Grootboom*, is dedicated to helping those rendered homeless in emergencies. The chapter covers those evicted from land or from unsafe buildings. Everyone agreed that the occupants' eviction fell under the definition of 'emergency'.

And Chapter 12 did not limit emergencies to those created by the City's own evictions. It covered all homeless emergencies – including those at the hands of private landlords like Blue Moonlight. The City insisted this was not its job. It argued that local government was not primarily responsible for providing access to adequate housing. That was national government's task. Its emergency housing budget was drawn up on this basis.

The court rejected the City's stand. It said its approach was not reasonable. In particular, it held that the City's budget was drawn up on an incorrect basis. The Housing Code does not preclude local government from making emergency provision for the homeless. On the contrary, it allows it. And this covers not only those rendered homeless by the City's own relocations and evictions, but also those evicted at the instance of private landlords. The City's complaints that it did not have the resources to fund emergency accommodation for all evictees, private and public, were therefore based on a misunderstanding of its duties. The City would have to re-budget.

So, was it reasonable for the City to differentiate within the category of emergencies between people relocated by the City itself, and those evicted by private landowners? And was it reasonable for the City inflexibly to include the first group, but exclude the second group entirely? The court said No. It held that all occupants rendered homeless by eviction – whether at the instance of local government or a private landlord – must receive emergency accommodation from government.

The court's decision has undoubtedly had a big impact. From now on, all inner-city residents will have some small cushion against the effects of being evicted. The ruling requires South Africa's cities and towns to rethink their budgets. In particular, they will have to rethink the resources allocated to the poorest urban households.

This is a dramatic intervention in government policy and budgets, but it is one the Constitution requires. The Constitution promises progressive realisation of access to adequate housing, within government's available resources. In *Blue Moonlight*, the courts were doing no more than giving effect to this promise.

IX The promise of socio-economic rights – and their limits

The court has given significant rulings on social and economic rights in addition to *Blue Moonlight*. It has held that a person's home cannot be sold off to pay a trifling debt. It has ruled that social grants must be extended beyond only citizens, to include all South Africa's permanent residents. It has given rulings making rental tenants more secure. Despite these decisions, some thoughtful commentators think the court has not gone far enough. They urge it to be more active in its interventions, and to do more to flex its judicial muscle. Indeed, on occasion some critics have bitterly denounced the court for refusing relief.

Commentators have also criticised the court's approach in flinching from specifying that each of the social rights has a claimable minimum core content.

Since *Soobramoney* and *Grootboom*, a decision the Constitutional Court gave on the right of access to water has been the focus of particular criticism. This was a case five residents of Phiri, one of the oldest areas of Soweto, brought to challenge the City of Johannesburg's free water policy. The applicants were all poor people living in separate households. The first applicant, Mrs Lindiwe Mazibuko, sadly passed away after the case was launched. She lived in a brick house on her mother's property. In the back yard there were two informal dwellings, for which the tenants paid low rentals. Altogether 20 people lived on the stand. The nub of her and the other applicants' case was that the City was not providing them and other poor people with enough free water.

Both the high court and the Supreme Court of Appeal sided with the applicants. They granted orders requiring the City of Johannesburg to increase the free allowance of water to its consumers. The Constitutional Court thought otherwise. It rejected the claim that the City's policy, which granted each household six kilolitres of water a month, was unreasonable. The court intervened to set aside the previous decisions. It said the other courts should not have second-guessed the City's water policies. It was not the business of courts to determine water allocations. So long as government was acting reasonably, courts should not interfere.

The court found that the City had gone to great lengths to explain how it came to make its water allocation to households, and how it made special provision for poor households. International experts gave conflicting evidence about whether what the City offered was enough. To add to the complexity of the litigation, the City adjusted its policies during the high court and appeal processes to take account of Mrs Mazibuko's complaints.

The City had ensured that its water policy was one of the most advanced in the world. The applicants demanded 50 litres of water per person per day free of charge. Aside from the fact that it was common cause that South Africa is water-stressed, and a developing country, no country in the world provided what the applicants claimed.

An argument that weighed strongly in the court's judgment is that the City's priority was to extend water provision to 750 000 people in informal settlements. At the time of the litigation, they had no access to water at all.

The City was scrupulous in offering full evidence of its policy. It conceded its shortcomings. The critical point was that its policy complied with what the court required in *Grootboom*. In these circumstances, the court said that for it to intervene would take it deeply into the realm of policy making on water provision. To do so would be second-guessing government's policies on social benefits. This it refused to do. Thus, while assessing government's policies from the standard of reasonableness has proven to be resilient in the face of South Africa's varying needs, it also imposes limits on how far the courts can tread into interfering with government's policies.

X Socio-economic rights – the risk of judicial overkill

The Constitutional Court has undoubtedly adopted a cautious approach. It was this that disappointed many commentators in the *Mazibuko* decision. The court's approach certainly contrasts with much more activist and interventionist approaches the courts of some other countries have adopted. The Supreme Court of India, for example, has given very detailed and prescriptive content to government obligations in socio-economic rights. It has granted strongly interventive remedies.

With health care rights, this seems to be the case also in Brazil and some other Latin American countries. In Brazil, it seems, the courts have been willing to order government to provide drugs directly to claimants, regardless of budgetary constraints. This approach, too, has been criticised. Evidence seems to suggest that litigation may actually have worsened health equity in Brazil. This is because the judicial intervention, and the constant risk of litigation, has skewed budget planning. Court decisions have diverted health resources. They have reduced government's capacity to provide cost-effective treatment for the poor. Instead, health budgets have had to provide for more expensive treatment for wealthier litigants. Huge portions of health budgets have to be set aside in advance, just in case judges make rulings in favour of those who manage to secure legal representation.

Some United States courts have also been notably interventive in granting orders against government to remedy social ills. In one case, seeking to desegregate schools in Kansas City, a judge specified the exact ratio of black students to white students that had to be attained in public schools. He ordered that a 6:4 ratio had to be met. But this ran into problems. It was impossible for the district in question to fill all the 'white' places in the designated schools, but until white children could be found, more black children could not be admitted to those schools. The result was that thousands of black children had to be placed on waiting lists, unable to attend the school of their choice, even though school spaces were available for them. The judge who issued the order eventually had to reconsider the plan.

It is these sorts of details, and their implementation, to which courts are particularly ill-suited. The Constitutional Court seeks to leave the details of policy formulation and its implementation strictly to the executive and legislative branches.

XI Socio-economic rights: the broader achievement

Even though the court's judgments have been cautious, the fact that the Constitution contains judicially enforceable socio-economic rights is a great achievement. Commentators across the world have hailed the South African courts' willingness to determine whether government's programmes are reasonable. They have also lauded the courts' caution about wading further into the policy field.

And even where the courts turn litigants away, as happened when Mrs Mazibuko unsuccessfully challenged her household's free water allocation, recourse to the courts has a beneficial effect on government and on citizens. In Mrs Mazibuko's case, Justice O'Regan, writing for the court, pointed out how litigation in this area is designed to hold the democratic arms of government to account. This kind of litigation, she said, 'fosters a form of participative democracy that holds government accountable and requires it to account between elections over specific aspects of government policy'.

This is because, when challenged on its policies, the government agency is obliged to explain why the policy is reasonable. Government must, she pointed out, disclose what it has done to formulate the policy: its investigation and research, the alternatives considered, and the reasons why the option underlying the policy was selected.

She emphasised that the Constitution does not require government to meet 'an impossible standard of perfection'. Nor does it require courts to take over the tasks of the democratic arms of government. 'Simply put,' she said, 'through the institution of the courts, government can be called upon to account to citizens for its decisions. This understanding of social and economic rights litigation accords with the founding values of our Constitution and, in particular, the principles that government should be responsive, accountable and open.'

Not only does court action require government to show that its chosen policy is reasonable, but it must show that the policy is being reconsidered consistently with its obligation to 'progressively realise' social and economic rights. An inflexible policy – one that is set in stone and never revisited – is unlikely, she noted, to be one that will progressively realise rights.

Justice O'Regan said the *Mazibuko* litigation in particular illustrated how court action concerning social and economic rights can exact a detailed accounting from government and, in doing so, impact beneficially on the policy-making process. During argument, Mrs Mazibuko's counsel had bemoaned the fact that the City had continually amended its policies as the case wound its way from high court to Supreme Court of Appeal to Constitutional Court. Justice O'Regan disavowed this criticism. In fact, she said, the effect of being brought to court 'was beneficial'. Forcing the City to explain why its free basic water policy was reasonable 'shone a bright, cold light on the policy that undoubtedly revealed flaws'. The continual revision of the policy in the ensuing years improved it – in a way that was entirely consistent with the City's duty to progressively realise the right.

The courts' decisions on socio-economic rights have undoubtedly shown how rights-directed litigation can improve the conditions of many socially vulnerable people, in ways that would not have been possible without these rights. The decisions also show how rights claims can be practically translated into material improvements to people's lives.

Mr Soobramoney's death without dialysis, and Mrs Grootboom's death without a house, do not mean we should give up on legal rights and on public interest litigation. It means only that we should do better.

XII Social grants, hand-outs and government charity

For a developing country, South Africa has a very extensive system of social welfare. A large proportion of social spending is dedicated to providing our country's poorest people with social grants. This system is one of the chief features of our complex and unequal democracy. In 1997 government published a planning paper on social development. It noted that a 'social security system is essential for healthy economic development, particularly in a rapidly changing economy, and will contribute actively to the development process. It is important for immediate alleviation of poverty and is a mechanism for active redistribution'.

In 2004 Parliament passed the Social Assistance Act. It established the South African Social Security Agency, SASSA, whose job is to ensure provision of comprehensive social security services against vulnerability and poverty. The legislation specifically directs SASSA to work within the constitutional legislative framework. The social grants SASSA distributes are created by the Social Assistance Act. They currently total six – an old age grant, a disability grant, a war veterans' grant, a care dependency grant, a foster child grant and a child support grant.

In his budget speech in 2013, finance minister Pravin Gordhan explained the massive growth in social spending over the preceding decade. This, he said, had financed 'a threefold increase in the number of people receiving social grants'. As a result, over 15 million people in South Africa now receive cash transfers from the state. The child support grant has been gradually extended to children up to the age of 18. This has meant that spending on social assistance has increased an average of 11% per year. In the 2014/15 financial year, it will increase to R120 billion.

On 30 September 2013 government announced the second increase within the year in disability grants, old age pensions, care dependency grants and war veterans' pensions. The increases were in addition to the child support grant and grant-in-aid increases, previously budgeted for.

Critics rightly caution that social grants heavily burden governmental spending. And they point out that social grants alone do not ensure people's dignity. People should also have access to a growing economy, to jobs, to training and to education. Indeed, the Constitution does not specify the ways in which those goals can be achieved. On the contrary, it is non-committal about the paths to social justice. It is neutral between different economic planning models. A national policy that favours job creation at the expense of other values would be as compatible with constitutionalism as one that does not.

But for many poor households in South Africa, social grants are their only form of income. The prime purpose of social grants is to improve standards of living, and they manifestly succeed. Grants also aim to redistribute wealth to create a more just and equal society. They are the prime means by which government is fulfilling its obligation progressively to realise the social and economic rights, access to which is guaranteed in the Constitution.

Most social grants are not much more in value today than R686. That is roughly the sum the unnamed benefactor handed to my mother and Jeanie and me in Bloemfontein in 1963. That act of human sharing transformed my life, and not simply by the material goods it enabled us to buy at a very hard time. It did so by allowing me to understand the imperative of social distribution. In our desperately unequal and still unjust society, social grants do that on our behalf. Through government, they extend to all some of the benefits of the prosperity many, but not enough, enjoy in a society that excludes far too many from its benefits.

Social grants are much more than hand-outs. And they do not

benefit only those who receive them. On the contrary, they enhance the dignity of even those who have the means to live without them. In themselves, they are not enough. But without them, none of us in South Africa, whether the rich, who sometimes sneer at them, and the poor, for whom they provide the minimum essentials of daily living, would have a claim to any dignity as moral citizens of a constitutional state.

Chapter Seven

Conclusion: The Promise and the Perils of Constitutionalism

I Twenty years of democracy and constitutionalism

As I sit at my desk in the Constitutional Court, writing the conclusion to this book, 2013 is nearly over. We are very nearly twenty years into our constitutional democracy. There is much in our country to feel sad and sober about. But there is also some basis for determined optimism.

Much has been achieved – perhaps more than those of us who tend to worry realise. While violent crime is still at disturbingly high levels, the endlessly upward wave that terrified us in the late 1990s has not come about. Compared to 1994, the murder rate in our country has almost halved. Though poverty is still pervasive, people's lives are mostly better. Government's housing programme has put many millions of South Africans into their own homes. In 1994, just over half of households had electricity. Now 85% do. In 1994, just more than one-third of six-year-olds were in school. Now 85% are.

The income of the average black family has increased by about a third. And, through the system of social grants totalling about R120 billion every year, the very poorest in our country are afforded some elements of a dignified material existence as well as access to a measure of social power – the same power Jeanie and I experienced when the anonymous lady's hand-out in Bloemfontein enabled us to buy necessaries.

What seems most important is that these gains have been achieved within a functioning constitutional democracy. Our political life is boisterous, rowdy, sometimes cacophonous and often angry. That much is to be expected. But after nearly two decades, we have more freedom, more debate, more robust and direct engagement with each other – and certainly more practically tangible social justice than we had twenty years ago.

But all is not well. On my journey to court in the mornings, I drive through my neighbourhood close to the universities of Wits and UJ, a former white working-class area that now features high-density student accommodation and some desperately overcrowded housing for poor people. On the edges of the inner city of Johannesburg, my journey takes me through Braamfontein, as I ascend Civic Hill and reach Constitution Hill, where the court building stands.

Listening to the morning talk shows, I often find myself sharing many callers' worries. Political debate is sometimes annihilatingly divisive. Race rhetoric still sometimes substitutes for performance. Gross inequality, largely racially structured, persists. Public schooling for poor black children seems to have gone backwards since the end of apartheid. Fragmentation and lack of leadership in important national institutions, like the SABC and the National Prosecuting Authority (NPA), seem to have reached dismaying proportions.

In many communities, anger that some have while they do not, is growing. 2012 saw the highest number of service delivery protests since 2004 – and very nearly nine out of ten (88%) were violent. More and more municipalities and national departments fail to fulfil basic auditing requirements. And the accounting chaos allows the tide of corruption to wash higher and higher. It threatens to engulf us. The shameless looting of our public assets by many politicians and government officials is a direct threat to our democracy and all we hope to achieve in it.

To many, the culture of high-minded civic aspiration that characterised our struggle for racial justice and our transition to democracy seems distinctly frayed, if not in tatters.

In all this, what does it mean that we are a constitutional state? It means not only that we project our highest aspirations into the Constitution. It also means that we place in it our best practical hopes. What we need to survive these tough times are honest leaders and an actively engaged public, together with practical sense and street wisdom.

The Constitution's lofty language and vaulting aspirations certainly won't see us through. But we don't need to rely on its high rhetoric. Quite the opposite. In a time of structural disintegration, social fraying and predatory looting, the Constitution continues to prove itself a viable framework for the practical play of power needed to secure our future beyond our current problems.

And 'framework' is the word I emphasise. The Constitution is not self-executing. It needs us to give it life – us, the citizens and inhabitants of South Africa, young and old, male and female, rural and urban, township and suburb dwellers. The Constitution creates the practical structures that enable the rest of us – you and me, together with principled, honest leadership, a committed government, an active citizenry and vigorous civil society institutions – to perfect our future.

II Two kinds of scepticism about the Constitution

As I drive to court in the mornings, and do my daily work, I do not ignore those who are sceptical about the whole business of constitutionalism. Their views claim respect and consideration.

Constitutional sceptics fall into roughly two camps. On the one side are those who think that rights and constitutionalism have diverted social power away from 'the people', who should rightly own it. The Constitution was a misguided compromise that fettered the people's power to radically transform our unjust society. Deputy minister Ngoako Ramathlodi expressed this form of scepticism most strongly. He said in 2011 that the constitutional transition was a victory for apartheid forces who wanted to retain 'white domination under a black government'. This was done 'by emptying the legislature and executive of real political power' and giving it to 'the judiciary and other constitutional institutions and civil society movements'.

More recently, the General Secretary of the National Union of Metalworkers of SA (NUMSA), Mr Irvin Jim, has said the clause in the Constitution protecting property rights should be 'dumped' so that radical change can be effected immediately. Scepticism of this sort was evident also when SAPS Commissioner Riah Phiyega said that criminals are brazen because we 'have the most beautiful Constitution that allows rights and rights are not limited'.

Sceptics in this camp say that the Constitution is too powerful to allow us to do what we must to make our society as it should be.

On the opposite side are sceptics who think that the Constitution is not powerful at all. This form of scepticism was most powerfully expressed in vigorous public debate triggered when Chief Justice Arthur Chaskalson died in December 2012. Mr Ken Owen and Mr RW Johnson suggested that constitutionalism is a mere guise under which radicals in the ANC and the SACP have seized for themselves as much power as they want, and through which they are distorting all state institutions in order to impose centralised control on the country. Sceptics in this camp suggest not only that the Constitution is not formidable enough, but that the whole constitutional project may have been a sham.

The two groups stand at opposite poles. The first say the Constitution is indeed powerful and that its effects are all too real because it is preventing the people from exercising the power that belongs to them– whether to stop criminals or to effect distributive reform. The second group say that, far from being a brake on radical exercise of power, the Constitution is a flimsy veneer and perhaps a con designed to license it.

Both groups of sceptics offer accounts of history that to me seem wrong. History is not likely to show that Mandela and the other negotiators either sacrificed the prospect of people's power to neo-liberal interests, or that they entered into constitutionalism as a front for claiming dictatorial power. Indeed, as described in chapter 3, the Constitution was not the product of elite, secret negotiation and compromise. Its coming into being was reflective of the vigorous debate and public participation that has come to mark our democracy.

But the sceptics' warnings are important nevertheless. They alert us to the limitations of rights-talk. They are impatient with the clogs and inhibitions the rule of law places on the exercise of power. And they warn us, rightly, that constitutionalism may prove ineffectual as a bulwark against authoritarianism. The sceptics' warnings are well directed.

Still, it seems to me that the Constitution remains the best path South Africans have to create a just and ordered future for ourselves. This is not a call for naive optimism. Instead, I offer a sober assessment of what constitutionalism means in our democracy after twenty years. My argument is that the Constitution is not just a document of high aspiration and idealism. It is a practicable, workable charter. And it has proved itself modestly but practically effective as a basis for the democratic exercise of power in our half-broken, half-fixed country.

I have five reasons for this cautiously upbeat assessment.

First reason for the Constitution – it has stood the test of twenty years

The Constitution has by no means yet proved itself. It hasn't yet stood the test of time. But it is on its way to doing so. We have had nearly two decades of tempestuous disputes, clashes of interests and contests. There have been conflicts between civil society and the state, between provinces and central government, between factions within the ruling ANC, dispossessed land claimants and urban tenants, on the one side, and landholders and property owners, on the other. All these clashes have been adjudicated within the Constitution's framework of values. Each time, those values have proved resilient and practically effective.

Second reason – the Constitution's distribution of powers is practical and effective

A second reason for believing in the Constitution is that the separation of powers it creates has proved good and practical. The executive, Parliament and the courts have settled into a working relationship. It is sometimes tense but it is reasonably effective. Judges are cautious when it comes to purely policy decisions (witness the reversal of the interdict against e-tolling), but they hold government strictly to account on its social delivery programmes.

Perhaps the best instance is the *Grootboom* decision. The Constitutional Court declared government's housing programme constitutionally invalid because it failed to make provision for the most desperately poor and vulnerable. The result was a radical overhaul of the state's entire housing programme. While still inadequate to the demands of a growing and loudly demanding population, housing delivery has undoubtedly been one of government's better successes. This has resulted from the judicially enforceable promise of access to housing in the Constitution.

An even more famous example is the Constitutional Court's order to President Mbeki's government, at the height of presidentially licensed AIDS denialism, to start making anti-retroviral drugs available to poor people at public health clinics. The national ARV treatment programme that resulted is a proud achievement. It was achieved through the Constitution's judicially enforceable promise of access to health.

This shows that claims that the Constitution would protect only privilege were too pessimistic. The promises in the Constitution, enforceable by the courts, have ensured a significant shift in resources (both government and non-government) to the poorest of the poor. That is right and just. And it is a proud achievement. It is one that may help ensure the success of constitutionalism and the rule of law in our country.

Third reason – people have claimed the Constitution as their own

Connected to this is a third reason for cautious optimism. This is that the notion of constitutionalism is extremely widespread in our country. Perhaps the most remarkable feature of our democracy is the extent to which nearly everyone claims the Constitution. Gay and lesbian youngsters from the rural areas, service delivery protestors in towns and cities, opposition parties and political factions within the ANC – all not only accept the legitimacy of the values and rights the Constitution sets out, but they claim them loudly for themselves. And they demand that the rights in the Constitution be realised, in their lifetimes, in their lives, now.

Fears that constitutionalism would be an elite phenomenon, confined to lawyers and armchair idealists, have proved completely wrong. Constitutionalism is one of the most powerful forces at all levels of our politics and national debate.

Fourth reason – the judiciary is still strong

A fourth reason for cautious optimism is the judiciary. Judges unavoidably have a central role in upholding the rule of law. So constitutionalism requires a strong and honest judiciary. Subject to some painful question marks, that is something I believe we still have in South Africa. That may change, especially if doubts grow about the personal integrity of senior judges, but, for now, we have a strong judiciary.

I feel no self-congratulation in saying this. The judiciary is frail and overworked. Questions have been raised about the honesty of some judges. And too often the police and courts give shockingly bad service to victims of crime and other litigants. This is frustrating for judges. They cannot investigate crimes. They cannot produce laboratory results on time. They cannot ensure that criminals are prosecuted competently and without fear or favour, as the Constitution demands. Nor can they deliver basic services, or put a stop to corruption.

But neither they nor the Constitution prevent any of this from being done. It is not the Constitution that prevents efficient police enforcement, detective work, investigative follow-up and prosecution. Nor does the Constitution prevent honest government and diligent delivery of basic services.

As my colleague Deputy Chief Justice Moseneke noted in May 2013, neither the Constitution nor the courts have prevented an effective programme of land reform and land redistribution. The much reviled 'willing-buyer, willing-seller' principle, that is said to inhibit land reform, is contained nowhere in the Constitution. All the Constitution outlaws are arbitrary deprivations of property. And all it requires is just and equitable compensation when government takes property. For that, all amongst us, shack dwellers and home owners, rich and poor, should be thankful.

Neither the Constitution nor judges can create social justice.

All they can do, when presented with cases, is what the Constitution tells them to do, and what by their judicial oaths they have undertaken to do. This is to dispense justice without fear or favour, impartially, and staying faithful to the high aspirations of the Constitution. That, I think, is more or less what the judiciary has been doing these last two decades.

The judges I know take certain fundamentals for granted. These are the value of independent institutions, the autonomous functioning of the judiciary, the need for utter integrity, the vital significance of the rule of law, and the supremacy of the Constitution. And, most importantly of all, they know that the high language of the Constitution's promises must be made real in people's lives.

Whether the litigants before us are private citizens or government, the Speaker of Parliament or the official opposition, a civil society group or a faction of political groupings – all are judged rigorously on the strength of their claims alone, measured only against the promises of the Constitution. A functioning, honest and robust judiciary, committed to the values of the Constitution, is not an insignificant achievement.

Fifth reason – the Constitution's fundamental values are right

There is a fifth reason why we can feel some measure of sober confidence. This lies in the fundamental structure and values of the Constitution. These are democracy, equality, a separation of power between independent institutions, and a commitment to social justice. The Constitution is a social democratic document. It demands that the state must include the poorest in our society in its planning. But, beyond that, it leaves space for government to pursue different economic theories, different paths of development and different conceptions of productive social investment.

The 'left' has never fully explored the radically egalitarian assertions in the Constitution's equality clause – including the promise that 'Equality includes the full and equal enjoyment of all rights and freedoms'. The 'right' has never fully explored the freedom of trade, occupation or profession enshrined in the Constitution.

The basic structure of the Constitution demands concern for the poor and the most vulnerable. It enjoins protection for the weak and for minorities without social or political power. This is right and necessary. Without it, constitutionalism and the rule of law would not be worth their name. In addition, the Constitution requires progressive realisation of basic social and economic rights. And it builds in protective institutional safeguards to support constitutional democracy through institutions such as an independent National Prosecuting Authority, a Public Protector and a Human Rights Commission (SAHRC).

But the Constitution stops there. Nothing in it prescribes what social remedies any democratically elected government is free to pursue to create jobs, to advance social equity and to give historical redress. Our Constitution gives government – of whatever party – power to advance the common welfare, to rectify injustices and to create social wealth. The basic values and structure of the Constitution are sound.

III Finale

For me, it has been a long journey since Queenstown and Laura's funeral. I have been a judge in democratic South Africa for nearly twenty years. After I had been an acting (temporary) judge for some months, President Mandela appointed me as a high court judge, in December 1994. The years since then have been a time of uncertainty, disquiet and occasional dismay. They have been years of gruelling hard work. But they have, for me, also been years of joy. I have seen a Constitution that started out as a piece of paper, borne aloft by the aspirational hopes of a visionary generation, evolve into a practically functioning charter for regulating power and making progress possible in our country.

After nearly twenty years, there is much about which we should feel disquiet and dismay. Our country is far from healed. Dishonest leadership, corruption and the destruction of independent state institutions could still wreck our ambitious constitutional project.

But we also have much about which we can feel at least a small measure of tentative pride. We have the most active and engaged citizenry on our continent. We have the loudest and most diverse media perhaps anywhere in the global south. Our national debate about values, about means and about goals is passionately serious.

We have not stood still since 1994. That is to the good. We have lost our virginal sense of innocence. We have lost our aspirational, wish-list way of planning. We now know the limits and the evils of power, including insidious looting of public assets for private gain. The whole undertaking is still at risk of ruin. But, after nearly twenty years, what we have is a battered, partly time-tested, mostly viable and certainly functioning constitutional democracy. We have a practical structure to create our future – and one that affords us a number of viable pathways to reach it.

The Constitution affords us a pathway to healing and integration. It offers our country what the law in my lifetime has offered to me. It offers us a framework within which to repair our country, to restore, redress and reconcile. It is up to us to claim the opportunities it offers. For the Constitution exists not only for high dreams and good times. It is there also for moments of dismay and sobriety. That is not a bad achievement for our first two decades. It is one that has a claim to our fierce commitment.

Notes

The quotation from former President Nelson Mandela is from his speech at the International Ombudsman Conference in Durban in 2001, accessed from an address by the Public Protector, Advocate Thuli Madonsela, in Pretoria on Tuesday 22 February 2011, available at http://www.pprotect.org/media_gallery/2011/23022011_sp.asp (accessed 19 November 2013).

CHAPTER ONE

I: A first encounter with the law

I tried to find the SAP69 criminal record for my father, Kenneth Hughson Cameron, but did not succeed.

II: A second encounter with the law – and a first lesson in lawyering

The story of the Dean of Johannesburg and Alison Norman is told in Denis Herbstein, *White Lies: Canon Collins and the Secret War Against Apartheid* (James Currey Publishers and HSRC Press, 2004) pp 160-167. Herbstein recounts that Ms Norman later admitted she perjured herself, encouraged by Father Trevor Huddleston, in denying ANC involvement. He sketches Judge-President Cillié as 'a dependable government appointee, of whom it was said that he had never been known to disbelieve the word of a senior police officer'. In the Dean's trial, 'He came up trumps again' (p 165).

The legal reports of the Dean's trial are published at *S v ffrench-Beytagh* 1971 (4) SA 333 (T) (ruling that the Dean was entitled to a copy of the statement he made to the security police); 1971 (4) SA 426 (T) (granting an order that evidence be taken from Ms Norman in London); 1971 (4) SA 571 (T) (a ruling on admissibility of evidence about a police witness's real political views); 1972 (1) SA 828 (T) (digest of trial judge's judgment convicting the Dean).

I have taken the account of the verdict in the Dean's trial, and women sob-
bing and singing 'Onward Christian Soldiers', from the Reverend Patrick
Comerford, 'In Retrospect: Canon Gonville Aubie ffrench-Beytagh (1912-
1991)', dated 23 April 2012, available at http://revpatrickcomerford.
blogspot.com/2012/04/in-retrospect-canon-gonville-aubie.html (accessed
25 April 2013).

III: The Dean takes his case to the appeal court

This history of the Supreme Court of Appeal, formerly the Appellate
Division of the Supreme Court of South Africa, which was founded in
1910, is available on the court's website, at http://www.justice.gov.
za/sca/historysca.htm (accessed 2 October 2013).

IV: A brave history – the 1950s appeal court confronts the apartheid government

The cases in which the Appellate Division of the Supreme Court nullified
the Separate Registration of Voters Act, 46 of 1951, and High Court of
Parliament Act, 35 of 1952, are *Harris v Minister of the Interior* 1952
(2) SA 428 (A) and *Minister of the Interior v Harris* 1952 (4) SA 769 (A).

The case in which the appeal court ruled 10-1 that the Senate gerry-
mandering passed muster is *Collins v Minister of the Interior* 1957 (1)
SA 552 (A). The dissenting judgment of Schreiner JA is at pp 571-581,
with the crucial reasoning at 572G and 580A. The final report of the
Truth and Reconciliation Commission (TRC) rightly describes the Senate shenanigan of 1956 as a 'constitutional fraud' (see volume 4, chapter 4, para 32, available at http://www.justice.gov.za/trc/report/final-
report/Volume%204.pdf (accessed 21 March 2013).

More than forty years later, the Supreme Court of Appeal quoted the dissenting opinion of Schreiner JA on form versus substance, as established legal doctrine, in *Nederduitse Gereformeerde Kerk in Afrika (OVS) v
Verenigende Gereformeerde Kerk in Suider-Afrika* 1999 (2) SA 156 (SCA)
at 170.

V : The appeal court wavers in defending liberties

The notorious appeal court decision denying Albie Sachs books, pens and
paper is *Rossouw v Sachs* 1964 (2) SA 551 (AD). The passage about not
relieving the tedium of detention is at p 565. The passage about the
courts taking Parliament's will as they find it in the words of legislation is at pp 563-564 (the court should 'determine the meaning of the

section upon an examination of its wording in the light of the circumstances whereunder it was enacted and of its general policy and object').

Courageous early critics of the Appellate Division's decisions adverse to liberty were AS Mathews RC and Albino 'The Permanence of the Temporary: An examination of the 90- and 180-day Detention Laws' (1966) 83 *SALJ* 16. John Dugard, himself a brave and powerful early critic of apartheid judges, has pointed out that this article contained 'no suggestion that the learned judges, particularly members of the Appellate Division, had merely "erred". On the contrary, judges were accused of intentionally endorsing the security laws in their harshest form. Both the partiality and the integrity of the judges were put in question' (see Dugard, 'Tony Mathews and criticism of the judiciary', chapter 1 p 4 in Marita Carnelley and Shannon Hoctor, *Law, Order and Liberty – Essays in Honour of Tony Mathews* (Scottsville, South Africa: University of KwaZulu-Natal Press, 2011).

The life of Chief Justice Ogilvie Thompson is described in Chief Justice Corbett's tribute to him, published in (1992) 109 *SALJ* 680.

On deaths in security police detention, AJ Christopher, *Atlas of Apartheid* (1994), pp 170-171, writes that from 1960 to 1990 some 78 000 people were detained without trial under security police legislation. 'One of the notable features of this legislation was the virtually unlimited power exerted by the Security Police over the detainees, and the consequent number of deaths in detention. In the 1960s, two or three detainees died each year, until the widely publicised death of Ahmed Timol in 1971. No more deaths were recorded until the Soweto riots of 1976. There then followed a horrific 26 deaths in two years. The international outcry over the much publicised death of Black Consciousness leader Steve Biko in 1977 again brought a halt to the deaths. However, in the 1980s, numbers of deaths once more began to rise until the end of the state of emergency. Thus some 73 people died in detention in the period [1960-1990], approximately 1 person per 1000 held.'

David Bruce, 'Interpreting the Body Count: South African statistics on lethal police violence', *South African Review of Sociology* 2005, 36(2), pp 141 and 142 note 2, available at http://www.csvr.org.za/docs/policing/interpreting.pdf (accessed 11 February 2013), reports that Dr Max Coleman's Human Rights Committee recorded 73 deaths of persons held in detention without trial under security legislation 1963-1990.

VI : The appeal court decides the Dean's appeal

The judgment of Chief Justice Ogilvie Thompson reversing the Dean's convictions and acquitting the Dean is published at 1972 (3) SA 430 (A). The appeal court's judgment is summarised in the SA Institute of Race Relations' *A Survey of Race Relations in SA* (1973) pp 95-96.

VII: Civil liberty, anti-apartheid activism and the Dean's judgment

For first-rate legal scholarship on the Terrorism Act and the apartheid state's injustices, as well as the Appellate Division's failure of nerve in security legislation, see AS Mathews, *Freedom, State Security and the Rule of Law* (1986), and John Dugard, *Human Rights and the South African Legal Order* (1978).

An excellent on-line overview of the Terrorism Act by Jonathan Cohen appears on the SA History Online website, http://www.sahistory.org.za/topic/1967-terrorism-act-no-83-1967 (accessed 1 February 2013).

VIII: White judges, the Defiance Campaign and attorney Mr Mandela

The tough law of 1950 was the Suppression of Communism Act, 44 of 1950. Attorney Mr Mandela was convicted of contravening section 11(b) because he advocated change 'by unlawful acts or omissions'. Section 11(i) stipulated a maximum sentence of ten years for contravening section 11(b).

My summary of the Defiance Campaign derives from the vivid account on the SA History Online website, http://www.sahistory.org.za/topic/defiance-campaign (accessed 11 February 2013), and the detailed facts set out in the judgment in *Incorporated Law Society v Mandela* 1954 (3) SA 102 (T) pp 103-107. Anthony Sampson's *Mandela – The Authorised Biography* (1999) provides a compelling account of the Defiance Campaign (pp 62-75).

Mandela's autobiography is available on-line at http://w.archive.org/stream/LongWalkToFreedom/PBI3231_djvu.txt (accessed 27 February 2013). This is where I found Mandela's assessment of Judge Rumpff, as well as his summary of the court's findings.

Judge Rumpff's best-known liberal judgments are his passionate anti-censorship dissent in *Publications Control Board v William Heinemann Ltd* 1965 (4) SA 137 (A) (where the court by a majority of 3-2 upheld a censors' ban on Wilbur Smith's *When the Lion Feeds*), and *Wood v Ondangwa Tribal Authority* 1975 (2) SA 294 (A), where he resurrected an ancient Roman law remedy to order a government tribal authority in Namibia/South-West Africa to release a detainee.

The judgment in *Law Society v Mandela* is reported as *Incorporated Law Society v Mandela* 1954 (3) SA 102 (T), judgment of Ramsbottom J (Roper J concurring), dated 28 April 1954. The stirring passages are at pp 108-109. Anthony Sampson's account of the Law Society case is on pp 79-80 of his Mandela biography.

Pollak on Jurisdiction continues to survive – a second edition by David Pistorius appeared in 1993 (Juta).

Sampson sets out Winston Churchill's assessment of the Defiance Campaign on p 75.

IX: Justice and the courts under apartheid – the Treason Trial

On Mandela remaining on the roll of practising attorneys, his friend, colleague and human rights lionheart, George Bizos, relates an anecdote recounting that 'whilst [Mandela was] incarcerated on Robben Island some ten years later, the Law Society once again filed an application to have his name removed from the roll. Mandela responded that he would need two weeks in the Pretoria Court library to adequately respond to their application. The Law Society quickly withdrew the application.' See George Bizos, presentation to Plato Week, School of Practical Philosophy, Johannesburg, 22 April 2013 – 'Law, Justice and Morality in South Africa: The Past and the Present', available at http://www.politicsweb. co.za/politicsweb/view/politicsweb/en/page71619?oid=371834&sn=-Detail&pid=71616 (accessed 26 April 2013).

The information on the first Schoeman who settled in the Cape is from Karel Schoeman, *'n Duitser aan die Kaap, 1724-1765: Die Lewe en Loopbaan van Hendrik Schoeman* (2004).

Sampson relates the anecdote about Mandela and the 'Hey, you' magistrate and Judge Quartus de Wet at p 80. The anecdote is repeated in Kenneth Broun, *Saving Nelson Mandela – The Rivonia Trial and the Fate of South Africa* (2012), p 21.

My account of the Treason Trial arrests and personalities, and the Drill Hall proceedings, draws on Anthony Sampson, *The Treason Cage – The Opposition on Trial in South Africa* (1958). He quotes the opening address of Vernon Berrangé QC on p 19. For the rest of the trial, I have also relied on Sampson's *Mandela* biography, pp 103-143.

The Criminal Procedure Act 51 of 1977 introduced a form of questioning by the presiding magistrate at an accused's first appearance that has led largely to the obsolescence of preparatory examinations, though under the statute they can still be held. See section 123.

I am indebted to the website African History, http://africanhistory.about.com/od/apartheid/a/TreasonTrial.htm (accessed 25 February 2013), for the summary of the Treason Trial judges' verdict.

X: Law and armed resistance to apartheid – the Rivonia Trial

This section draws heavily on the gripping account of the trial by Joel Joffe, the attorney for the Rivonia accused, *The State v Nelson Mandela: The Trial that Changed South Africa* (2007).

In addition to the Rivonia accused listed in the text, two further accused were arraigned, but not convicted – Jimmy Kantor (whom the prosecutor, Percy Yutar, vindictively prosecuted as the brother-in-law and law partner of Harold Wolpe, who was arrested and supposed to stand trial with the Rivonia accused, but sensationally escaped from custody with Arthur Goldreich), and Bob Hepple, who agreed to give evidence against the accused, but managed to slip out of the country, into exile abroad, without doing so.

Joffe tells the stories of both Kantor and Hepple. Hepple's arresting personal account is available at http://www.sahistory.org.za/archive/rivonia-story-accused-no11-bob-hepple (accessed 1 March 2013).

On Mandela's military training, see the authoritative account on the Nelson Mandela Foundation's website, http://www.nelsonmandela.org/news/entry/nelson-mandelas-military-training (accessed 8 October 2013).

Joffe recounts the quashing of the indictment in chapter 3, pp 41-57.

Information on Operation Mayibuye is from Joel Joffe, and from the website http://law2.umkc.edu/faculty/projects/ftrials/mandela/mandelaoperationm.html (accessed 27 April 2013), which carries the document's full text, as well as from the on-line version of Nelson Mandela's autobiography, http://w.archive.org/stream/LongWalkToFreedom/PBI3231_djvu.txt (accessed 27 April 2013). The translation of Mayibuye as 'let Africa come back' also comes from Mandela's autobiography.

The statute the prosecution relied on for the main charge against the accused was the Sabotage Act, 76 of 1962.

Joffe's assessment of Judge-President De Wet is on p 35 of his book.

Information on Bram Fischer is from Stephen Clingman, *Bram Fischer: Afrikaner Revolutionary* (David Philip, 1998), and Martin Meredith, *Fischer's Choice: A Life of Bram Fischer* (Jonathan Ball, 2002).

Quashing the indictment: Joffe chapter 3; Broun, *Saving Nelson Mandela –
The Rivonia Trial and the Fate of South Africa* (2012) chapter 6.
The passage from Joffe on the importance to the trial of Operation Mayi-
buye is on p 146 of his book.

XI: Law and the struggle for justice under apartheid – the legacy for democracy

The *Law Society v Mandela* judgment was distinguished and not followed
when Judge-President De Wet (Judges Hill and Boshoff concurring)
struck Bram Fischer off the roll of advocates on 2 November 1965 in
Society of Advocates of South Africa v Fischer 1966 (1) SA 133 (T). But
even in doing so, Judge De Wet said, 'I regret I cannot agree' with the
submissions for Fischer. And De Wet managed to envisage a time when
Fischer might reapply for admission as an advocate. 'It is impossible
for the court to foresee what will happen in the future,' he said. 'We are
concerned with the laws in force at the present time and with the structure of society as it exists in this country at the present time.' Even
apartheid-supporting judges did not envisage 1 000 years of apartheid
supremacy.
Quotes reflecting Mandela's assessment of the legal system are from his
biography by Anthony Sampson. Sampson cites Mandela's remark about
a 'race-blinded white oligarchy' on p 129.
The two judgments that put an effective end to the enforcement of the
pass laws are *Komani NO v Bantu Affairs Administration Board, Peninsula
Area* 1980 (4) SA 449 (A) and *Oos-Randse Administrasieraad v Rikhoto*
1983 (3) SA 595 (A). For the significance of the cases, and the impact
of Arthur Chaskalson's advocacy, see the tribute Geoff Budlender paid
to Chaskalson on his untimely death on 1 December 2012, available at
http://groundup.org.za/content/tribute-arthur-chaskalson (accessed
28 February 2013).
Geoff Budlender, the instructing attorney in Mrs Komani's case, recalled
in his tribute to 'the finest advocacy I have ever heard' that Chaskalson 'constructed a brilliant and novel argument which was so persuasive that Chief Justice Rumpff – hostile from the outset – became frustrated ... But he could not find the flaw in the argument, because there
was none. Ultimately, the Appellate Division unanimously decided in
favour of Mr and Mrs Komani.'
The Moutse case, in which John Dugard was the lead advocate, is *Mathebe
v Regering van die Republiek van Suid-Afrika* 1988 (3) SA 667 (A).
The KwaNdebele women's vote case is *Machika v Staatspresident* 1989 (4)

SA 19 (T). Of this case, Geoff Budlender, the instructing attorney from the Legal Resources Centre, in an email communication to me dated 28 February 2013, recalled: 'One of my all-time favourite cases. The clients were wonderful. And it really did stop independence in its tracks – and the outcome played a significant role in bringing an end to the civil war in KwaNdebele. I have greatly enjoyed attempting to explain to non-SA audiences how under apartheid you could complain that authorised racist subordinate legislation was invalid because it infringed the right to gender equality – and that a conservative judge could uphold the argument.'

XII: The apartheid judiciary and the Truth and Reconciliation Commission

On the Truth and Reconciliation Commission, see David Dyzenhaus, *Judging the Judges, Judging Ourselves: Truth, Reconciliation and the Apartheid Legal Order* (Oxford, Hart Publishing, 1998), and Deborah Posel and Graeme Simpson, *Commissioning the Past – Understanding South Africa's Truth and Reconciliation Commission* (Witwatersrand University Press, 2002).

For a critical assessment of the judiciary's involvement in apartheid, and its non-participation in the Truth and Reconciliation Commission, see David Dyzenhaus, above. For a more upbeat assessment of the Bloemfontein appeal court's achievements under apartheid, see Stacia L Haynie, *Judging in Black and White: Decision Making in the South African Appellate Division, 1950-1990* (Peter Lang Publishing, 2003).

The history of the TRC process is recounted in three Constitutional Court judgments: see *Azanian People's Organisation (AZAPO) v President of the Republic of South Africa* ZACC 16; 1996 (4) SA 672 (CC); *Du Toit v Minister for Safety and Security* [2009] ZACC 22; 2009 (6) SA 128 (CC) paras 17-30 (available at http://www.saflii.org/za/cases/ZACC/2009/22.html (accessed 18 March 2013)) and *The Citizen 1978 (Pty) Ltd v McBride* [2011] ZACC 11; 2011 (4) SA 191 (CC) paras 49-78, available at http://www.saflii.org/za/cases/ZACC/2011/11.html (accessed 25 November 2013).

The five senior judges' submission to the TRC was published in (1998) 115 *South African Law Journal* 21. Justice Langa's submission was published in (1998) 115 *South African Law Journal* 36.

The TRC's report deals with lawyers and judges in volume four, chapter four, available at http://www.justice.gov.za/trc/report/finalreport/Volume%204.pdf (accessed 18 March 2013).

XIII: Apartheid law and the constitutional transition

The most arresting defence of the rule of law as intrinsically curbing power is EP Thompson's postscript to *Whigs and Hunters: The Origin of the Black Act* (1975).

XIV: Law as a reparative project

No notes.

CHAPTER TWO

I: Illness and shame

On HIV as a retrovirus, there is an informative summary at http://www.chm.bris.ac.uk/webprojects2002/levasseur/hiv/hiv3.htm (accessed 6 March 2013).

William Shakespeare, Sonnet 129, lines 9-12. Lust is 'Mad in pursuit, and in possession so; /Had, having, and in quest to have, extreme; /A bliss in proof, and proved, a very woe; /Before, a joy proposed; behind, a dream.'

II: The mass epidemic of AIDS reaches South Africa

The history of the National Union of Mineworkers is recounted at http://www.num.org.za/new/history/ (accessed 24 March 2013).

III: Friday 2 February 1990

For my description of the Johannesburg High Court building, and the statue of Carl von Brandis, I am indebted to the anonymous author of the vivid material posted at http://www.gauteng.net/attractions/entry/the_johannesburg_high_court/ (accessed 9 March 2013).

The judgment setting aside the magistrate's ruling forbidding cross-examination in the Kinross fire inquest is reported as *National Union of Mineworkers v Government Mining Engineer* 1990 (2) SA 638 (W).

My account of the Kinross mine disaster draws on Judge Goldstein's reported judgment, and on the information on the South African History Online site, http://www.sahistory.org.za/dated-event/mine-disaster-kills-177 (accessed 7 March 2013).

The then mining legislation was the Mines and Works Act, 27 of 1956.

IV: AIDS and the path to democracy

My account of the post-1990 negotiations has benefited greatly from the South African History Online website, including http://www.sahistory. org.za/dated-event/talks-between-government-and-anc-negotiations-proceed (accessed 9 March 2013). See also Allister Sparks, *Tomorrow Is Another Country: The Inside Story of South Africa's Road to Change* (1995) and Patty Waldmeir, *Anatomy of a Miracle* (1997).

My sources for the account of train violence are the Report of the Truth and Reconciliation Commission, chapter 2, available at http://www.justice.gov.za/trc/report/finalreport/Volume%202.pdf (accessed 9 March 2013), as well as an archived SABC news report available at http://www.sabctrc.saha.org.za/glossary/train_violence.htm&tab = glossary (accessed 9 March 2013). Studying the East Rand townships of Thokoza and Katlehong, researcher Gary Kynoch has recently presented a 'more fractured, less partisan picture' of responsibility for the violence, one that rejects 'the one-dimensional morality play that still retains hegemonic status', and that 'transcends the dominant narrative that African National Congress (ANC) supporters in the townships were under relentless attack by state security units known as the "third force", along with the co-opted impis of the Inkatha Freedom Party (IFP)'. The author's evidence 'indicates that Inkatha was responsible for much of the violence, but that ANC-affiliated militants also conducted murderous campaigns. Some police commanders and their units initiated violence for political ends, but different police and military groups operated independently and lacked a uniform political orientation. Some favoured the IFP, some backed the ANC, while others were divided or indifferent.' He concludes that 'the narrative that casts the ANC as victims of a state-orchestrated onslaught versus the Inkatha sell-outs who opportunistically sided with the white government (and its security forces) does not accurately capture events on the ground in Thokoza and Katlehong'. See Gary Kynoch, 'Reassessing Transition Violence: Voices From South Africa's Township Wars, 1990-4', *African Affairs*, 2013, 112 (447), pp 283–303, downloaded for me from http://afraf.oxfordjournals. org/ at the University of Pretoria on March 11, 2013. Kynoch is, however, critical of Anthea Jeffery's account, which attributes responsibility for the attacks largely to the ANC: see *People's War: New Light on the Struggle for South Africa* (2009).

My recollection of the injuries Soneni Ncube of CALS sustained in the Sebokeng violence was refreshed by personal email communication from her on 13 March 2013.

The CODESA opening declaration of intent is available at http://www.nelsonmandela.org/omalley/index.php/site/q/03lv02039/04lv02046/05lv02047/06lv02049/07lv02052.htm (accessed 11 March 2013).

V: The trial of Barry McGeary

The AIDS confidentiality trial was Case No 90/25317, *McGeary v Kruger*, Witwatersrand High Court, 16 October 1991 (judgment of Levy AJ, unreported). The judgment is noted in (1992) 8 *South African Journal on Human Rights*, p 154, where it is recalled that Mr Acting Justice Levy found that what led to fears of increase in the prevalence of HIV was the 'spread of the disease amongst persons practising normal sexual behaviour, presumably originating from homosexuals or bisexuals'.

VI: The media and AIDS

Cathy Stagg, a journalist who covered the trial for the *Sunday Times* newspaper, reflects on the media coverage in a fiction piece, 'Closer to God in a Garden', in Maire Fisher (ed), *Women Flashing: A Collection of Flash Fiction From Women's Writing Workshops* (2005).

VII: Preparing a future democracy for AIDS

The conscription case is *End Conscription Campaign v Minister of Defence* 1993 (1) SA 589 (T) (judgment of Eloff JP, van der Walt and van Dyk JJ concurring).

Nelson Mandela's speech to the national AIDS conference at Nasrec on 23 October 1992 is available at http://www.sahistory.org.za/archive/speech-nelson-mandela-national-conference-aids-%C2%A0nasrec-23rd-october-1992 (accessed 11 March 2013).

The full Nelson Mandela/HSRC Study of HIV/AIDS report, the South African National HIV Prevalence, Behavioural Risks and Mass Media Household Survey, 2002, by Olive Shisana and Leickness Simbayi (editors) is available at http://www.hsrcpress.ac.za/product.php?productid=2009 (accessed 13 March 2013). The 2005 survey, South African National HIV Prevalence, HIV Incidence, Behaviour and Communication Survey, 2005, by Shisana O, Rehle T, Simbayi L, Parker W, Zuma K, Bhana A, Connolly C, Jooste S, Pillay V (editors) is available at http://www.hsrcpress.ac.za/product.php?productid=2134 (accessed 13 March 2013).

Facts and figures on the HIV epidemic are from UNAIDS and the national Department of Health, specifically UNAIDS Epidemiological Fact Sheets, 2004, available at http://data.unaids.org/Publications/Fact-Sheets01/southafrica_en.pdf (accessed 8 March 2013), and see the website of the Department of Health, http://www.doh.gov.za/list.php?-type = HIV%20and%20AIDS (accessed 3 October 2013).

See, too, JP Swanevelder, HGV Kistner, A van Middelkoop, 'The South African HIV Epidemic, reflected by Nine Provincial Epidemics, 1990-1996', available at http://archive.samj.org.za/1998%20VOL%2088%20 Jan-Dec/9-12/Articles/10%20October/17%20THE%20SOUTH%20 AFRICAN%20HIV%20EPIDEMIC,%20REFLECTED%20BY%20 NINE%20PROVINCIAL%20EPIDEMICS,%201990-1196,%20J%20 P%20Swaneve.pdf (accessed 8 March 2013).

VIII: The appeal court decides Barry McGeary's appeal

The appeal court judgment setting aside the judgment of Levy AJ is *Jansen van Vuuren NO v Kruger* [1993] ZASCA 145; 1993 (4) SA 842 (AD); [1993] 2 All SA 619 (A) (28 September 1993), available at http://www.saflii.org/za/cases/ZASCA/1993/145.html (accessed 13 March 2013). My account of events during argument was kindly confirmed by email communication from Mr Peter A Solomon, SC, on 14 March 2013, and from my colleague Justice Louis Harms, retired Deputy President of the Supreme Court of Appeal, on 25 March 2013.

CHAPTER THREE

I: Judicial office and mortal frailty

On 'long-term non-progressors', see a study by Elahi and others, 'Protective HIV-specific CD8 + T cells evade Treg cell suppression', explaining how some people with HIV delay disease progression to AIDS. This study was published in the on-line edition of *Nature Medicine*, 17 July 2011, and can be purchased at http://www.nature.com/nm/journal/v17/n8/pdf/nm.2422.pdf%3FWT.ec_id%3DNM-201108 (visited 14 March 2013). I have relied for my understanding of it on a news release by the Fred Hutchinson Cancer Research Center dated 25 July 2011, available at https://www.fhcrc.org/en/news/center-news/2011/07/control-HIV.html (accessed 14 March 2013). For a helpful summary of the science on 'elite controllers' (people with detectable levels of HIV, but whose levels do not rise significantly, even without treatment), see Babbage, Science and Technology, 'AIDS treatment – Visconti's coup',

14 March 2013, available at http://www.economist.com/blogs/babbage/2013/03/aids-treatment (accessed 18 March 2013).

Information on pneumocystis pneumonia, or PCP (which used to be called pneumocystis carinii pneumonia), is available at http://www.ncbi.nlm.nih.gov/pubmedhealth/PMH0001692/ (accessed 27 September 2013).

II: The judiciary in transition from apartheid to democracy

On the Bloemfontein appeal court's record under apartheid, see Stacia L Haynie, *Judging in Black and White: Decision Making in the South African Appellate Division, 1950-1990* (Peter Lang Publishing, 2003).

The interim Constitution is available at http://www.info.gov.za/documents/constitution/93cons.htm (accessed 11 March 2013). The provision on transitional arrangements and the judiciary, section 241(2) and (3), summarised in the text, is available at http://www.info.gov.za/documents/constitution/93cons.htm#SECTION241 (accessed 16 March 2013). The provision on the jurisdiction of the Constitutional Court is section 98, available at http://www.info.gov.za/documents/constitution/93cons.htm#CHAP7 (accessed 16 March 2013). President Mandela's power to appoint the first President of the Constitutional Court derived from section 97(2)(a), available at the same place. Section 105(1)(a) provided that the Chief Justice would preside at meetings of the JSC. The President of the Constitutional Court was a member in terms of section 105(1)(b).

For judicial jostling about the pre-eminence of the Constitutional Court in all matters related to the Constitution, see *Pharmaceutical Manufacturers Association of South Africa: In re Ex Parte President of the Republic of South Africa* [2000] ZACC 1; 2000 (2) SA 674 (25 February 2000), paras 20-56, available at http://www.saflii.org.za/za/cases/ZACC/2000/1.html (accessed 16 March 2013).

My information that Chief Justice Ogilvie Thompson insisted that Judge Corbett be appointed as a judge of appeal is based on my recollection of personal communications to me by Judge Corbett. See also Ellison Kahn's introduction to Kahn (editor), *Quest for Justice – Essays in Honour of Michael McGregor Corbett* (1995). The dissent of Judge Corbett was in *Goldberg v Minister of Prisons* 1979 (1) SA 14 (A)). The appeal court adopted the dissent as correct in *Minister of Justice v Hofmeyr* [1993] ZASCA 40; 1993 (3) SA 131 (A), available at http://www.saflii.org/za/cases/ZASCA/1993/40.html (accessed 16 March 2014).

President Mandela's speech on 11 December 1996, at the state banquet to mark Chief Justice Corbett's retirement, is available at http://www.anc.org.za/show.php?id = 3503 (accessed 16 March 2013).

III: Joining the judiciary

Details on Joe Slovo's life and his death are available on the South African History Online website at http://www.sahistory.org.za/people/joe-slovo (accessed 19 March 2013).

The annual salary of a judge of the high court in 1997/1998 was R356 805 – circular from JN Labuschagne, Head, Ministerial Services, referenced 3/15/1/1(HMS) and dated 16 March 1998. I am indebted to Ms Wilma Mostert, registrar of my colleague Judge AN Kruger of the high court, Bloemfontein, for kindly locating this information for me. Household income for late 1990s sourced from 'South Africa Survey 1999/2000', South African Institute of Race Relations, 296 (2000). The ensuing section draws on the research undertaken for and references collected in Geffen, N. and Cameron, E. 2009. The deadly hand of denial: Governance and politically-instigated AIDS denialism in South Africa. CSSR Working Paper 257, available at: http://www.cssr.uct.ac.za/sites/cssr.uct.ac.za/files/pubs/WP257.pdf (accessed 19 March 2013).

IV: ARV treatment and openness with the public

I have sourced Zackie Achmat's speech at the funeral of Simon Nkoli in December 1998 from the transcript of Beat-It (a popular television programme promoting treatment awareness and literacy) celebrating five years of the TAC, available at http://www.beatit.co.za/archive-documentaries/five-years-of-tac (accessed 18 March 2013).

On the internal uprising in which Simon Nkoli participated, see the South African History Online website, available at http://www.sahistory.org.za/township-uprising-1984-1985 (accessed 19 March 2013).

Nathan Geffen, an insider, tells the story of the Treatment Action Campaign in *Debunking Delusions* (2010). More information on the book is available at http://www.quackdown.info/debunkingdelusions/ (accessed 19 March 2013).

V: President Mbeki questions the science of AIDS

For an account of President Mbeki's flirtation with AIDS denialism, on which this chapter draws, see Geffen, N. and Cameron, E. 2009. The deadly hand of denial: Governance and politically-instigated AIDS denialism in South Africa. CSSR Working Paper 257, available at: http://www.cssr.uct.ac.za/sites/cssr.uct.ac.za/files/pubs/WP257.pdf (accessed 19 March 2013).

For President Thabo Mbeki's life, the indispensable source is the biography by Mark Gevisser, *Thabo Mbeki: The Dream Deferred* (2007).

Figures on HIV prevalence in 1990 and in 1999, when President Mbeki took office, are taken from 'National HIV and Syphilis Antenatal Seroprevalence Survey in South Africa, 2005', Department of Health (2006), available at http://www.doh.gov.za/docs/reports/2005/hiv.pdf (accessed 21 March 2013). The official figures for the period 1990 to 2005 are tabulated on p 10.

I have relied for some information on AZT on the extensive and densely referenced entry in Wikipedia, available at http://en.wikipedia.org/wiki/Zidovudine (accessed 20 March 2013). The Concorde Trial reported the deficiencies of AZT as a monotherapy, finding that there was 'no significant difference in progression of HIV disease' between those taking AZT and those not: see 'Concorde: MRC/ANRS randomised double-blind controlled trial of immediate and deferred zidovudine in symptom-free HIV infection. Concorde Coordinating Committee', published in *The Lancet* 1994 Apr 9; 343(8902):871-81, accessible from http://www.ncbi.nlm.nih.gov/pubmed/7908356 (visited 20 March 2013).

President Mbeki's address to the National Council of Provinces on 28 October 1999 is available at http://www.info.gov.za/speeches/1999/991028409p1004.htm (accessed 19 March 2013).

Statistics for Thailand are available at http://www.unaids.org/en/regionscountries/countries/thailand/ (accessed 5 October 2013).

Statistics for Nigeria are available at http://www.naca.gov.ng/ (accessed 5 October 2013).

For President Mbeki's comparison of AIDS denialism to persecuted fighters for knowledge, see his letter of 3 April 2000 to President Clinton, Prime Minister Blair, President Schroeder and others, http://www.pbs.org/wgbh/pages/frontline/aids/docs/mbeki.html (accessed 21 March 2013).

President Mbeki's correspondence with opposition leader Tony Leon is posted on a website dedicated to propounding the denialist position on AIDS, http://www.virusmyth.com/aids/news/letmbeki.htm (accessed 23 March 2013).

President Mbeki's speech in which he accuses treatment activists, following AIDS science, of regarding Africans as lustful germ carriers, was the Inaugural ZK Matthews Memorial Lecture, delivered at the

University of Fort Hare, 12 October 2001, available at http://www.unisa.ac.za/contents/colleges/docs/2001/tm2001/tm101201.pdf (accessed 20 March 2013).

President Mbeki's address at the opening session of the 13th international AIDS conference in Durban on Sunday 9 July 2000 is available at http://www.info.gov.za/speeches/2000/000714451p1001.htm (accessed 21 March 2013).

For the history and effects of President Mbeki's denialist postures see Nattrass, N, *The Moral Economy of AIDS in South Africa* (2004); Cameron, E, *Witness to AIDS* (2005); Nattrass, N, *Mortal Combat: AIDS Denialism and the Struggle for Antiretrovirals in South Africa* (2007); Gevisser, M, *Thabo Mbeki: The Dream Deferred* (2007); Feinstein, A, *After the Party* (2007); Cullinan, K and Thom, A, *The Virus, Vitamins and Vegetables – The South African HIV/AIDS Mystery* (2009); and Geffen, N, *Debunking Delusions* (2010).

For a conservative estimate of the cost in human life of presidential flirtation with denialism, see Pride Chigwedere and others, 'Estimating the Lost Benefits of Antiretroviral Drug Use in South Africa', 49 *Journal of Acquired Immune Deficiency Syndromes* (2008) 410-415, which can be accessed via http://libra.msra.cn/Publication/14190500/estimating-the-lost-benefits-of-antiretroviral-drug-use-in-south-africa (visited 21 March 2013).

On the negotiations that led to the interim Constitution, see LM du Plessis and HM Corder, *Understanding South Africa's Transitional Bill of Rights* (Juta, 1994); Carl F Stychin, *A Nation by Rights* (Temple University Press, 1998); Richard Spitz and Matthew Chaskalson, *The Politics of Transition – a Hidden History of South Africa's Negotiated Settlement* (Witwatersrand University Press, 2000).

VI: The courts, presidential policy-making and the new Constitution

The Restitution of Land Rights Act, 22 of 1994 is available at http://www.info.gov.za/acts/1994/a22-94.pdf (accessed 21 March 2013).

The explanation of the transitional agreement for the Constitutional Court's vetting of the final Constitution subject to Constitutional Principles is from the first certification judgment (*Certification of the Constitution of the Republic of South Africa*, 1996 [1996] ZACC 26; 1996 (4) SA 744 (CC), para 13), available at http://www.saflii.org/cgi-bin/disp.pl?file = za/cases/ZACC/1996/26.html&query = certification (accessed 21 March 2013). The Constitutional Principles are set out as Annexure 2 to this judgment.

Information on the Natives' Land Act 27 of 1913 can be obtained from the

South African History Online website at http://www.sahistory.org.za/dated-event/native-land-act-was-passed (accessed 21 March 2013).

Section 71(2) of the interim Constitution provided that 'The new constitutional text passed by the Constitutional Assembly, or any provision thereof, shall not be of any force and effect unless the Constitutional Court has certified that all the provisions of such text comply with the Constitutional Principles'.

The Constitutional Court certified the amended text of the final Constitution as complying with the Constitutional Principles in *Certification of the Amended Text of the Constitution of The Republic Of South Africa, 1996* [1996] ZACC 24; 1997 (2) SA 97, available at http://www.saflii.org/cgi-bin/disp.pl?file = za/cases/ZACC/1996/24.html&query = certification (accessed 25 March 2013).

VII: The new Constitution and the fundamental right to health care

The right to health care is contained in sections 27 and 28 of the Constitution. In part, these provisions read –

27(1) Everyone has the right to have access to –

  (a) health care services, including reproductive health care;

   . . . .

  (2) The state must take reasonable legislative and other measures, within its available resources, to achieve the progressive realisation of each of these rights.

   . . . .

28(1) Every child has the right –

   . . . .

  (c) to basic nutrition, shelter, basic health care services and social services.

Uslaner, EM (2008). *Corruption, Inequality, and the Rule of Law*. Cambridge: Cambridge University Press. On socio-economic rights, see too Sandra Liebenberg, *Socio-Economic Rights: Adjudication Under a Transformative Constitution* (2010) and Kirsty McLean, *Constitutional Deference, Courts and Socia-Economic Rights in South Africa* (2009).

CHAPTER FOUR

I: Pretoria High Court, Monday morning, 26 November 2001

The best on-line resource for the 1914 rebellion seems to be http://en.wikipedia.org/wiki/Maritz_Rebellion (accessed 25 March 2013).

On the 1922 mineworkers' rebellion, see http://www.sahistory.org.za/topic/rand-rebellion-1922 (accessed 25 March 2013). See, too, Rodney Warwick, 'White on White Violence: The 1922 Rand Revolution' (15 March 2012), available at http://www.politicsweb.co.za/politicsweb/view/politicsweb/en/page71639?oid = 286744&sn = Detail and on the SA History Online website at http://historymatters.co.za/white-on-white-violence-the-1922-rand-revolution-by-rodney-warwick (both accessed 25 March 2013).

On Judge Schreiner sentencing Robey Leibbrandt to death, see the digitised newspaper coverage preserved at http://trove.nla.gov.au/ndp/del/page/622157?zoomLevel = 1 (accessed 25 March 2013), and on Afrikaner responses to South African involvement in the Second World War generally, see Rodney Warwick, 'Afrikaners and the Second World War' (6 March 2012), available at http://www.politicsweb.co.za/politicsweb/view/politicsweb/en/page71639?oid = 284445&sn = Detail&pid = 71639 (accessed 25 March 2013). The appeal court dealt with the legal issues arising from Leibbrandt's trial in *Rex v Leibbrandt* 1944 AD 253. (Prime Minister Jan Smuts commuted Leibbrandt's death sentence to life imprisonment, and on coming into power in 1948 the National Party government released him.)

II: The law, the Constitution and the crisis of death from AIDS

In this entire chapter I have drawn heavily on the minutely documented statistical and other evidence presented by the applicants, and not denied by the respondents, in *TAC v Minister of Health*. Most of the case papers are available at http://www.tac.org.za/Documents/MTCTCourtCase/MTCTCourtCase.htm (accessed 25 March 2013).

The estimated deaths from AIDS in 2000 are from the now-celebrated article by Pride Chigwedere and others, 'Estimating the Lost Benefits of Antiretroviral Drug Use in South Africa', published on line in the *Journal of Acquired Immune Deficiency Syndromes* (JAIDS), 20 October 2008, at table 1, p 412.

For President Mbeki's question in Parliament in September 2000 whether a virus can cause a syndrome, see http://www.aegis.org/DisplayContent/?SectionID = 370502 (accessed 29 March 2013), and the follow-up article by the then spokesperson for the ANC, Mr Smuts Ngonyama, 'A virus cannot cause a syndrome' in *Business Day*, 4 October 2000, available on the denialist website Virusmyth, at http://www.virusmyth.com/aids/news/bdmbeki.htm (accessed 29 March 2013).

On 4 November 2004, the University of Cape Town conferred an outstanding leadership award on President Mbeki. The Vice-Chancellor,

Professor Njabulo Ndebele, commended President Mbeki for his 'thoughtful steadfastness' in the face of activism: 'It could be said that you lead with pain and resolve, helped on by your enormous sense of responsibility.' See http://www.politicsweb.co.za/politicsweb/view/politicsweb/en/page71656?oid = 270558&sn = Detail (accessed 28 March 2013). In *The Dilemmas of Leadership* (2004), Professor Ndebele commended President Mbeki's 'steadfast and intelligent refusal to be trapped in a web of assumptions' about AIDS. He suggested that 'it seems possible to argue that HIV/AIDS does not constitute a major and serious threat to society because, given the reporting restrictions on HIV/AIDS-related deaths, the prevalence statistics did not bear out the contention that it was such a threat'. Quoted by Seepe, Sipho, 'Educated jesters of Mbeki's court', *Business Day*, 18 September 2006, available at http://ccs.ukzn.ac.za/default.asp?3,28,11,2794 (accessed 28 March 2013).

III: The crisis of infants and HIV

The doctor from the Cecilia Makiwane Hospital is quoted by Mark Heywood, then head of the AIDS Law Project, and now head of SECTION27, in his presentation at the Barcelona international AIDS conference in 2002, available at http://www.tac.org.za/Documents/MTCTCourtCase/MTCTCourtCase.htm (accessed 27 March 2013).

IV: The breakthrough of hope – anti-retroviral protection for babies

See 'WHO: New data on the prevention of mother-to-child transmission of HIV and their policy implications. Conclusions and recommendations.WHO technical consultation on behalf of the UNFPA/UNICEF/WHO/UNAIDS Inter-Agency Task Team on Mother-to-Child Transmission of HIV. Geneva, 11-13 October 2000. Geneva, World Health Organisation, 2001,WHO/RHR/01.28', available at http://whqlibdoc.who.int/hq/2001/WHO_RHR_01.28.pdf (accessed 25 March 2013).

V: Combivir, plus Nevirapine – my own drug combination in 2000

Information on Combivir can be obtained at http://www.aidsmeds.com/archive/Combivir_1083.shtml (accessed 27 March 2013)

VI: Infants born with HIV – government digs in its heels

The experts' recommendation regarding pilot sites was that 'There is currently no justification to restrict use of any of these regimens to pilot project or research settings'. See page 9 of the meeting summary at http://whqlibdoc.who.int/hq/2001/WHO_RHR_01.28.pdf (accessed 5 October 2013).

VII: The activists consider the courts – the legacy of Soobramoney and Grootboom

Soobramoney v Minister of Health (Kwazulu-Natal) [1997] ZACC 17; 1998 (1) SA 765 (CC), available at http://www.saflii.org/za/cases/ZACC/1997/17.html (accessed 26 March 2013).

Government of the Republic of South Africa v Grootboom [2000] ZACC 19; 2001 (1) SA 46 (4 October 2000), available at http://www.saflii.org/za/cases/ZACC/2000/19.html (accessed 11 October 2013).

In Edwin Cameron, 'What You Can Do with Rights', [2012] *European Human Rights Law Review*, issue 2, pp 148-161, in overviewing the court's socio-economic rights cases generally, I cite international commentators who have praised the *Grootboom* decision.

VIII: The Biko case in medical memory

The description of Steven Bantu Biko's condition is based on evidence set out in the judgments in the two court cases cited below, as well as the evidence of Professor Peter Folb at the TRC – see http://www.justice.gov.za/trc/media/1997/9706/s970617j.htm (accessed 27 March 2013).

In *Veriawa v President, SA Medical and Dental Council* 1985 (2) 293 (T), the Pretoria High Court (Boshoff JP, O'Donovan J concurring) set aside the decision by the SAMDC refusing to institute disciplinary proceedings against the Biko doctors under the Medical, Dental and Supplementary Health Service Professions Act, 56 of 1974. Further information on the case is in *Tucker v SA Medical and Dental Council* 1980 (2) SA 207 (T), where Coetzee J dismissed an attempt by Dr Tucker to thwart the early stages of the investigation into his conduct.

The evidence that the Council considered appealing against Judge-President Boshoff's ruling was given before the TRC by Dr Len Bekker on behalf of the Medical Council – see http://www.justice.gov.za/trc/media/1997/9706/s970617j.htm (accessed 27 March 2013).

For the impassioned resolution adopted by the Wits University medical school, see the letter by its Dean, Professor Phillip Tobias, published in the *British Medical Journal* of 19 July 1980, p 231, available at http://www.ncbi.nlm.nih.gov/pmc/articles/PMC1713643/?page=1 (accessed 27 March, 2013).

For the disciplinary outcomes against Drs Lang and Tucker, see 'Pretoria doctor loses his license', *New York Times*, 17 October 1985 http://www.nytimes.com/1985/10/17/world/pretoria-doctor-loses-his-license.html; 'Steve Biko: Ten years after', *Mail & Guardian*, 11 September 1987 http://mg.co.za/article/1987-09-11-steve-biko-ten-years-after; 'Biko's doctor apologises for death of black activist', *Observer-Reporter*, 21 October 1991, carried in microfiche at http://news.google.com/newspapers?nid = 2519&dat = 19911021&id = A4FeAAAAIBAJ&sjid = 7mENAAAAIBAJ&pg = 2252,7025467; 'Doctor apologises to Biko family', SAPA, 17 June 1997 http://www.justice.gov.za/trc/media/1997/9706/s970617j.htm (all accessed 27 March 2013).

For Professor Peter Folb's apology to the Biko family at the TRC hearings on 17 June 1997, see http://www.justice.gov.za/trc/media/1997/9706/s970617j.htm (accessed 27 March 2013).

The final report of the TRC indicates (volume 4, chapter 5, p 113) that 'Dr Lang was found guilty of improper conduct on five counts and was suspended for three months (ironically, this suspension was conditionally suspended for two years and so had no impact on Dr Lang's practice of medicine). Dr Lang continued to be employed as a district surgeon by the Department of Health and was, in fact, promoted to chief district surgeon in Port Elizabeth in Dr Tucker's place.' http://www.justice.gov.za/trc/report/finalreport/Volume%204.pdf (accessed 27 March 2013).

IX: The claimants decide to act

The doctors' letter of demand is included in the court papers.

X: The TAC claimants make their case for court intervention

The TAC papers are available at http://www.tac.org.za/Documents/MTCTCourtCase/MTCTCourtCase.htm (accessed 27 March 2013).

XI: Government's response in the court case

The TAC website asserts that the state respondents in the case refused a request for electronic copies of their papers. The TAC therefore typed up two of the opposing affidavits, namely those of Dr Jonathan Bernhard Levin and Dr Philip Chukwuka Onyebujoh. Those are available at http://www.tac.org.za/Documents/MTCTCourtCase/MTCTCourtCase.htm (accessed 27 March 2013).

XII: The TAC rejoins to government's response

For an overview of the court papers, see Mark Heywood, 'Current Developments – Preventing Mother-To-Child HIV Transmission in South Africa: Background, Strategies and Outcomes of the Treatment Action Campaign Case Against the Minister of Health, (2003) 19 *SA Journal on Human Rights* pp 278-315. Heywood claims that 'Although intimidating in volume, once deconstructed it was clear that the government papers were full of deception and contradiction. Health Department officials sought to undermine established science and scientific institutions. There seemed to be very little of a sense of urgency to come to the assistance of pregnant women with HIV or to resolve the dilemmas expressed by hundreds of doctors in the TAC papers about not being able to treat women properly. Sometimes the lack of compassion is quite startling' (p 298).

XIII: *The Pretoria High Court hears the TAC case*

See Heywood (2003) 19 *SA Journal on Human Rights* 278.

For the family connection of Marumo Moerane SC to President Mbeki (they are cousins), see Mark Gevisser, *Thabo Mbeki: The Dream Deferred* (2007).

XIV: *The Pretoria High Court decides the TAC case*

The judgment of Mr Justice Botha is reported only in an on-line subscription service, http://www.lexisnexis.co.za/ – *Treatment Action Campaign & others v Minister of Health & others* [2002] JOL 9482 (T). It can be downloaded from the TAC website at www.tac.org.za/Documents/MTCT-CourtCase/mtctjudgement.doc (accessed 5 October 2013).

My account of judgment hand-down is taken from Mark Heywood (2003) 19 *SA Journal on Human Rights* 278 at 301.

XV: *Government appeals to the Constitutional Court – the spectre of Castro Hlongwane*

The document 'Castro Hlongwane, Caravans, Cats, Geese, Foot & Mouth and Statistics – HIV/AIDS and the Struggle for the Humanisation of the African', dated March 2002, is available on the denialist website Virusmyth at http://www.virusmyth.com/aids/hiv/ancdoc.htm (accessed 28 March 2013).

For President Mbeki's endorsement of the views in the Castro Hlongwane document, see Mark Gevisser, *Thabo Mbeki: the Dream Deferred* (2007).

The judgment of Mr Justice Botha dated 11 March 2002 ordering the immediate implementation of the main part of his order of 14 December 2001, notwithstanding the pending appeal, is available at http://

www.saflii.org/za/cases/ZAGPHC/2002/3.html (accessed 28 March 2013).

The Constitutional Court's reasons for its order dated 4 April 2002, dismissing government's interim appeal, were given on 5 July 2002 and are available at http://www.saflii.org.za/za/cases/ZACC/2002/16.html (accessed 28 March 2013).

XVI: The Constitutional Court and the perils of the Nevirapine case

For the history of the Constitutional Court, and its past and present judges, see http://www.constitutionalcourt.org.za/site/thecourt/history. htm (accessed 28 March 2013).

For the number of persons hanged each year in Pretoria, see Professor Jolandi le Roux, 'The impact of the death penalty on criminality', conference paper presented at 'Convergence of Criminal Justice Systems: Building Bridges – Bridging the Gaps' hosted by the International Society for the Reform of Criminal Law (The Hague, The Netherlands, August 2003), available at http://www.isrcl.org/Papers/LeRoux.pdf (accessed 7 October 2013). Professor Le Roux says: 'A total of 4 288 persons have been executed in South Africa since 1911. A chronological analysis shows that the highest number of executions occurred in 1987 (a total of 164). The number of people executed declined from 164 in 1987 to 117 in 1988, and only 53 people were executed in 1989. This decrease in the number of executions was mainly due to widespread petitions circulated to save convicted criminals on death row' (p 5). Since 1989, there have been no executions in South Africa – President De Klerk announced a moratorium on executions in his speech on 2 February 1990.

XVII: Constitutional supremacy, the rule of law and the separation of powers

The first two provisions of the Constitution of the Republic of South Africa read thus:

1. Republic of South Africa
   The Republic of South Africa is one, sovereign, democratic state founded on the following values:
   a. Human dignity, the achievement of equality and the advancement of human rights and freedoms.
   b. Non-racialism and non-sexism.
   c. Supremacy of the constitution and the rule of law.
   d. Universal adult suffrage, a national common voters roll, regular

elections and a multi-party system of democratic government, to
ensure accountability, responsiveness and openness.

2. Supremacy of Constitution

This Constitution is the supreme law of the Republic; law or conduct inconsistent with it is invalid, and the obligations imposed by
it must be fulfilled.

The Constitution Seventeenth Amendment Act, 2102, was assented to
and gazetted in *Government Gazette* 36128, 1 February 2013.

The leading legal philosopher I quote is John Gardner, professor of jurisprudence at Oxford University. I have adapted his words from his
paper 'Strict liability in private law: some rule of law anxieties' at
page 4. Professor Gardner's full original quote is: 'The ideal of the rule
of law is the ideal according to which the law should be capable of
guiding those who are subject to it. People should not be ambushed
by the law; it should be possible for them reliably to anticipate the legal
consequences of their actions and reliably to obtain or to avoid those
consequences by following the law. So understood, the ideal sets a wide
range of disparate standards for all legal systems to live up to. The ones
that mainly concern us here are standards for legal norms to live up to.
Legal norms should not, according to the ideal of the rule of law, be
secret, retroactive, unclear, impossible to conform to, or forever in a
state of flux; and particular legal norms (rulings) should be applications of general legal norms (rules). Legal norms that do not live up to
these standards, as Lon Fuller famously explained, are not truly capable of being followed.' Professor Gardner in turn was drawing on a
famous essay by Joseph Raz, 'The Rule of Law and its Virtue', in *The
Authority of Law: Essays on Law and Morality* (OUP, 2009).

The statute that empowered the continued and indefinite detention of
Robert Sobukwe and others, by ministerial decree, was the General
Law Amendment Act, 37 of 1963. It authorised the Minister of Justice
to prohibit the release of a prisoner, convicted under certain security
statutes, if he considered that the person, on release, would be likely to
further the achievement of prohibited statutory objectives. The Minister's power to prohibit a prisoner's release in this way had to be renewed annually by Parliament.

Information on Robert Sobukwe and the Pan Africanist Congress can be
obtained from the SA History Online website, http://www.sahistory.
org.za/topic/pan-africanist-congress-timeline-1959-2011 (accessed 18
May 2013).

Section 167(5) of the Constitution provides that the Constitutional Court makes the final decision on whether a parliamentary or provincial statute, or conduct of the President, is constitutional, and must confirm any order of invalidity made by another court, before that order has any force.

A previous draft amendment, that would have given the Minister of Justice authority over the courts, was the Constitution Fourteenth Amendment Bill of 2005, published in *Government Gazette* of 14 December 2005. This proposed to insert into the Constitution a clause providing that 'The Cabinet member responsible for the administration of justice exercises authority over the administration and budget of all courts'. The Seventeenth Amendment put paid to this.

XVIII: The rule of law and the power of judges

On the Roman law of the Twelve Tables, see the entry in Encyclopaedia Britannica Online at http://www.britannica.com/EBchecked/topic/610934/Law-of-the-Twelve-Tables (accessed 18 May 2013).

On the Roman Praetor, see the entry at http://www.historyteacher.net/GlobalHistory-1/Readings/RomanLaw&TwelveTables.htm (accessed 17 May 2013).

The statute that abolished Latin as a requirement to qualify as an advocate in South Africa was the Admission of Advocates Amendment Act, 55 of 1994.

Section 34 of the Bill of Rights, access to courts, provides that everyone has the right to have any dispute that can be resolved by the application of law decided in a fair public hearing before a court or, where appropriate, another independent and impartial tribunal or forum. Section 35(3) gives every accused person the right to a fair trial, which includes the right 'of appeal to, or review by, a higher court'.

The e-tolling judgment is *National Treasury v Opposition to Urban Tolling Alliance [OUTA]* [2012] ZACC 18; 2012 (6) SA 223 (CC) (20 September 2012), available at http://www.saflii.org/za/cases/ZACC/2012/18.html (accessed 20 May 2013). The excerpts quoted are from paras 44 and 67-68.

In October 2013, the Supreme Court of Appeal dismissed the substantive challenges against e-tolling in *Opposition to Urban Tolling Alliance v South African National Roads Agency Limited* (90/2013) [2013] ZASCA 148 (9 October 2013), available at http://www.justice.gov.za/sca/judgments/sca_2013/sca2013-148.pdf (accessed 9 October 2013).

On the Constitutional Court's 'meaningful engagement' orders, see Geoff

Budlender's Bram Fischer Memorial Lecture, 2011, available at http://
www.lrc.org.za/papers/1654-2011-11-11-bram-fischer-memorial-lecture-
peoples-power-and-the-courts-by-geoff-budlender (accessed 18 May
2013). The first order was given on 19 February 2008, in *Occupiers of
51 Olivia Road, Berea Township and 197 Main Street Johannesburg v City
of Johannesburg* [2008] ZACC 1; 2008 (3) SA 208 (CC).

XIX: President Mandela, the rule of law and the separation of powers

The case in which the Constitutional Court overruled President Mandela's proclamation, and declared that the legislature could not delegate
its legislative authority to him, is *Executive Council of the Western Cape
Legislature v President of the Republic of South Africa* [1995] ZACC 8;
1995 (4) SA 877 (22 September 1995), available at http://www.saflii.
org/za/cases/ZACC/1995/8.html (accessed 29 March 2013).

Other pre-Nevirapine cases mentioned in which the Constitutional Court
ruled against government include *Mohamed v President of the Republic
of South Africa* 2001 (3) SA 893 (CC), available at http://www.saflii.
org/za/cases/ZACC/2001/18.html (accessed 29 March 2013) (depor-
tation and 'rendering' of foreign nationals); *National Coalition for Gay
and Lesbian Equality v Minister of Justice* 1999 (1) SA 6 (CC), available
at http://www.saflii.org/za/cases/ZACC/1998/15.html (accessed 29
March 2013) (same-sex offences); *August v The Independent Electoral
Commission* [1999] ZACC 3; 1999 (3) SA 1 (CC), available at http://www.
saflii.org/za/cases/ZACC/1999/3.html (accessed 7 October 2013) (prisoners' votes).

I mention the Nuneham Park meeting between exiled ANC lawyers and
internal lawyers and judges in *Witness to AIDS* (2005) on p 125 (www.
witnesstoaids.com).

XX: The Constitutional Court decides the Nevirapine case

The Constitutional Court judgment in the Nevirapine case is *Minister of
Health v Treatment Action Campaign* (No 2) [2002] ZACC 15; 2002 (5)
SA 721; 2002 (10) BCLR 1033 (5 July 2002), available at http://www.
saflii.org/za/cases/ZACC/2002/15.html (accessed 7 October 2013).

XXI: A historically momentous judgment and order

On the silence of international diplomats, former Canadian ambassador
Stephen Lewis vividly recalled in December 2011 how in 'all those
years of denialism' there was 'not a single voice at the most senior

levels of the United Nations – Under-Secretaries-General, the Secretary-General himself. Not one of them said publicly to Thabo Mbeki, "You're killing your people". Oh, to be sure, it was said in private by everyone. They took Thabo Mbeki aside and begged him to reverse course. He didn't budge an inch. Around him, in every community in South Africa, and in communities throughout a continent heavily influenced by South Africa, were the killing fields of AIDS. As we come to this thrilling moment of progress, I can't forget the millions who died on Thabo Mbeki's watch, while those who should have confronted him before the eyes of the world stood mute.' See Stephen Lewis, 'Remarks to ICASA 2011, Addis Ababa', 6 December 2011, available at http://www.aidsfree-world.org/Publications-Multimedia/Speeches/Stephen-Lewis-remarks-to-ICASA-2011.aspx (accessed 29 March 2013).

XXII: The rule of law and life-saving treatment for AIDS

The figure of two million people in South Africa on ARV treatment is from mid-2012 – see the presentation by Dr Olive Shisana, head of the HSRC, available at http://www.hsrc.ac.za/en/media-briefs/hiv-aids-stis-and-tb/plenary-session-3-20-june-2013-hiv-aids-in-south-africa-at-last-the-glass-is-half-full (accessed 7 October 2013).

The Constitutional Court's employment discrimination decision is *Hoffmann v South African Airways* [2000] ZACC 17; 2001 (1) SA 1 (CC) (28 September 2000), available at http://www.saflii.org/za/cases/ZACC/2000/17.html (accessed 29 March 2013).

The transcript of health minister Dr Manto Tshabalala-Msimang's threat on SABC News, 24 March 2002, that government would not respect the court order on Nevirapine is available at http://www.beatit.co.za/archive-documentaries/law-and-freedom-part-2-a-nice-country (accessed 7 October 2013):

News reader: The fight against HIV/AIDS is coming to the courts, the whole issue between government and the TAC regarding the roll-out of nevirapine. A very controversial issue. To discuss this we are joined now by our Health Minister doctor Manto Tshabalala-Msimang. Dr Tshabalala-Msimang: My own opinion is that the judiciary cannot prescribe from the bench. News reader: Will you stand by whatever the court decides? Dr Tshabalala-Msimang: No, I think the courts and the judiciary must also listen to the regulatory authorities both from this country and the United States. News reader: So are you saying no? Dr Tshabalala-Msimang: Yes I'm saying no. I am saying no.

Justice Kate O'Regan, 'A Forum for Reason: Reflections on the Role and Work of the Constitutional Court', the Helen Suzman memorial lecture, November 2011, available at http://www.hsf.org.za/resource-centre/lectures/HSF%20Memorial%20Lecture%202011.pdf (accessed 29 March 2013).

CHAPTER FIVE

I: First intimations of difference

On the Hindu festival Rath Yatra, see http://www.swaminarayan.org/festivals/rathyatra/ and http://hinduism.about.com/od/rathyatra/a/rathyatra.htm (both accessed 7 October 2013).

On 'covering' – which is to 'downplay a disfavored trait so as to blend into the mainstream' – see Kenji Yoshino, *Covering – The Hidden Assault on Our Civil Rights* (Random House, 2006).

The SABC's 1968 'The Broken Link' programmes have been archived, and some are now available online, in podcast: see http://www.sabc.co.za/wps/portal/SABC/springbok (accessed 14 May 2013). I am indebted to Ms Retha Buys, senior archivist for Springbok radio at the SABC, for the information that Brian Chilvers was the producer, and that the programmes on homosexuality flighted as follows: 'Homosexuality: Who's to blame' #5 – 21 July 1968; 'Homosexuality: Compassion or Compulsion' #6 – 28 July 1968; 'Lesbians: The Mandy Story' #7 – 4 August 1968; 'Lesbians' #8 – 11 August 1968.

II: The Constitution and national diversity

The Constitution is available, in all eleven official languages, on the Constitutional Court's website, http://www.constitutionalcourt.org.za/site/home.htm (accessed 14 May 2013).

The figures in the text from the 2011 census are rounded off from http://www.info.gov.za/aboutsa/people.htm (accessed 22 May 2013) and from http://www.statssa.gov.za/Census2011/Products/Census_2011_Census_in_brief.pdf (accessed 22 May 2013). The census gives the number of people signifying adherence to the Zion Christian Church (ZCC) as 4 971 932, and to 'other Apostolic churches' as 5 609 070.

III: Constitutional diversity – citizenship, national flag and language

Information of the Pan South African Languages Board can be obtained from http://www.pansalb.org.za/ and https://en.wikipedia.org/wiki/ Pan_South_African_Language_Board (both accessed 20 May 2013). The statement that English is the most widely understood language, and the second language of the majority of South Africans, is from http://www.info.gov.za/aboutsa/people.htm (accessed 22 May 2013), although the particular statement I draw on ('Although English is the mother tongue of only 8,2% of the population, it is the language most widely understood, and the second language of the majority of South Africans') misstates the percentage of first-language English speakers, which is correctly given as 9.6% in the table that immediately follows.

The languages in which the Constitutional Court may be addressed are regulated by Rule 13(4) of the rules of the court, available at http:// www.constitutionalcourt.org.za/site/thecourt/rulesofthecourt.htm (accessed 14 May 2013).

On South Africa's Roman-Dutch common law, and customary law, section 39(3) of the Constitution provides that the Bill of Rights does not deny the existence of other rights or freedoms recognised or conferred by the common law or customary law, to the extent that they are consistent with the Bill.

Section 211 of the Constitution recognises the institution, status and role of traditional leadership, according to customary law, subject to the Constitution, and provides that 'The courts must apply customary law when that law is applicable, subject to the Constitution and any legislation that specifically deals with customary law' (section 211(3)).

IV: Diversity – sexual orientation and the rich harvest of history

For the argument that protecting lesbian and gay equality was a test case for constitutionalism as a whole, see my inaugural lecture delivered at the University of the Witwatersrand 27 October 1992, published in (1993) 110 *South African Law Journal* 450, and cited with approval by the Constitutional Court in *National Coalition for Gay and Lesbian Equality v Minister of Justice* [1998] ZACC 15; 1999 (1) SA 6 at paras 20 and following, available at http://www.saflii.org/za/cases/ZACC/1998/ 15.html (accessed 21 May 2013).

On Cecil Williams, Nelson Mandela's driver on the day he was arrested, see SA History Online, http://www.sahistory.org.za/people/cecil-williams (accessed 21 May 2013).

The SA History Online site has no biography of Simon Nkoli. A good short overview of his life can be obtained on Wikipedia, http:// en.wikipedia.org/wiki/Simon_Nkoli (accessed 21 May 2013).

To the account of the inclusion of sexual orientation in South Africa's Constitution in the main text should be added the account by Mr Peter Tatchell, who interviewed Ruth Mompati, a senior member of the ANC's national executive, in London in 1987, eliciting causally pivotal anti-gay comments, which at the instance of Mr Tatchell the ANC through Mr Thabo Mbeki later repudiated. Mr Tatchell explains his role in these events on his website, http://www.petertatchell.net/lgbt_rights/history/anc.htm (accessed 21 May 2013). Ms Mompati herself later recalled the interview and disavowed her anti-gay statements in a moving foreword to Neville Hoad, Karen Martin and Graeme Reid, *Sex and Politics in South Africa – The Equality Clause / Gay and Lesbian Movement/ the Anti-apartheid Struggle* (Cape Town: Double Storey, 2005).

V: Diversity – the sharp lessons of history

On the Burundian genocide of 1972, see René Lemarchand and David Martin, *Selective Genocide in Burundi* (July 1974), available at http://www.burundi-agnews.org/agnews_selectgenobur.htm (accessed 15 May 2013).

On the Rwandan genocide of 1994, see Fergal Keane, *Season of Blood: A Rwandan Journey* (1997), and for a deeply moving personal account, see Théogène Niwenshuti, 'Bringing colour into life again', in Sean O'Toole, *über(W)unden – Art in Troubled Times* (2012).

The most arresting account of the Biafran tragedy is to be found in Chinua Achebe's memoir, published shortly before he died on 21 March 2013, *There Was a Country: A Personal History of Biafra* (2012).

The statement in the text about the ANC's experience from the Mozambican and Angolan wars of liberation is taken from the ANC's website. See 'Affirmative Action and the New Constitution – why we need affirmative action', available at http://www.anc.org.za/show.php?id=283 (accessed 22 May 2013). The passage on which I have drawn reads: 'Our experience of living through and supporting the radical transformations in Angola and Mozambique had taught us that sometimes the processes that brought the greatest rewards to the poor and the oppressed in the short term, caused them the greatest hardship in the long run. Real victory for the people meant being able to deliver – not just promises and abstractions, but houses, jobs, electricity, water, schools and clinics, real freedom and real choices in the fullest sense. We wanted democracy to be associated with a better life and peace, not with poorer living standards and civil war.'

VI: The Constitutional Court rules on how far diversity must be protected

The full name of the Equality Act is the Promotion of Equality and Prohibition of Unfair Discrimination Act, 4 of 2000. Equality Courts are
created by chapter 4, sections 16-23.

The nose-stud case is *MEC for Education: Kwazulu-Natal v Pillay* [2007]
ZACC 21; 2008 (1) SA 474 (CC) (5 October 2007), available at http://
www.saflii.org/za/cases/ZACC/2007/21.html (accessed 22 May 2013).
The 'parade of horribles' quotation from Langa CJ is at para 107. For
comment on the judgment, see Lourens du Plessis, 'Religious Freedom and Equality of Difference: A Significant Development in Recent
South African Constitutional Case-Law', *PER/PELJ* 2009 volume 12
number 4; and Elda de Waal, Raj Mestry and Charles J Russo, 'Religious and Cultural Dress at School: A Comparative Perspective', *PER/
PELJ* 2011 volume 14 number 6.

The case of the dreadlocked Rastafarian pupil from Welkom, Free State,
is reported at http://www.timeslive.co.za/thetimes/2013/05/20/vic-
tory-for-expelled-pupil (accessed 7 October 2013).

VII: The nose-stud case and political diversity

The judgment by Chief Justice Mogoeng is *Oriani-Ambrosini, MP v Sisulu,
MP Speaker of the National Assembly* [2012] ZACC 27; 2012 (6) SA 588
(CC) (9 October 2012), available at http://www.saflii.org/za/cases/
ZACC/2012/27.html (accessed 21 May 2013). The main quotation from
it is from para 43.

VIII: The broken promises, and the hope, of constitutional diversity

Perhaps the most important research to date about the meaning of the
Constitution's promises in the lives of rural township gays is contained in Graeme Reid, *How to be a Real Gay – Gay Identities in Small-
town South Africa* (UKZN Press, 2013). Reid concludes (p 188f) that
political and legal changes in South Africa have allowed new forms of
citizenship to emerge. The promise of constitutional equality and subsequent legal changes have affected the lives of small-town township
gays. He rejects the view that the benefits of change remain the preserve of the affluent. Without the Constitution and the sweeping legal
changes it introduced, different ways of being gay could not have been
expressed. There are indications of 'a new sense of belonging, of citizenship, which comes from a new emancipation – the abolition of laws
that were oppressive in terms of race, and equally importantly ... sexual orientation'.

For the murder of Thapelo Makhutle, and the arrest and court appearance of his alleged killer, see http://www.mambaonline.com/article.asp?artid=7050 (accessed 21 May 2013).

CHAPTER SIX

I: A random act of kindness

The inflation-calculating website is http://inflationcalc.co.za/ (accessed 27 May 2013). I did my calculation at http://inflationcalc.co.za/?-date1 = 1963-01-01&date2 = 2013-05-27&amount = 10, which rendered the information that 'R 10.00 from January 1963 would be worth R 686.00 in April 2013' (27 May 2013).

II: Social justice, remedial measures and the Constitution

The equality clause in the Constitution, section 9, reads in full as follows:
Equality
Everyone is equal before the law and has the right to equal protection and benefit of the law.

Equality includes the full and equal enjoyment of all rights and freedoms. To promote the achievement of equality, legislative and other measures designed to protect or advance persons, or categories of persons, disadvantaged by unfair discrimination may be taken.

The state may not unfairly discriminate directly or indirectly against anyone on one or more grounds, including race, gender, sex, pregnancy, marital status, ethnic or social origin, colour, sexual orientation, age, disability, religion, conscience, belief, culture, language and birth.

No person may unfairly discriminate directly or indirectly against anyone on one or more grounds in terms of subsection (3). National legislation must be enacted to prevent or prohibit unfair discrimination.

Discrimination on one or more of the grounds listed in subsection (3) is unfair unless it is established that the discrimination is fair.

III: The Constitutional Court decides its first affirmative action case

Minister of Finance v Van Heerden [2004] ZACC 3; 2004 (6) SA 121 (CC) (29 July 2004), available at http://www.saflii.org/za/cases/ZACC/2004/3.html (accessed 27 May 2013).

IV: 'First-order rights', social rights and the promise of equality

The famous aphorism about the majestic equality of the law is attributed to Anatole France: 'The law, in its majestic equality, forbids the rich as well as the poor to sleep under bridges, to beg in the streets, and to steal bread', from *Le Lys Rouge [The Red Lily]* (1894), chapter 7. I got this from Wikiquote – see http://en.wikiquote.org/wiki/Anatole_France (accessed 9 October 2013).

The pivotal work showing that the distinction between 'first-order' and socio-economic rights is false is Henry Shue, *Basic Rights: Subsistence, Affluence, and US Foreign Policy* (2nd ed) (Princeton University Press, 1996). See also Sandra Fredman, *Human Rights Transformed: Positive Rights and Positive Duties* (Oxford University Press, 2008).

The electoral cases from early 2009 are *Richter v Minister for Home Affairs* [2009] ZACC 3; 2009 (3) SA 615 (CC), available at http://www.saflii. org/za/cases/ZACC/2009/3.html (accessed 28 May 2013), and *A Party v Minister for Home Affairs* [2009] ZACC 4; 2009 (3) SA 649 (CC), available at http://www.saflii.org/za/cases/ZACC/2009/4.html (accessed 28 May 2013).

TAC case: the Constitutional Court acknowledged the limits of judicial intervention in socio-economic rights cases in *Minister of Health v Treatment Action Campaign* (No 2) [2002] ZACC 15; 2002 (5) SA 721, para 38, available at http://www.saflii.org/za/cases/ZACC/2002/15. html (accessed 30 May 2013).

V: Social and economic rights in the South African Constitution

Quotation from the water case, *Mazibuko v City of Johannesburg* [2009] ZACC 28; 2010 (4) SA 1 (CC), available at http://www.saflii.org/za/cases/ZACC/2009/28.html (accessed 30 May 2013).

VI : The right to life and the right of access to health care

Soobramoney v Minister of Health (Kwazulu-Natal) [1997] ZACC 17; 1998 (1) SA 765 (CC); (27 November 1997), available at http://www.saflii. org/za/cases/ZACC/1997/17.html (accessed 29 May 2013).

VII : Mrs Grootboom's house and the right of access to adequate housing

Government of the Republic of South Africa v Grootboom [2000] ZACC 19; 2001 (1) SA 46 (CC) (4 October 2000), available at http://www.saflii. org/za/cases/ZACC/2000/19.html (accessed 11 October 2013).

About a month before the judgment was handed down, the court issued an order made by agreement between the parties, providing for interim shelter and facilities for Mrs Grootboom and the Wallacedene community: see *Grootboom v Government of the Republic of South Africa – Constitutional Court Order* [2000] ZACC 14 (21 September 2000), available at http://www.saflii.org/za/cases/ZACC/2000/14.html (accessed 10 October 2013).

VIII: *From* Grootboom *to* Blue Moonlight

City of Johannesburg Metropolitan Municipality v Blue Moonlight Properties 39 (Pty) Ltd [2011] ZACC 33; 2012 (2) SA 104 (CC); 2012 (2) BCLR 150 (CC), available at http://www.saflii.org/za/cases/ZACC/2011/40.html (accessed 30 May 2013).

IX: *The promise of socio-economic rights – and their limits*

The ruling that you cannot sell off a home for a trifling debt is *Jaftha v Schoeman* [2004] ZACC 25; 2005 (2) SA 140 (CC) (8 October 2004), available at http://www.saflii.org/za/cases/ZACC/2004/25.html (accessed 31 May 2013), extended in *Gundwana v Steko Development CC* [2011] ZACC 14; 2011 (3) SA 608 (CC) (11 April 2011), available at http://www.saflii.org/za/cases/ZACC/2011/14.html (accessed 31 May 2013).

The ruling extending social grants to permanent residents is *Khosa v Minister of Social Development* [2004] ZACC 11; 2004 (6) SA 505 (CC) (4 March 2004), available at http://www.saflii.org/za/cases/ZACC/2004/11.html (accessed 31 May 2013).

The tenants' rights ruling is *Maphango v Aengus Lifestyle Properties* [2012] ZACC 2; 2012 (3) SA 531 (CC) (13 March 2012), available at http://www.saflii.org/za/cases/ZACC/2012/2.html (accessed 31 May 2013).

For criticism of *Mazibuko*, see Sandra Liebenberg, *Socio-Economic Rights: Adjudication Under a Transformative Constitution* (Cape Town: Juta, 2010) at p 467, and Pierre de Vos, 'Water is life (but life is cheap)', http://constitutionallyspeaking.co.za/water-is-life-but-life-is-cheap/, 13 October 2009 (accessed on 31 May 2013) (saying *Mazibuko* judgment to some extent 'represents a retreat for the court from its hey-day when (in the TAC case) it ordered the state to take steps to make Nevirapine available', and that the court endorsed 'the neo-liberal paradigm of water provision adopted by the city, a policy which would often deny poor people access to adequate water because they would be unable to pay for the water needed to live'); David Bilchitz, 'What is reasonable to the court is unfair to the poor', *Business Day*, 16 March 2010. See also Redson Kapindu, 'The desperate left in desperation: a court in retreat – *Nokotyana v Ekurhuleni Metropolitan Municipality* revisited' *Constitutional Court Review*, (2010) vol 3, 201-222, at 201.

Jackie Dugard and M Langford, 'Art or Science? Synthesising Lessons from Public Interest Litigation and the Dangers of Legal Determinism', *South African Journal on Human Rights*, (2011) vol 27, 39-64 (pointing out that the public impact litigation process in *Mazibuko* 'delivered much more than the judicial decision', suggesting that the limitations on judicial process and decision making can be overcome through litigation and social mobilisation).

X: Socio-economic rights – the risk of judicial overkill

For an illuminating discussion that criticises India and Brazil, and by contrast lauds the approach of the South African Constitutional Court, see Jeff King, *Judging Social Rights* (Cambridge University Press, 2012), especially pp 81-5.

The Kansas City case is *Jenkins v State of Missouri* 593 F.Supp. 1485 (W.D. Mo. 1984). In *Missouri v. Jenkins*, 515 U.S. 70 (1995), the United States Supreme Court, by a majority of 5 to 4, overturned a District Court ruling that required the state of Missouri to correct racial inequality in schools by funding salary increases and remedial education programmes.

XI: Socio-economic rights: the broader achievement

Jeff King, *Judging Social Rights* (Cambridge University Press, 2012) p 105 considers the South African model of constitutionally expressed socio-economic rights to be 'the exemplar to work from'.

XII: Social grants, hand-outs and government charity

In this section I have drawn heavily on 'Everything you need to know about social grants' by Issa Saunders, published in GroundUp newsletter of 6 March 2013, available at http://groundup.org.za/content/everything-you-need-know-about-social-grants (accessed 31 May 2013). See also Gabrielle Kelly, 'We need to change how we think (and talk) about social grants', GroundUp, 10 October 2013, available at http://groundup.org.za/content/we-need-change-how-we-think-and-talk-about-social-grants (accessed 10 October 2013).

The legislation creating SASSA is the South African Social Security

Agency Act, 9 of 2004, available at http://www.info.gov.za/view/DownloadFileAction?id = 67983 (accessed 31 May 2013).

SASSA implements grants under the Social Assistance Act, 13 of 2004, available at http://www.info.gov.za/view/DownloadFileAction?id = 67950 (accessed 31 May 2013).

The research and writing of Dr Jonny Steinberg provide eloquent support for the power of social grants to afford recipients the means of economic independence and dignity. See 'Grants encourage liberation, not dependence', *Business Day*, 23 August 2013, available at http://www.bdlive.co.za/opinion/columnists/2013/08/23/grants-encourage-liberation-not-dependence (accessed 10 October 2013).

CHAPTER SEVEN

This Conclusion is adapted from my address to the Sunday Times Alan Paton Literary Awards dinner in Johannesburg on 29 June 2013, and is available at http://www.constitutionalcourt.org.za/site/judges/justicecameron/Sunday-Times-Literary-Award-address-Saturday-29-June-2013.pdf (accessed 21 October 2013).

I: Twenty years of democracy and constitutionalism

Most of the statistics I mention here are taken, with gratitude, from Jonny Steinberg, 'Oscar Pistorius: the end of the rainbow', *The Guardian*, 24 May 2013, available at http://www.guardian.co.uk/world/2013/may/24/oscar-pistorius-end-of-rainbow (accessed 11 October 2013). The figure of R120 billion for social grants comes from the 2013 Budget Speech by the Minister of Finance, Pravin Gordhan, available at http://www.moneyweb.co.za/moneyweb-2013-budget/2013-budget-speech (accessed on 11 October 2013). I got the figure of 88% for violent service delivery protests from Trevor Neethling, 'Police not backing down on violent protests, says Minister', *Business Day*, 8 August 2012, available at http://www.bdlive.co.za/national/2012/08/08/police-not-backing-down-on-violent-protests-says-minister (accessed on 11 October 2013).

II: Two kinds of scepticism about the Constitution

See Ngoako Ramatlhodi (deputy minister for correctional services), 'ANC's fatal concessions – Constitution is tilted in favour of forces against changes', *The Times*, 1 September 2011, available at http://www.times-live.co.za/opinion/commentary/2011/09/01/the-big-read-anc-s-fatal-concessions (accessed 11 October 2013). I quote deputy minister Ramatlhodi also in Edwin Cameron, 'What you can do with rights – Fourth Leslie Scarman Lecture' (25 January 2012), *European Human Rights Law Review* pp 149-161 available at http://www.constitutional-court.org.za/site/judges/justicecameron/scarman.pdf (accessed on 11 October 2013).

Matuma Letsoalo, 'Numsa targets land reform, the Constitution – and Pravin' *Mail & Guardian*, 4 June 2012, available at http://mg.co.za/article/2012-06-04-no-compensation-numsa-targets-land-reform-the-constitution-and-pravin-gordhan (accessed 11 October 2013).

For the full interview with General Phiyega, see 'Who polices the police', broadcast on Al Jazeera on 16 March 2013, available at http://www.aljazeera.com/programmes/south2north/2013/03/2013314105953174623.html (accessed 11 October 2013). See also: 'Constitution remarks haunt Phiyega', *News24*, 26 March 2013, available at http://www.news24.com/SouthAfrica/News/Constitution-remarks-haunt-Phiyega-20130326 (accessed on 11 October 2013).

Mr Ken Owen and Mr RW Johnson: see the debate following the death of former Chief Justice Arthur Chaskalson: Ken Owen, 'Chaskalson's influence was decisive', *Business Day*, 7 December 2012, available at http://www.bdlive.co.za/opinion/letters/2012/12/07/letter-chaskalsons-influence-was-decisive (accessed 11 October 2013) (stating that 'This constitution has allowed the development of a party oligarchy' and 'the drift towards democratic centralism, which is a duplicitous term for the old communist ideas of a "vanguard party" and a "dictatorship of the proletariat"' and 'has permitted the persistence of the pre-liberation African National Congress-SACP culture of violent mass demonstrations' and 'preserved the notion that political ends may be achieved by making parts of the country "ungovernable"'); RW Johnson, 'Chaskalson a loyal fellow traveller', *Business Day*, 12 December 2012, available at http://www.bdlive.co.za/opinion/letters/2012/12/12/letter-chaskalson-a-loyal-fellow-traveller (accessed 23 August 2013).

First reason for the Constitution – it has stood the test of twenty years

The case where ANC factions in the Free State turned to the Constitutional Court is *Ramakatsa v Magashule* [2012] ZACC 31; 2013 (2) BCLR 202 (CC), available at http://www.saflii.org/za/cases/ZACC/2012/31.html (accessed 11 October 2013).

Second reason – the Constitution's distribution of powers is practical and effective

Grootboom: *Government of the Republic of South Africa v Grootboom* [2000] ZACC 19; 2001 (1) SA 46 (CC) (4 October 2000), available at http://www.saflii.org/za/cases/ZACC/2000/19.html (accessed 11 October 2013).

TAC: *Minister of Health v Treatment Action Campaign* (No 2) [2002] ZACC 15; 2002 (5) SA 721; 2002 (10) BCLR 1033 (5 July 2002), available at http://www.saflii.org/za/cases/ZACC/2002/15.html (accessed 11 October 2013).

Third reason – the people have claimed the Constitution as their own

On the extraordinarily wide dissemination and internalisation of the Constitution, see Graeme Reid, *How to be a Real Gay – Gay Identities in small-town South Africa* (UKZN Press, 2013).

Fourth reason – the judiciary is still strong

For the Constitutional Court's contribution to the fight against corruption, see its judgment finding that government is constitutionally obliged to create independent corruption-busting entity: *Glenister v President of the Republic of South Africa* [2011] ZACC 6; 2011 (3) SA 347 (CC); 2011 (7) BCLR 651 (CC) (17 March 2011), available at http://www.saflii.org/za/cases/ZACC/2011/6.html (accessed 11 October 2013).

Deputy Chief Justice Dikgang Moseneke, '100 years after the Native Land Act of 1913: How the Constitution has embraced land reform and property rights' (15 May 2013) (unpublished address at the 45th anniversary convention of the South African Property Owners' Association).

Section 25(1) of the Constitution provides that 'No one may be deprived of property except in terms of law of general application, and no law may permit arbitrary deprivation of property'. Section 25(2) provides that 'Property may be expropriated only in terms of law of general application – (a) for a public purpose or in the public interest; and (b) subject to compensation, the amount of which and the time and manner of payment of which have either been agreed to by those affected or decided or approved by a court'.

Private citizens: *Hattingh v Juta* 2013 (3) SA 275 (CC), available at http://www.saflii.org/za/cases/ZACC/2013/5.html (accessed 11 October 2013); *Mayelane v Ngwenyama* 2013 (4) SA 415 (CC), available at http://www.saflii.org/za/cases/ZACC/2013/14.html (accessed 11 October 2013); *Glenister v President of the Republic of*

South Africa 2011 (3) SA 347 (CC), available at http://www.saflii.
org/za/cases/ZACC/2011/6.html (accessed 11 October 2013).

Government: *New National Party of South Africa v Government of the
Republic of South Africa* 1999 (3) SA 191 (CC), available at http://
www.saflii.org/za/cases/ZACC/1999/5.html (accessed 11 October 2013); *Government of the Republic of South Africa v Grootboom*
2001 (1) SA 46 (CC), available at http://www.saflii.org/za/cases/
ZACC/2000/19.html (accessed 11 October 2013).

Speaker of Parliament: *Oriani-Ambrosini, MP v Sisulu, MP Speaker of
the National Assembly* 2012 (6) SA 588 (CC), available at http://
www.saflii.org/za/cases/ZACC/2012/27.html (accessed 11 October
2013).

Political parties: *Democratic Alliance v President of South Africa* 2013
(1) SA 248 (CC), available at http://www.saflii.org/za/cases/
ZACC/2012/24.html (accessed 11 October 2013).

Civil society groupings: *Minister of Health v Treatment Action Campaign (No 2)* 2002 (5) SA 721 (CC), available at http://www.saflii.
org/za/cases/ZACC/2002/15.html (accessed 7 October 2013); *Centre for Child Law v Minister for Justice and Constitutional Development* 2009 (6) SA 632 (CC), available at http://www.saflii.org/za/
cases/ZACC/2009/18.html (accessed 11 October 2013), and
*Abahlali Basemjondolo Movement SA v Premier of the Province of
Kwazulu-Natal* 2010 (2) BCLR 99 (CC), available at http://www.
saflii.org/za/cases/ZACC/2009/31.html (accessed 11 October 2013).

Party factions: *Ramakatsa v Magashule* 2013 (2) BCLR 202 (CC),
available at http://www.saflii.org/za/cases/ZACC/2012/31.html
(accessed 11 October 2013).

Fifth reason – Constitution's fundamental values are right

Equality includes the full and equal enjoyment of all rights and
freedoms: section 9(2) of the Constitution.

Freedom of trade, occupation or profession: section 22 of the Constitution.

Independent national prosecuting authority: section 179 of the Constitution.

Public Protector: section 182 of the Constitution.

South African Human Rights Commission: section 184 of the Constitution.

Abbreviations

AIDS – Acquired Immune Deficiency Syndrome

ALP – AIDS Law Project

ANC – the African National Congress, founded in 1912, and banned by the apartheid government between 1960 and February 1990

ARVs – anti-retrovirals – medical treatment to suppress activity of HIV in the human body

CALS – Centre for Applied Legal Studies, a human rights research and litigation centre founded at the University of the Witwatersrand by John Dugard in 1978, where I worked from 1986 to 1994

CODESA – Convention for a Democratic South Africa, the negotiations for a democratic transition and constitution that took place near Johannesburg between December 1991 and 1993

COSATU – Congress of South African Trade Unions

HIV – the human immunodeficiency virus, which causes AIDS

HSRC – the Human Sciences Research Council

IFP – Inkatha Freedom Party, founded by Chief Mangosuthu Buthelezi

JSC – Judicial Service Commission, established by section 105 of the interim Constitution, and functioning now under section 178 of the Constitution

KZN – KwaZulu-Natal province

LRC – Legal Resources Centre, a public interest law firm founded by Felicia Kentridge, Arthur Chaskalson and others in 1979

MCC – the South African Medicines Control Council

MEC – Member of the Executive Committee (the political executive in charge of a provincial government department)

MK – uMkhonto weSizwe – the Spear of the Nation – the armed wing of the ANC

MP – Member of Parliament

NACOSA – the National AIDS Council of South Africa, founded in 1992 to formulate AIDS policy for democratic government in South Africa

NPA – National Prosecuting Authority, established under section 179 of the Constitution

NNRTIs – non-nucleoside reverse transcriptase inhibitors, a class of anti-retroviral drugs

NUM – the National Union of Mineworkers, founded in 1982 by Cyril Ramaphosa

NUMSA – National Union of Metalworkers of South Africa

PAC – Pan Africanist Congress

TRC – the Truth and Reconciliation Commission, founded as part of the constitutional settlement in 1994 to consider human rights violations during apartheid, amnesty for perpetrators, and reparations for victims

SACC – South African Council of Churches

SAHRC – South African Human Rights Commission

SAMDC – South African Medical and Dental Council, the body established under the Medical, Dental and Supplementary Health Service Professions Act 56 of 1974 to regulate medical practice in pre-democracy South Africa

SAPS – the South African Police Service

SASSA – the South African Social Security Agency

SERI – Social and Economic Rights Institute of South Africa

UNAIDS – the joint United Nations agency dealing with responses to the worldwide AIDS epidemic

UCT – University of Cape Town

UJ – University of Johannesburg

Wits University – the University of the Witwatersrand, Johannesburg

WHO – World Health Organisation, one of the sponsoring organisations of UNAIDS, headquartered in Geneva

Acknowledgements

I am deeply grateful to those of my friends and colleagues and law clerks who read the whole or part of the manuscript. They made many valuable suggestions for improving it. I am particularly grateful to my law clerks for helping with research and references.

My family members are separately acknowledged.

In South Africa: Laurie Ackermann, Samir Ali, Nurina Ally, Claire Avidon, Leo Boonzaier, Geoff Budlender, Busisiwe Deyi, Nick Ferreira, Nathan Geffen, Tony Hamburger, Johan Jansen van Vuuren, Zelda Kruger, Carole Lewis, Christopher Mann, Gcina Malindi, Gilbert Marcus, Michael Mbikiwa, Caroline Nichols, Gerrit Olivier, Jean Richter, Wim Richter, Renee van der Riet, Stef Venter and Lwando Xaso.

Abroad: Mark Behr (Memphis), Sappho Dias (London), John Dugard (Den Haag), Ietje Dugard (Den Haag), Sandra Fredman (Oxford), Rob Garris (Rockefeller Foundation, NYC), Jeremiah Johnson (New York City), Sydney Kentridge (London), Chris McConnachie (Oxford), Elena Ongania (Bellagio), Pilar Palacia (Bellagio), Hanneke Smulders Ritzen (Bellagio), Jonathan Watt-Pringle (London), Margy Jenkins Wax and Al Wax (Bellagio) and Robert Wintemute (London).

A very special thank you is due to my former law clerk, Claire Avidon. At a late stage, and at an exceptionally busy time in her practice as an attorney, she devoted a hard-reading weekend to meticulously proofreading the whole manuscript. She found omissions and inconsistencies and roughnesses of style, as well as one important statistical inconsistency, that none of the rest of us picked up. She also suggested several important improving additions. As a result, the final manuscript benefited enormously from her scrupulous care and attention.

I am very greatly indebted to George Claassen, an author in his own right, for meticulously and imaginatively produced indexes, which I believe will greatly enhance the value of the book. He was actively aided in the late stages of preparing the indexes by my foreign law clerk, Thomas Scott, and my sister Jeanie, to both of whom I am also hugely grateful.

The best bit about writing this book was Bellagio. During March 2013, the Rockefeller Foundation of New York afforded me a writing residency at its centre there, on Lake Como, Italy. It proved to be a lifetime experience. The month I spent there was joyful and productive. I was able to write in peace and serenity amidst very great beauty, while sharing memorable mealtimes and walks (and occasional jailbreaks) with extraordinary people. I wrote almost half the book there. Without that time, the book could not have been completed.

And I am greatly indebted to the two special readers whom my publishers appointed, Alison Lowry and Hannes van Zyl, for generously professional encouragement at a critical stage. My debt to my publisher, Erika Oosthuysen, is long and intense. It goes back to *Witness to AIDS*. She has been personally generous, supportive and constantly encouraging.

I acknowledge two final debts – to my family, Jean, Wim, Marlise and Marc, and Graham and Andrea; and to my current colleagues in the Constitutional Court; as well as to former colleagues Kate O'Regan and Zak Yacoob, and to two dearly missed deceased colleagues, Arthur Chaskalson and Pius Langa.

About the Author

Edwin Cameron has been a Justice of South Africa's highest court, the Constitutional Court, since 1 January 2009.

Cameron was educated at Pretoria Boys' High School, Stellenbosch and Oxford, where he was a Rhodes Scholar and won the top academic awards and prizes. During apartheid he was a human rights lawyer. President Mandela appointed him a judge in 1994. Before serving in the Constitutional Court, he was a Judge of the Supreme Court of Appeal for eight years, and a Judge of the High Court for six.

Cameron was an outspoken critic of then-President Thabo Mbeki's AIDS-denialist policies, and in 2005 wrote a prize-winning memoir, *Witness to AIDS*, about his own experience of living with AIDS. Published in South Africa, the United Kingdom, the United States and in translation in Germany and China, *Witness to AIDS* was co-winner of the Sunday Times Alan Paton Literary award for non-fiction.

Cameron chaired the governing council of the University of the Witwatersrand for more than ten years (1998-2008), and remains involved in many charitable and public causes. He has received honours for his legal and human rights work, including a special award by the Bar of England and Wales in 2002 for his 'contribution to international jurisprudence and the protection of human rights'. He is an honorary fellow of the Society for Advanced Legal Studies, London, and of Keble College, Oxford (2003), as well as an honorary bencher of the Middle Temple, London (2008). He holds honorary doctorates in law from King's College London (2008), the University of the Witwatersrand, Johannesburg (2009), Oxford University (2011) and the University of St Andrews (2012).

For more information, see www.witnesstoaids.com and http://www. constitutionalcourt.org.za/site/judges/justicecameron/index1.html.

Index of Persons

329

Index of Subjects

electronic tolls (e-tolls) 186-187, 279, 309

End Conscription Campaign 29

End Conscription Campaign v Minister of Defence 295

England 18, 97, 124

English 13, 183, 206, 209-211, 313

environmental rights 249-250

equality 37, 39, 58, 79, 107, 119, 134, 137, 177, 180, 216-217, 223-224, 227-229, 237-245, 256, 258, 282-283, 291, 301, 307, 310, 313-317, 319, 323

Equality Act 223, 237, 315

Equality Court 223

European Convention on Human Rights 137

Executive Council of the Western Cape Legislature v President of the Republic of South Africa 310

first-order rights 244-245, 247-248, 317

Fischer's Choice: A Life of Bram Fischer, 290

flag, national 210

Fluconazole 115, 163

Fort Hare, University of 167, 299

franchise 38, 247

Fred Hutchinson Cancer Research Center 296

Freedom Charter 37, 42

Free State Republic 17

Ga-Rankuwa hospital 150

Gauteng 141, 150, 185

gay (homosexuality) 9, 119, 122, 128, 201, 206, 208, 213-219, 228-229, 280, 310, 312-316, 322

Gazankulu 53

gender 57, 204-205, 213, 215, 218, 228

Geneva 114, 148-149, 166

Germiston 53-54

Glenister v President of the Republic of South Africa 322

Goldberg v Minister of Prisons 297

Government of the Republic of South Africa v Grootboom 169, 190, 194, 197, 259, 261-262, 264, 267, 279, 304, 318, 322-323

Grahamstown 25, 154

grand apartheid 54-55

Greek 183, 211

Grey College, Bloemfontein 232

Groote Schuur Minute 77, 90

Gugulethu 52

Gujurati 211

Gundwana v Steko Development 318

Harris v Minister of the Interior 1952 286

Hattingh v Juta 322

health care 84, 93-94, 119, 122, 128, 131, 137-138, 146, 151-152, 161, 169, 193, 249-252, 255-256, 268, 317-318

Hebrew 211

High Court of Parliament Act 286

high treason 38-39

Hillbrow 38, 113, 262

Hindi 211

Hindu 202, 223-224

HIV (see also AIDS) 64-70, 72, 81-89, 91-96, 98-103, 105, 112-115, 120-122, 124-126, 129-131, 138, 140-150, 154, 158-159, 161-169, 171-173, 192, 194-196, 198-199, 216, 258, 293, 295, 297, 299-300, 303, 306, 311

343

On *Justice: A Personal Account*

Brave, compelling and illuminating . . .

SUE GRANT-MARSHALL, *Business Day*

Powerful and very meaningful. A really different and special and hopeful addition to our legal literature, and a courageous autobiographical contribution.   JUSTICE LAURIE ACKERMANN

It is impossible to read this book without a lump in the throat – for it is a celebration of all that is great about our country South Africa, a reminder that wounds can be healed through just laws and our great Constitution. However, throughout the book, there is a sobering reminder of the darkest chapters of our history and how these resulted in profound personal losses and sacrifices. Nonetheless, we are reminded of our individual responsibility and power to influence the course of history.

What makes Edwin Cameron an extraordinary South African is not only his personal journey and the obstacles he has overcome – death of loved ones, poverty, AIDS – but his passion for constitutionalism and justice. In this book, he takes us on an incredible journey that is both personal and political. We are reminded of the triumph of the human spirit against oppression and are encouraged to bring to life our progressive Constitution, through our everyday decisions and how we live our lives.   REDI TLHABI

On *Witness to Aids*

Dealing as it does with life and death, Cameron's book is among the most substantial contributions to the concepts of national identity, community and solidarity, that we have had since 1994.   JONNY STEINBERG

A powerful personal story written with eloquent simplicity, understated humility and profound insight.   MALEGAPURU WILLIAM MAKGOBA

Relentlessly brilliant and hopeful . . . it is a text to live by.

NADINE GORDIMER

Remarkable . . . it offers a coherent and enlightened view of the many debates about HIV and AIDS, but it also reminded me of something Toni Morrison, Nobel Literature laureate, said in her Nobel lecture in 1993:

> The vitality of language lies in its ability to limn the actual, imagined and possible lives of its speakers, readers, writers . . . Be it grand or slender, burrowing, blasting, or refusing to sanctify; whether it laughs

out loud or is a cry without an alphabet, the choice word, the chosen silence, unmolested language surges toward knowledge . . .

Witness to AIDS indeed surges toward knowledge.

ANGELA MUVUMBA

Anyone who has been lucky enough to hear Cameron speak will be familiar with his elegant, lucid style, and this book . . . is a moving, important work. MICHELE MAGWOOD, *Sunday Times*

Superb – a relentlessly honest, solidly-argued, meticulously referenced, perceptively illustrated, at times philosophical and frequently gripping narrative ... Complex and at times painful issues are pursued with sensitivity, reason and balance. SHARON DELL, *Natal Witness*

Cameron addresses the taboo questions of race, sexual orientation, poverty and stigma in the context of the HIV/AIDS epidemic, writing almost always from a personal perspective, but with an unconditional commitment to social justice. ZACKIE ACHMAT

Although the most moving sections . . . are those on Cameron's personal life, what stays with one are his reflections on the role of stigma, race and sexuality in South Africa. JOHANNES DE VILLIERS, *Die Burger*

This book, a mixture of memoir and action statement, is proof of his sharp intellect, searing honesty, sensitivity and passion for justice . . . unusual. JUSTICE KIRBY, *Australian Law Journal*

Cameron represents the 'Force of the True' and this force is shiny and tolerant, bright and compassionate, and hopeful.

LOREN ANTHONY, *Sunday Times Lifestyle*

Spellbinding analysis . . . a must-read.

WERANI CHIRAMBO, *Bonela Guardian*

Masterly . . . an authentic South African story of hope and humanity.

ME COETZEE, *Volksblad*